A DICTIONARY OF EPONYMS AND ANTHROPONOMICS

A DICTIONARY OF EPONYMS AND ANTHROPONOMICS

(Based on Telugu Inscriptions)

Dr. A.V.D. SARMA

AKANSHA PUBLISHING HOUSE
NEW DELHI • GUWAHATI • VISAKHAPATNAM

AKANSHA PUBLISHING HOUSE
4649-B/21, Ansari Road
Daryaganj, New Delhi - 110 002
Phones: 011-23263193, 9811582779, 0943116718
Fax: 011-23263193
Email: ektabooks@yahoo.com

A Dictionary of Eponyms and Anthropnomics

First Published 2017

ISBN 978-81-8370-297-3

[The responsibility for the facts stated, conclusions reached etc. is entirely of the Author. The publisher is not responsible for them, whatsoever.]

PRINTED IN INDIA
Published by M.P. Misra for Akansha Publishing House, New Delhi.

Contents

Preface

The undertone of this work is to lift the weft off of an otherwise ubiquitous subject – the eponyms (surnames) and anthroponomics (personal names) pertaining to a particular region of the country i.e., Andhra and its language i.e., Telugu. It was not an altogether unsounded aspect of the onomatology either of this or other regions of the country and its multiple languages. To further upbuoy it from the matrix and larva stage to an iridescent level–a thought provoking attempt is proffered to the scholar-researcher while remaining legible to the common reader. Reconnecting ancient roots through in a pellucid recap remains as the guerdon of this work. Its docket is as inclusive as possible based on a sound substratum and parure material the main resource having recumbented on epigraphy.

To finis, it is oblilgatory to record that this work is the resultant flowering and fruition of a Major Research Project favoured by the University Grants Commission, New Delhi, that flavoured during the period 2009-11. As such, sincere thanks are due to that institution and also to the Maharajah's College (Autonomous), Vizianagaram– my alma mater that generously hosted me as always it's wont.

The usual disclaimers apply.

(A.V.D. SARMA)

Acknowledgements

I gratefully acknowledge the sanction of a Major Research Project by the University Grant Commission, New Delhi which academically and economically enabled the present work.

I am also thankful to Mr. M.P. Misra, Akansha Publishing House, New Delhi for undertaking publication of this work.

Dr. A. V. D. Sarma,
Principal Investigator

Transliteration Method

అ (a), ఆ (ā), ఇ (i), ఈ (ī), ఉ (u), ఊ (ū)
ఋ (r̥), ఎ (e), ఏ (ē), ఐ (ai̥), ఒ (o), ఓ (ō), ఔ (au);
ం (ṃ), ఁ (v̄), ః (ḥ); క (k), ఖ (kh), గ (g),
ఘ (gh), ఙ (ŋ), చ (c), ఛ (ch), జ (j), ఝ (jh),
ఞ (n̄), ట (ṭ), ఠ (ṭh), డ (ḍ), ఢ (ḍh), ణ (ṇ),
త (t), థ (th), ద (d), ధ (dh), న (n), ప (p),
ఫ (ph), బ (b), భ (bh), మ (m), య (y), ర (r),
ఱ (r̲), ల (l), ళ (ḷ), వ (v), శ (ś), ష (ṣ), స (s),
హ (h), ఴ (l̲).

Abbreviations

(Castes & Sub-sects)

AD	:	Ārāma Drāviḍa
Ad.N	:	Adwita Niyōgi
AK	:	Āruvēla Kamma
AN	:	Āruvēla Niyōgi
Ar	:	Āarādhyula
AS	:	Ādi Śaiva
ASP	:	Adi Śaiva Pūjāri
BKN	:	Baḍa Kannaḍa Niyōgi
Br	:	Brāhmin
CV	:	Chattaḍa Vaiṣṇava
D	:	Draviḍa
DD	:	Dimili Ḍrāviḍa
DK	:	Dhenu Karna (VS)
DV	:	Drāviḍa Vaiṣṇava
GV	:	Gōlkonḍa Vyāpāri
Ka	:	Kamma

Kan	:	Kaṇvulu
KD	:	Kōnasīma Drāviḍa
Kh	:	Khastriya
KKV	:	Karaṇa Kamma Vaidīki
KKV	:	Karaṇakamma Vyāpāri
KN	:	Kāsalanāṭi
KNV	:	Kāsalanāṭi Vaidīki
Kp	:	Kāpu
LN	:	Lingadhāri Niyōgi
M	:	Mulikināṭi
M Dh	:	Madhwas
MV	:	Mulikināṭi Vaidīki
N	:	Nandavarika
NN	:	Nandavarapu Niyōgi
NV	:	Niyōgi Vaishṇava
PD	:	Pēruru Drāviḍa
Pg N	:	Prāgnāṭi Niyōgi
PNN	:	Pākanāti Niyōgi
Ps N	:	Pradhama Śakha Niyōgi
Pu D	:	Pūdvru Drāviḍa
Re	:	Reddy
Ren	:	Rēṇuka
S	:	Śaiva
SA	:	Śivarchaka
SB	:	Śaiva Brāhmaṇa

SK	:	Śankha Karṇa
SK	:	Śiṣhṭu Karaṇam
SV	:	Śri Vaiṣṇava
TD	:	Tummaguṇṭa Drāviḍa
TG	:	Telagāṇya
UA	:	Udbhatāchārya
V	:	Viadīki
VB	:	Viswabrāhmaṇa
Vel	:	Velnāṭi
VK	:	Viswakaraṇa (VS)
VN	:	Vēgināṭi
VR	:	Vēmanārādhya
VS	:	Vira Śaiva
VV	:	Velanāṭi Vaidiki
Vy	:	Vykhānasa
Vs	:	Vaisysa
Yag	:	Yāgñavalkya
YS	:	Yajus Śākha

General

CV	:	Chāḷukya Vikrama Era
Dt.	:	District
p.: pp	:	page : pages
Pe.N	:	Personal Ṇame
Pl.N	:	Place Name
S	:	Saka Era

vol.: vols.	:	Volume; Volumes.

Books and Journals

ABS	:	Āndhradēsa Charitra Bhūgoḷa Sarvasvamu, vols.
ARE	:	Annual Report on Epigraphy
APAS	:	Andhra Pradesh Archaeological Series
ASSP	:	Āndhra Samsthānamulu Sāhitya Pōṣhanamu (Doṇappa)
CII	:	Copper Plate Inscriptions Indicarum
Cp of Ap	:	Copper Plate Inscription of Andhra Pradesh Government Museum
CTI	:	Corpus of Telangana Inscriptions
DED	:	Dravidian Etymological Dictionary
EAN	:	Epiraphia Āndhrica
EI	:	Epigraphia Indica
ETI	:	Early Telugu Inscriptions
HAS	:	Hyderabad Archaeological Series
IA	:	Indian Antiquary
IAP	:	Inscriptions of Andhra Pradesh
IMP	:	Inscriptions of the Madras Presidency
ISGO	·	Inscriptions of the Suryavamsi Gajapatis of Orissa
IVR	:	Inscriptions of the Vijayanagara Rulers, vol. IV, Telugu Inscriptions (1351-1665 AD)
JAHRS	:	Journal of Andhra Historical Research Society

MER	:	Madras Epigraphical Report
NAD	:	Nallore District Inscriptions
SAVK	:	Sangraha Āndhra Vijnana Kōsamu, vols.
SAS	:	Samagra Āndhra Sāhityam; vols (Ārudra)
SII	:	South Indian Inscriptions, vols.
SED	:	Sanskrit English Dictionary
TS	:	Telugu Samskruti. vols.

Note: The above illustrative list reveals that most of the Brahmin sub-sects are (i) profession and ritual oriented such as Niyōgi, Vyāpāri and Vaidiki (ii) related to the regions to which they belonged to such as Valnāṭi, Vēgināṭi, Kāsalnāti–a practice as old as that of the time of Paṇini (iii) religious oriented such as Madhva, Śaiva and Vaiṣṇava. Again within the Śaiva sub-sects one find different affiliations like Lingdharis (those who were the Linga, the icon of Śiva). Again one has to notice subtle distinction between a Pūjāri and Archaka. Though both of them are concerned with the workship of the deity, the former has to do only with 'Pūja' (offering flowers etc.) while the latter has to engage in total worship of the deity etc., All these minute differentiation in the socio-religious hierarchy have to some extent reflected in the processs of obtaining their respective surnames.

1

Introduction

Where fore

If the name is the sense of a man the surname is the essence of his family. Of course, the Sanskrit dictum '*Yathā nāma tatha guṇāḥ*'' may not always work out and so as the dictum '*Yathra ākrūta tatha guṇāḥ*'. Be that as it may, the very fact that our Nation builders such as Bose (Subhas Chandra), Gandhi (Mohandas Karamchand), Nehru (Jawaharlal), Patel (Vallabhbhai) et al. are instantly remembered by mere reference to their surnames (eponyms) more than to the fuller version of their names emphasizes the persistent relevance of the family name–'Iṅṭi pērlu' in Telugu.

The romance of a name lingers in its flavour and leaves its fragrance for those who choose to inhale it in thc realm of muse.

The concept of a physical world is dotted with name of even minutest part of an atom and molecule. The Eskimos had nearly 52 names for snow because it was so important to them.

The name as well as the surname is a complex socio-cultural code. When decoded they give information on customs, sanctions, superstitions, power (opponent or latent), authority, status and face value of a cultural entity.

Indian system of name giving is considered to be highly specialized. It has a rich and vibrant tradition. Besides bestowing a personal name to an individual, a surname or cognomen is suffixed or prefixed, the latter being the usual practice in Andhra, in order to assign membership of a cohesive group. The surname may be a totemic name representing a lineage, a clan, a descent but reflective of individuals socio-religious, economic and cultural standing within a group. After all, as K.A. Nilakantha Sastry (1892-1976) has put it "Names are the Music of History." They form a unique and prescient variety of literature (Sāhitya) when fine tuned with proper notational background will yield instant pleasure in the pursuit of knowledge in the aesthetic as well as in the educative sense. While poetry is the art of giving different names to the same thing; mathematics is the art of giving the same name to different things.

Thus, while onomastic studies can be an indispensable tool especially in the contextuality of any given country – including of course India – serious enquiries and methodological inquests in this regard have yet to gain momentum assigning their rightfully deserving place in the realm of knowledge. That lacuna prompted the current exercise.

Earlier Forays

Whereas, there are no doubt macro and general studies pertaining to Toponyms – an important branch of onomastics available in University level theses and journals like that of Place-Names Society of India (Est. 1978) emphatic researches in its equally important branches, Eponymic and Anthroponomic have still to be furthered particularly with regard to Āndhradēśā which has Telugu as its mother tongue that has also been recently sanctified with the classical status by the Government of India.

There are studies of general as well as of focused nature at the all India and regional levels. Mention may be made of Maneka Gandhi's 'Hindu Names' (Penguin, 1993) which "started with the realization that I did not know the meaning of my name (intro)". 'A Dictionary of Personal Names in the Indian History from the earliest to 1947' by Krishna Lalkhera (New Delhi 2002) is an index to personal names based on the history and culture of the Indian people edited by R.C.

Mujumdar and A.D. Pusalkar et al. Tej Ram Sharma's 'Personal and Geographical Names in the Gupta Inscriptions (Concept, Delhi, 1978) is in the words of Lallangi Gopal has adopted a 'fresh approach and imparted a living warmth to the socio-cultural life of the period'. Similarly, Bhabatarn Datta's 'A Linguistic Study of Personal and Surnames in Bengal' (University of Calcutta, 1981) was also felt as a very welcome contribution by linguists like Sukumar Sen. Shibani Roy and S.H.M. Razvi's 'Encyclopedia of Indian Surnames' (Delhi, 2002) is a work representative cataloguing of Indian eponyms. M.V. Vishnu Namboodri's 'Nattarivum Nama patanavum' (Kottayam, 2010) in Malyalam is considered "as a good reference material for researchers" (*Hindu*, 24th August, 2010, p.14).

In Telugu

Undoubtedly, Yarlagedda Balagangadhara Rao laid firm foundations to the onomastic studies pertaining to Andhradesa. His Inṭipērlu (Mangalagiri, 2000) and the thesis under his stewardship by Tella Satyavati 'Teluguvāri Inṭipērlu' (Guntur, 1987) ranks high in this category. Earlier there are learned articles like 'Telugu Personal Names: A structural analysis' by Andre F.S. Joberg and that of eminent scholars in Telugu like Chilukuri Narayana Rao (1890 - 1952), Korada Mahadeva Sastry and Tumati Donappa (1926 – 1996). Studies in Indian Place Names (Bharatiya Sthalanama Patrika) – a Journal is offering a ready platform to the seasoned as well as the budding scholars in the field. For example, Mahadev N. Katti 'A Sample Dictionary of Personal Names' (Vol.XIX,1998); E.M.S. Prasad 'Immigrant Deccan Brahmanas of Andhra Pradesh -- A case study of Surnames' (Vol. XII, 1991) and that of the present author 'Eponyms of Andhra Madhva Brahminas – A Study' (Vol.XXIV, 2010).

So much so

The typically Indian genius for systematization and elaboration of its fund of knowledge in all spheres encompassed the naming process taking due account of the prescriptive norms and prohibitive rules prescribed in the grammatical works, the *Gṛhyasutras* and the *Smṛtis* which elaborated in subsequent times and led to the composition of separate treatises on various aspects and problems connected with and to giving names.

Whether animate or inanimate, every object or person will carry a name for the simple purpose of common identification from yet another. Obviously they have no choice in it for it is bestowed by others. So also in the case of a family name for one inherits it. While the personal name suggests about the socio-cultural background of the family, the family name reveals the roots of it. However, on the ground that caste names are an impediment to social justice and holistic development there are pleas that names should be just generic (Ambumani Ramdoss, 'What is in a Names', *The Hindu*, 27th August, 2010, p.11). Therein it is observed that in India we have names according to different states, languages, castes etc. Names like Menon; Nair (Kerala); Mudaliar, Gowndar, Iyer (Tamil Nadu); Gowda, Hegde, Rai (Karnataka); Reddy, Naidu, Setti (Andhra Pradesh); Patnaik, Panda (Orissa); Naik, Sinde (Maharashtra); Patel, Desai (Gujarat); Chatterjee, Mukharjee, Sen (West Bengal). In the BIMARU states, the names are endless – Sharma, Varma, Bhat, Chauhan, Mishra, Yadav, Paswan, Meena. These are all considered invariably caste, sub-caste, class or sect names.

In Andhra, is first Chief Minister Tanguturi Prakasam Pantulu (1892-1957); the harbinger of social reform movement Kandukuri Veeresalingam Pantulu (1848-1919) and Raghupati Venkata Ratnam Naidu (1862-1939) only to cite a few, have had name endings denoting a particular caste.

The social revolution of eliminating caste names began two generations ago in Tamil Nadu and the question is if it can do why not the rest of the country? A laudable and ponderable suggestion indeed. However, what is disturbing is that even modern women of the current generation – public personalities whether on celluloid of tinsel world or in real politics are found to be fond of suffixing their names with caste name tags!

The above observations highlighten the academic necessity to look beyond the names. Thus, despite the Shakespearean injunction, for those who wish to probe, there are many things in a name.

In so much as

Originally intended to be 'A Socio-cultural History of medieval Andhra through A study of Eponyms and Anthroponomics gleaned from Telugu Lithic Inscriptions (Ca 6th Century A.D. through Ca 14th Century A.D.), it metamorphosised as a 'Dictionary of eponyms and Anthroponomics – from Telugu Inscriptions the time frame remaining the same – çourtesy the discussion with the peer committee of the University Grants Commission which favoured the endeavour with the sanction of a major Research Project (2009-2011).

The Sources

'Ekam Sat Vipra Bahuda Vadanti'. In other words while opinion can be free, the fact has always to be sacred. Thus, the core material is culled from the Telugu lithic records complimented by C.P's published in the volumes of South Indian Inscriptions and the Journals Epigraphia Indica, Epigraphica Andhrica and the District-wise Inscriptions edited and published so far by the Department of Archeology and Museums, Government of Andhra Pradesh.

The data is also gathered from catalogues of surnames such as Musunari Venkata Sastry, "Viprula Inṭi Pērlu – Sākhalu" (Deepak Book Centre, Rajahmundry, 1980); Vajrapani, "Brāhmaṇula Inṭipērlu (Bharani Publications, Vijaywada, 2008); Garre Satyanaryana Gupta "Ārya Vysya Gōtramulu, Ruṣhulu, Pravaralu, Inṭipērlu". P.B. Veeracharyulu, "Viśwa Brāhmaṇa Gōtramulu" (Rohini Publications, Rajahmundry, 1995); Chillagattu Srikanth Kumar, "Kāpulu" (Vijayawada. 2002). Sadinneni Ranga Rao, "Kammavāri Inṭipērlu, Vāḍuka Gōtramulu" (Tenali, 1993). etc.

Composers of Inscriptions without Surnames

In inscriptions one comes across a long list of the pedigree of the donor coupled with flattering accounts about their accomplishments in war and peace. It is surprising that the composers themselves do not mention their surnames leading to the conclusion that they were not felt worth mentioning or such a practice has yet to find a wider currency during their times. For example : Achitēndra (Anmakoṅd a

Praśasti); Nandimitra (Ganapeswaram Inscription); Anantasūri (Pānugallu Inscription); Bālasaraswati (Ippagallu Inscription).

Poets and Authors without Surnames

The names given together with one or other of their important works.

1.	**Adharvaṇāchārya**	(Adharvaṇa Chandam).
2.	**Nannechōḍa**	(Kumāra Sambhavam)
3.	**Mallikārjuna Panditārādhya**	(Sivstatvasarvam)
4.	**Śivadēvayya**	(Puruṣhārdhasāram)
5.	**Śripati Pandita**	(Śrikarabhāṣhyam)
6.	**Gōkarṇa**	(Gōkarṇa Chandam)
7.	**Appana Mantri**	(Chārucharya)
8.	**Baddena**	(Neetisastra Muktāvaḷi)
9.	**Manchena**	(Keyūrrabāhu Charitra)
10.	**Mārana**	(Mārkandēya Purāṇam)
11.	**Vidyānādha alias Agasthya**	(Pratāparudra yaśōbushaṇam)
12.	**Appayārya**	(Jinēndra kalyāṇābhyudayam)
13.	**Gangādēvi**	(Madhura Vijayam)
14.	**Viśwanātha**	(Sowgandhikāharaṇam)
15.	**Narasimha**	(Kādambari Kalyana Nāṭakam)
16.	**Rudradēva**	(Neetisāram)
17.	**Jāyapa**	(Nrutta Ratnāvaḷi)
18.	**Mallikārjuna Bhaṭṭu**	(Bhāskara Rāmāyaṇam)
19.	**Kumara Rudradēva**	(Bhāskara Rāmāyaṇam)
20.	**Ayyalārya**	(Bhāskara Rāmāyaṇam)
21.	**Gowrana**	(Hariśchandra Charitra)
22.	**Śarabhānka**	(Śarabhānka Linga Śatakam)
23.	**Krishnamāchāryulu**	(Simhagiri Vachanamulu)
24.	**Dōnayāmātya**	(Sasyānandam)
25.	**Kondanāmatya**	(Neeti Tarāvaḷi)
26.	**Viśvēśwarakavi chandra**	(Chamtkāra Chandrika)

27. **Errāpragaḍa** (Harivamśam)
28. **Anantāmātya** (Bhōjarājēyam)
29. **Vamanabhaṭṭabhaṇa** (Vemabhupala Charitram)
30. **Śrinadha** (Śringāranaiṣhadham etc.)

Poets and Authors with Surnames

In the following list it can be noticed that invariably the surnames happen to be the personal names of either their fathers or forefathers– a prominent predecessor.

1. **Bhāskaruni** Kētana (Kādambari).
2. **Gouranagāri** Bhyarava Kavi (Śriranga Mahatmyam)
3. **Bopparāju** Ganganna (Bhāgavatam – Sḥaṣhṭa Skandam)
4. **Dēchanagāri** Śankara Kavi (Harischandra Kāvyam)
5. **Kūchirāju** Erranna (Kokkokam)
6. **Vāśirāju** Rāmayya (Bruhannārdiyam)
7. **Siddhirāju** Timmarāju (Paramayōgi Vilāsam)
8. **Ayyalarāju** Rāmabhadra (Rāmābhyudayam)
9. **Madayyagāri** Mallana (Rajaśēkhra Charitra)
10. **Tippayyagāri** Bhānu Kavi (Panchatantram)
11. **Bycharāju** Venkaṭanātha (Panchatantram)
12. **Rāmarāju** Rangapparāju (Sambōpākhyānam)
13. **Jakkarāju** Venkaṭakavi (Kamoudakam)
14. **Gangarāju** Chowḍayya (Sāmudrika Śāstram)
15. **Bhāvana** Pemmana (Aniruddha Charitra)
16. **Jytarāju** Mummayya (Vishnu Katha Nidhanam)

17.	**Kanchirāju**	Sūrayya (Kannappa Charitra)
18.	**Dōmarāju**	Sōmayya (Bharta Śātram)
19.	**Pōtarāju**	Verayya (Tripura Vijayam)
20.	**Muddarāju**	Pedarāmanna (Rāghava Pāndaveya Vykhya)
21.	**Śripati**	Bhāskarakavi (Chitta Śatakam)
22.	**Bhadrakavi**	Lingakavi (Dēvānga Purāṇam)
23.	**Peddirājugāri**	Rāmarāju (Śeetamma Satakam)
24.	**Naranngāri**	Sūranna (Vanamāli Vilāsam)
25.	**Śridhara**	(Sridhara Chandam)
26.	**Bhyravakavi**	(Śriranga Mahatmyam)
27.	**Manumanchibhaṭṭu**	(Hayalakṣhaṇa Vilāsam)
28.	**Īswarapaṇi Bhaṭṭu**	(Paratatva Rahasyam)
29.	**Dēvarāraju Bhaṭṭu**	(Harischandra Kāvyam)
30.	**Rājanādha Kavi**	(Sāluvābhyudayam)
31.	**Śrikrishna dēvarāya**	(Āmuktamālyada)
32.	**Dhūrjaṭi**	(Śrikālahasti Mahatmyam)
33.	**Bhaṭṭumūrti alias Rāmarajābhūṣhaṇa**	(Narasabhupālēyam) (Vasuchaṛitra)
34.	**Tirumalāmba**	(Varādambika Pariṇayam)
35.	**Hari Bhaṭṭu**	(Matsya Purāṇam)
36.	**Viśvēśwarakavi**	(Viśvēśwara Chandam)
37.	**Īkāmranādha**	(Pratāpa Charitra)
38.	**Pōlamarāju**	(Parvata Puraṇam)
39.	**Pōtarāju**	(Bethāḷa Panca Vimśati)
40.	**Siddhana Pragaḍa**	(Śākuntalam)
41.	**Pedakemparāya**	(Ganga Gowri Vilāsam)
42.	**Bhāskarāchāryulu**	(Vāsavi Mahatyam)
43.	**Rājalingakavi**	(Kurma Purāṇam)

If verified at random the above category from the times of Nannayya, (11th century) the Ādikavi (First poet) in Telugu through circa 1650 A.D. the practice of adopting surnames gradually gained currency. It is perplexing as to why they who by their original creative temperament are given to write elaborately about their Vamśa (which is often equated with the surname), parents, gurūs (teachers) and patrons did not specifically state their surnames. The only tentative conclusion that can be drawn will be that sporting surnames was perhaps not very common and that popular until the advent of the late medieval period in the Andhra society. However, it must be pointed out here that in the recent past researchers have indeed affixed surnames to some of them such as Nannayya, Tikkanna and Erranna, hailed as the *Kavitrāya* (poet trimuvalet) of Telugu literature.

Place / Surname Suffixes

S. No.	*Grāma Namantya Rūpam*	*Village / Surname*	*Caste / Śākha / sect*
1	*2*	*3*	*4*
1	Ada	Tumarada	V.Vy
2	Anki	Jaladanki	A.N.
3	Angi	Meelangi	A.N
4	Antla	Gorantla	Ka
5	Akki	Nutakki	Br
6	Aka	Upamaka	A.D
7	Alam	Nandyala & Nandala	Kh
8	Api < Epi	Pothapi	Nan
9	Bada	Dowllthabada	MDh
10	Bakam	Puthabakam	
11	Bandi	Rallabandi	V.Vy
12	Bala	Rebala	Re
13	Charla	Macharla	A.N.
14	Cherla	Kancherla	PN
15	Chedu	Karamchedu	V.Vy
16	Chili	Yelamanchili	V.Vy
17	Chinta	Rentachinta	V.Vy
18	Dapi	Medapi	PN
19	Devi	Mopidevi	AN
20	Dindi	Kalidindi	A.N. & Kh
21	Dinne	Nemalladinne	P.N
22	Durthi	Kundurthi	A.N.
23	Durgam	Hosadurgam	Vy

(Contd...)

1	*2*	*3*	*4*
24	Gara	Angara	Ka
25	Gedda	Kamarajugadda	A.N.
26	Gama	Nandigama	A.N.
27	Gala	Munagala	V.Vy
28	Gali	Suragali	Cha
29	Gundam	Mokshagundam	Mu
30	Gudi	Choragudi	A.N.
31	Guptam	Devaguptam	A.N.
32	Gummi	Palagummi	A.N.
33	Gula	Madugula	V.Vy & TG
34	Gonda	Tarigonda	Nan
35	Gotla	Kaligotla	A.N.
36	Gallu	Edupugallu	A.N.
37	Giri	Mangalagiri	A.N.
38	Jarla	Nallajarla	PN
39	Jada	Ajjada	P.D
40	Jala	Yamijala	TG
41	Jella	Veiella – Vejendla	PN
42	Katla	Appikatla	A.N.
43	Karla	Kakarla	A.N. & Ka
44	Kani	Kakani	Ka & V.Vy & AN & PN
45	Kurthi	Cheemakurthi	AN & TG
46	Kera	Maddikera	PN
47	Kella	Tanikella	V.Vy
48	Kond	Kokkonda	A.N
49	Kondi	Akondi	A.D
50	Kolanu	Vavilakolanu	G.Vy
51	Kota	Dharanikota	V.Vy
52	Manchi	Kattamanchi	Re
53	Manda	Maremanda	MDh
54	Maddi	Janamaddi	Vy
55	Madaka	Jammalamadaka	V.Vy & A.N.
56	Maddali	Kurumaddali	A.N.
57	Malli	Nedurumalli	Re
58	Malla	Pemumalla	A.N.
59	Mani	Nemani, Vadlamani	P.D
60	Mala	Mallemala	Re
61	Manu	Kakumanu	A.N.
62	Meda	Gundimeda	A.N.
63	Mela	Tarimela	Re

(Contd...)

1	*2*	*3*	*4*
64	Mera	Bammera	A.N.
65	Mella	Garimella	Ve & AN
66	Milli	Adusumilli	V.Vy
67	Molu	Nidumolu	A.N.
68	Mudi	Kondamudi	A.N.
69	Parthi	Palaparthi	A.N.
70	Palli	Devulapalli	The & K.K & Ve
71	Paka	Tallapaka	Nan
72	Pala	Dhulipala	A.N.
73	Pudi	Mangipudi	Ve
74	Pirala	Aripirla	K.K. & MDh
75	Puram	Itchapurapu	
76	Pattanam	Tirumalabukkapatnam	Vy Kha
77	Patnam	Kalipatnam	A.N.
78	Nandi	Paranandi	Ka
79	Nagaram	Bhoganagara/ Bhagaasaagarapu	MDh
80	Nava	Unnava	A.N.
81	Nnada	Ponnada	VB
82	Nuthala	Ravinuthala	AN
83	Olu	Vangolu	L.N & A.N.
84	Palem	Ullipalem	A.N.
85	Pragada	Tallapragada	A.N.
86	Prolu	Gollaprolu	A.N.
87	Rangi	Pandrangi	A.N.
88	Rala	Duggirala	A.N. & V.Vy
89	Revu	Vadrevu	A.N.
90	Rella	Kurella	Br
91	Sala	Ghantasala	A.N. & V.Pujarlu
92	Thili	Attili	Vy
93	Ttisa	Pattisa (Pra)	V.Vy
94	Uru	Kandukuri	P.N & Vvy
95	Utla < Utla	Pillutla	V.Vy & Nam
96	Vamthsa	Avamthsa	Vy
97	Varam	Dharmavarm	A.N.
98	Vali	Kavali	A.N.
99	Valli	Khandavalli	A.N. & Ve. Vy & Sai
100	Vada	Bejawada	Re
101	Vay	Vathsavayi	Kh
102	Villi	Bikkavilli	V.Vy
103	Vennu	Kolavennu	A.N.

(Contd...)

1	*2*	*3*	*4*
104	Vella	Chiruvella	PN
105	Velugu	Nandivelugu	A.N.& Ādiśaivulu
106	Volu	Nidadavolu	A.N.

Surnames in the Inscriptions

S. No	*Surname*	*Inscription Period C.E.*	*Inscription*	*Source*
1	*2*	*3*	*4*	*5*
1.	Rekadi	668/9	E.M.VII,185-191	Budaraju Radhakrishna, Pracheenandra Sasanalu (CE1100) p.174, 467 here afterwards PAS.
2	Pandiri +	668/9	E.I.VII,185-191	" p.174, 378
3	Nitta +	7th Century	Vol.III, 1152&55	" p.210,361
4	Kottali +	725	-	" p.282
5	Pittaluri	742-98	-	" p.389
6	Purranulli	8th Century		" p.391
7	Kallegunna	825 approx	SII X, 639	" p.54&267
8	Pulveri	972		" p.90 & 393
9	Yalamkari	"		" p.90 & 454
10	Rakunna	"		" p.90 & 468
11	Lepara	"		" P.90 & 470
12	Chintanipu	1060	Domta plates of Ananthavarma Vijrahastha	Copper plate inscriptions of A.P. Govt. Museum, Vo.I, p.141, here afterward C.P of A.P
13	Kari	1060	Ananthavarma Chodaganga	"
14	Adapa	1061	C.P. No.8 of 1913/14	Bhavaraju Venkata Krishna Rao, History of the Eastern Chalukyas of Vengi, p.376
15	Kona	1082	SII IV No.1161	P.A.S. p.134 & 291
16	Janakota	1087	" No.1016	P.A.S. p.142 & 323

(Contd...)

1	*2*	*3*	*4*	*5*
17	Chagi	1088	N.I. III,1072	P.A.S. p.142 & 32
18	Nannuri	1089/89	"	P.A.S. p.143 & 356
19	Talarasi	1095	N.I.I IV, No1300	P.A.S. p.155 & 329
20	Badiya	1069	N.I.I. X, No1144	P.A.S. p.122 & 412
21	Chevali	1212	N.I.I. X, No.259	Āndhradēśa Charitra Bhūgōla Sarvasvamu, Vol.I,p.248
22	Kamepalli	1264	N.I.I. X, No.259	
23	Palli	1264	Alapadu grant of Ellana deva	C.P. of A.P. Vol. I, p.115
24	Vudayagiri	1264	"	"
25	Kondapalli	1264	"	"
26	Somayajula	1292	Inscription No.35	Corpus of Teleangana Inscriptions, Part IV, (Hyderabad ,1973) p.79
27	Kotela	1299	" 36	" " p.81
28	Attili	1315	S.I.I. X, No.510, 511	Andhradesa Charitra Bhūgōla Sarvasvamu, Vol.I, p.151,157
29	Muppireddi	"	"	"
30	Cherupilla	"	"	"
31	Anisetti	"	"	"
32	Vodala	"	"	"
33	Kamineni	"	"	"
34	Chenganeni	"	"	"
35	Adukula	"	"	"
36	Motupalli	"	"	"
37	Kotikalapudi	1415	S.I.I. IV, No.69	" p. 624
38	Kaluvakolini	1464	Recherlavari Sasanam	Corpus of Telangana Inscription, Part IV. p. 98-99
39	Madabhusi	"	"	"
40	Ambala	"	"	"
41	Mangoli	"	"	"
42	Varanasi	"	"	"
43	Ramadugu	"	"	"
44	Undrukendela	"	"	"

(Contd...)

1	*2*	*3*	*4*	*5*
45	Durbaka	1506	Srisailam Plates of Santhaya linga	Epigraphic Andhrika Vol., p.48
46	Thundipalli	"	"	"
47	Nethi	"	"	"
48	Thangaduri	"	"	"
49	Cheerala	"	"	"
50	Ayala Somayajulu	"	"	"

Personal and Surname Suffixes

Anna :

E.g.: Kāka; Timma; Pullūru; Mogili; Hanuma
Elder brother; Father
Normally occurs as the suffix of personal names.
Tamil : Annan; Malayalam : Annan; Tulu : Anne
D.E.D. 122

Appa = Elder sister :

Occurs as a suffix to both masculine and feminine personal names. At some instances 'Gāru' – honorific is found attached. Tamil : Appau, Appa; Malayalam : Appau; Kannada : Appa; Tulu : Appe
D.E.D. 154.

Arasu :

< Kannada Arasu < Sanskrit Rāja
Occurs in the context of personal names of those who are employed in the royal courts, such as Ministers.

Ākula :

Synonym of Kūra (curry). Which also takes the form of Gūra, Gūrla.
Eg : Koyya; Chēma; Tōṭa; Pala; Pulla; Batchchali;

Ambika :

An honorific suffix to the names of women of status (SII, X, 112, S1065) E.G. Aytambika

1. Mother; 2. Sensitive; compassionate; loving; a good woman; the harvest in the most productive season. Another name for Parvati (Maneka, p.17)

Aka < Akka : An honorific suffix to the female names
Eg : Pēraka (SII, IV, 676; S1073)
Per + Akka = Pērakka;
Per = Elderly; Akka = Elder sister

Appa : The elder sister
Eg : Vijayāditya Dēva Chakravarthi appa Śri Gōmathi Dēvi (SII, VI, 1257, S1177)
Gomati : 1. rich cattle; milky
2. a river personified as a goddess supported to be the incarnation of Kauili the sister of Visvamitra and the wife of sage Ṛcika (Śkanda Purana) (Maneka, p.140)

Amma : An affix to the masculine names
E.g.: Tātamma : Tātatamma

Amamgāru > Ammagāru : Respectable suffix the female names
E.g.: Rudrayadēva Ammamgāriki (SII, VI, 603, Date.).
Amma = mother; Gāru – commonly used as a respectable suffix to both masculine and feminine names.

Ayya : Father, commonly found as a suffix to masculine names. Also used as a suffix to the names of respectable class of women especially Kshatriya ladies in the Circars.

Ayyamgāru : A respectable suffix to a person.
Eg. : Śrimath Kāśisvara 'Śiva Ayyamgāru' (SII, X, 396, Ś1183)

Ayyaru : A suffix to smartha Brahmin masculine names (SII X, to 93, (600 – 700 AD)

Ayyavarlu : A respectable person.
Kondala Doḍḍāchāryula Ayyavārlu (NI, P.8, Ś1573)

Arasu : A title generally used at the end of the names of high royal (Kannada Arasa) dignitaries and ministers.
E.g.: Saluva timm**arasa**yya (SII, 702, S1440)

Amḍi : Suffix to masculine names of the community of smiths Viśvakarma kula sambhavunḍu nu ..... Nūkāmḍi (SII, IV, 673, S 1069)

Acāryuḍu : A temple priest
A conductor of religious ceremonies in a temple.
A teacher.
(SII, IV, 1129, S1100)
Śri Viśveśvara Gōḷakamyachārya
(SII, X, 395, S 1189)
Śri Nārāyaṇa nambi achāryunaku, (SII, VI, 82).

Acāryulu : A title assumed by artificers
Suffix to the names of artificers, blacksmiths, goldsmiths etc.
Eg. : (SII, V, 1214, S 12131)
(SII, X, 16, S 1033)

Anḍi : Suffix to women's names
Eg. : Sōmānḍi (SII X 13)

Ārādhyulu : A title bestowed on those Brahmins who are of the Lingayat caste. Saivite spiritual teacher; one who is adorable.
SII, VI, 118, S 1208

Ārya : An esteemed person; An honorific suffix to the names of Brahmins.
(SII, X 248, S 1131)

Āḷu : A suffix to masculine names, an individual; a grownup
Kanada: Āḷḷ person in general, a servant.
Tamil : Āḷ
Eg. : Rēvanakālu, (E.I. XXVII – 42 A) (600-700 AD)
Erikal Mutturājulla kunḍi – kaḷḷu
(E.g. : XXVII, 42-B, 600-700 AD)

Battuḍu : A suffix to masculine names of the five classes of artificers in general. E.g.: Lingabattuḍu (SII, IV, 951)

Battina / Battini / Battu / Battuni / Battula

A vikrui form of the Sanskrit Bhakta (devotee).

Often occurs among the carpenters, smiths, potters as an honor fix.

Brahma : A suffix of the title added to the names of Brahmins (E.g.: VI, 10, S 1024)

Bhaktuḍu : Suffix to the names of Brahmins

E.g. : Basuvābhaktud?u (SII, IV, 102 Ś 1440)

Bhaṭṭopādhyayulu :

(Bhaṭṭa+upādhāya) Suffix to the names of learned Brahmin teacher; title of Brahmin teacher.

Bhattu / Bhattaru / Bhatla / Bhotla

Bhaṭṭu : A Brahmin who professes a knowledge of Vedas or belongs to a family in which they have been taught. A title of respect or distinction used at the end of proper names.
Eg. : Vaggiya Ṣhadangabhaṭlu. (SII X, 6, S 965)
Kommana-bhaṭlu, Datta-bhaṭlu (SII X, 89, S 1054)
A Brahmin who professes the knowledge of Vedas. A title of respect or distinction used with Brahmin names.
E.g. : Nanniya-bhaṭṭu, (Eg. : IV, 43, S 975)
Bhāskara bhaṭṭa (Eg. V, 10, S 10243).

May be a stumped form of Bhattaraka, a learned man, proficient in Vedic knowledge.

E.g., Adhytra -1, Annadana, Naga, Simham, Hemadri.

Normally occurs among the Vaidiki Brahmins.

Bhatta, masculine nominative singular; A learned man < Skt.Bhatta; I.A.12, 91-95, 945 -70 AD, Potana-bhatta.

Bhattu (mas, nom. sg.sg.)

SII 5.1118 A.D. 1083. Madhava-bhattu; occurring as an appellation to masculine names.

Bhatla (masculine general oblique plural) Janniya bhatla, SII 10.8; AD 1061.

In Telugu this surname suffix appears as Bhatla, its variant. Bhotla in the sense of the family of such and such a learned man (bhatta) or of a particular place. Most of the Andhra Brahmin sub-sects share this surname suffix.

Kuppam (KN); Kuchi (AD; VV); Kesava (V); Kesa (AN); Kondu (TG)

Konam (KK); Gangadhara (KN); Ganapati (KN); Gadu (TG); Gopala (Vel)

Chamdru (P & N); Chintamani (MDh); Chenu (VV; TG; KK); Jakkana (KK)

Jaggu (VV); Jannamu (TG); Jonnabha (VV; TG); Tippa (VV); Tripurari (TG)

Pandi (VV); Divakara (V); Devam (PSN); Yellam (VN; TG)

Bhattaru with the core element Dingaru (which itself a surname) with the same meaning as bhattu is found among the Vykhasanas.

Bhōjaka - Bōkta temples to a community called as bōyas.

Botu / Botula / Boni / Boyani / Boyina / Bola / Bōya / Bōyani :

Different forms of 'Boya' – a tribe.

< Pakrit Bhoyaga < Sanskrit Bhojaka, Bhokta.

E.g.: Vanigraboyadve (EI. VIII, 238, 67340)

Somayajula Vellelkkibol, Marlabol (EI. VIII, 1)

In the medieval period 'Boyas' are often associated with the temples for supplying ghee for the maintenance of the perpetual lamps to the deities, by maintaining the Cows, Buffaloes, Sheep etc., donate to the temple.

Bhupati

Lord of the earth. King
Normally occurs among the Kshatriya or Raju community.
There is also a surname. Bhupati-raju.

Cheṭṭi / Seṭṭi

From Sanskrit Śrēṣhti meaning the best.

Dāsu

A variant of the classical form Dāsari and is traceable to Sanskrit Dāsah, meaning slave, servant. Often assured by the Vaishnava mendicants.

Dēva

God; overlord. Employed in respect of the deity or the temporal king who is traditionally considered as the shadow of God on earth. 'Na Viṣnu Prudhvipati '

Dēvara, of Dēva

A respectable appellation in Kannada

Dēvi : A honorific suffix to the married women's name. A respectable title applied to a lady of the first rank.
Eg. : Proliraju penḍlamu mudigonḍamadēvi (SII X, 13).
< Sanskrit Dēvi
E.g., Akkala – Ganga – Gowri -
Respectful suffix to the female names.

Dēvula

Plural form of Dēva.
E.g. : Dharaṇi Dēvula

Dēvula as plural form of Dēva is contrary to lakshana. Correctly it should be Dharaṇi Devuḍu meaning a God on earth.

Dāsi : A suffix to the names of Brahmin in the sense of a servant a devotee to God.
E.g. : Śrikrshna Dāsi, Tiruvengaḷdāsi
(SII, V. 1233)

Ēri : A suffix to masculine names
E.g.: Divakara Peddēri; SII X, 9 S 983

Gavi – seṭṭi The title assumed by the vaisya caste.

E.g.: Vaisya vamsulu ... (SII, X, 82, Ś 1046)

Gupta : The suffix to the masculine names of vaisya (the third caste)
E.g.: Kannaya – Gupta
Kanna + ayya; Kanna < Kanha : Krishna
SII, VI, 651.

Gāri

From the term 'Gāru' meaning respectful. Normally as a suffix to personal name.

Gōni / Gouni

From Gowda Sanskrit Grama kūṭa. In Telugu inscription occurs as Gāmunḍa.

Inṭi : meaning House, dwelling place.
E.g: Koṭṭa (New); Chinna (small); Naddimi (middle)
Pāta (old); Mūla (corner); Mēraka (upland)

Jiyya : A priest of the Śaiva temple; suffix to their names.
E.g.: Pōta Jiyya;
(SII V, 589; S 1269)
Konḍa; Komma; Gōpa; Brahma; Malla; Yella

Jōsyula

< Sanskrit Joutiṣhka; popular in the north India as Jōṣhi one who

predicts the future of a person either by studying the palm or the birth chart.

Jyosyulu : Astrologer
Sanskrit = E.g.: Vāśishṭa Gōtram Goutama Jyosyulu
Jyotiṣhika (SII, IV, 1355)

Kāyala

Plural of Kāya, meaning a kind of vegetable.
E.g. : Kandi, Kobbari, Cinta etc.

Kūcci/Kūci/Kūcei/Guaci

Literally means a child, particularly mere so in the sense of a dear child; endeared.

E.g.: Kēśava Kūci son of Kāmadēva peddi SII X, No. 281., Ś 1156

Kūti

Connected with Kūḍu meaning food; rice.
Compare Kannada Kulu; Tulu kulu, Malayalam kul. D.E.D 1592.

Kūra

Leaves of a tree or plant used to prepare a side dish

Tamil Kari from which the English curry arrived.

Makhi : A sacrificer; a title at the end of the Brahmin names.
E.g. : Śri Singa-yajva perumāḍi – makhi. (EI V.9 (S 1352)

Misruḍu : An honorary suffix to the names of scholars.
Śri Dēvaraja-misrōyam (NI (P.I. Ś 1312).

Mamci / Manci

Mamci : Suffix to the proper names of Brahmins.
E.g.: Kāśyapa gōthrulyna Āravelli Māra pōta-mamci-gāru.

Manci : E.g., Kattamanci

Probably derived from Kannada 'Benchi' meaning a place where water gets accumulated naturally. Also occurs as a personal name is inscriptions.

E.g. Arivelli Marapota Manccigaru

Mantri

See preggada

Malla

Occurs as a suffix to the male names.

< Prakrit Malla a Sanskrit Madva

Generally means a wrestler.

Often occurs among the Kamma and Komati (merchant) communities.

Na / Ni / Nāyani / Needi / Needu / Nēṭi

A stumped form of nēni which in turn derived from Nāyani meaning a leader.

E.g. : Akkina – Muppa –

Mostly found in the Kamma community and partially among the Brahmins.

Nādha / nādham / nādhuni

< Sanskrit Nādha

E.g. : Gōpinādhuni, Viśwanātha, Jagannādha

Ojhalu : Teacher; an honorific suffix the Brahmin names.

Oju/Oju/Vajjula

<Prakrit ojju – upajhaya < Sanskrit Upādhāya

Besides the Brahmins, some of the artisan communities (Pañcaṇamvāru) assured the suffix 'oju'. Rarely occurs in the name suffix of the Barbars. Kondoju supposed to have excelled in the court of Krishnadēvarāya of Vijayanagar dynasty.

Pamdituḍu : A learned person. The suffix to the names of Brahmins
Gokina pamḍitula koḍuku permāḍi pamḍitulu
(SII, VI, 183, S1073)

Panḍya < Panḍa:

Temple Brahmin priest. Suffix to the names of such Brahmins.
Kālabōla Panḍya (SII, IV, 1120, S 1076)

Pāmgu : A beautiful woman. Suffix to the names of dancing girls.
(SII X, 171, Ś 1092)

Peddi : A respectable person. A honorific suffix to the Brahmin names
E.g.: Nāgadēvapeddi (SII X, 281, S 1156)

Pōti : A suffix to feminine names
E.g.: Nāgapōti (I.A. VIII, 77-78)

Pōri : A young woman. A suffix to female names
(Inscriptional Glọssary, p. 202)

Pregada / Preggeda :

A Brahmin, an officer, a minister
E.g. : Era-preggada (SII X, 73, S 1037)
Preggeḍa - SII XI, 119 S 1069
Pergeḍa - SII IX, 3

Pātra / Pātruni :

One who is worthy as a minister; A kind of office. Particularly under the Sūryavamsi Gajapathis of Orissa.
E.g.: Kamsa nārāyaṇa biruda pātra Rāmajiyana (SII VI, 734, Ś1301).
Balabhadhra Pātruni; Ganṭi Mahāpātruni

Panḍa

< Sanskrit panḍa meaning knowledgeable, Panḍita

Occurs among the Brahmin Priests. E.G Puri Panḍa. Here 'Puri' (Oriya) stands for city or town.

Purāṇa Panḍa meaning one who is proficient in reading or interpreting the puranas

Pati

< Sanskrit Pati meaning the overlord
E.g.: Sabhāpati, leader of the Assembly.
Madhavapati, leader among the Madhava faith.

Rāju / Rājula

Literally meaning king.

Occurs as a suffix associated with personal names that are become surnames. Besides the Kshtriyas most of the Niyogi Brahmin sport after it is a suffix to their surnames.

E.g.: Maitrāvaruṇa Gōtrulu, Āpasthambha sūtrulu Dūbaguṇṭa Sūrama rāju (NI, Kandukur, 16, S 1352).
Now popular among the Niyōgi Brahmana sub sect.
Also found among the Velama and Bhaṭrāju communities.

Rāyani

Sanskrit Rajat. Raya in Kannada means Rāja

Rao / Rāvu : It is a title frequently occurring after 13th century A.D.
<Pakrit : Ravo < Sanskrit Rāju
More often among the Velama community.

Riṣhi : Eg. : Kāma
A hyper standardization of Arasu

Śarma : A suffix to the Vaishnava Brahmin names
E.g.: Vaishnava brahmanana .... Kulasēkhara Krs?na - Śarma etc., (SII, V, 1231, S 1077)

Śāstry < Śāstrin:

A learned man; he who has mastered Śāstras.
E.g.: Chiṭṭamūri Timmanabhaṭṭu Śāstrulavāriki (EI, XXI, 42 S 1257).

Śiṣtuḍu : An eminent and distinguished person. A righteous or honest person. A suffix to the Brahmin names.
E.g.: Kamdūri Singaya – śiṣta; Rāmaya – śiṣta etc., (EI, XI, 3, Ś 1334)

Śrauti : A Brahmin who observes Vedic rites. A title affixed to the Brahmin names.
E.g.: Vallbhāchārya – Śrauti. (EI, V, 9; Ś 1352)

Ṣaḍamgavi : The person who is proficient in six Vedangas i.e. (1) Science of proper articulation (2) Prosody (3) Grammar (4) Etymological explanation of different words (5) Astronomy and (6) Rituals or Ceremonies.
E.g.: Kommiya – S?ad?amgavi (SII, X, 9, Ś 483)
Appaya – S?ad?mgavi etc., (EI, V, 10, Ś 1024)

Sahasra : An honorific suffix to the names of Brahmins.
E.g.: Bharta – sahasra, Ayypana – sahasra, Cheluva–sahasra
(EI, V, 10, Ś 1024)

Sumati : A standing designation of the followers of Dwita school.
(Śrikurman Inscription of Narahari Ti?rtha, EI, VI, 25, S 1203)

Seṭṭi (Śreṣhṭi) :

The title assumed by the oil monger caste.
E.g.: Bolli-seṭṭi ... Telikavēvuru (SII X, 221)

Sōmayāji : A title assumed by a Brahmin who has celebrated a sacrifice.
E.g.: Dāmōdarabhaṭṭa – sōmayāji etc.
(EI V, 10, Ś 1024)

Sanskrit: Upādhāya (EI XXX 111; 52, Ś 1380)

Siri : An honorific term used as prefix and suffix to the names of distinguished persons.
E.g.: Siri – camtamula ..... Mahā-Kamdasiri (EI, XX-1)
<Sanskrit = Rāju

Sāni : Chief of the cavalry and elephant horses.
<Prakrit : Sāhiṇi> In sanskritic tradition the wife of the king is addressed as Swamini, which percolated into Telugu as Sāni.
E.g.: Eurukala-sāni; Mudusalisāni; Reddysāni.
Apart from the Kāpus and Reddys it is also found as a surname suffix among the Brahmins.
E.g.: Allasāni Peddana, a Nandavarika Gōtrin, son of Gādayamatya, the Andhra Kavita Pitāmaha (Grand father of Telugu poetry).

Swami : A learned Brahmin; a righteous Brahmin.

Trivēdibhaṭṭa : A suffix to the Brahmin names denoting proficiency in the three Vedas.
E.g.: Datta Trivedibhaṭṭah : (Eg.SII V.10, S 1024)

Vēdi : A learned man. A suffix to the names of a Brahmana.

E.g.: Guntūri Nāgayadvēdi (EI, V, 9 S 1352)

Velamaḍu : A cultivator; suffix to the names of cultivator caste. (Tamil : Vettan) E.g.: Śrikaraṇam pratāpaganga velamḍuna chinnama - nāyaka (SII, V, 1054, S 1056)

Kavi

Poetry is an important branch of literature. Poets are considered as the unacknowledged legislators of the world – "Nā rishi Kurutē Kāvyam." Monier-Willams (SED, P.264, column 2) enumerates several meaning of the word Kavi "gifted with insight, intelligent, knowing, enlightened, wise, sensible, prudent, skilful, cunning, sage, seer, prophet, a singular, bard, poet (but in this sense without any technical application in the Vedas)."

In Telugu 'Kavi' generally means a poet and there were families who acquired this literary title as a suffix to their surnames. From about 18th through 20th centuries there were occasional acrimonious debates whatever poetry is the exclusive possession of one or the other sub-sects among the Andhra Brahmins. The following examples disapprove any such assumptions. These adjectives are also indicative of the variety, caliber, status, expertise, specialization and multifaceted facets of the poets.

Kavi; poet (N); Kavi –konḍala (PS); Aghōra = Not terrific (AN);
Kadha = Story (AN); Kavita = Poetry (Vel); Kavi – dhāṭi = forceful poet (V)
Kavi – mukku = Nose. There is an interesting anecdote that Nandi Timmana wrote a beautiful poem on 'Mukku' (nose) and from then onwards was known as Mukku Timmana (Early 16th centuty).
Kavi-rāṇamu = Royal poet; Kavi-rāyani = Royal poet; Kavi-vege = of Kavi (MDh)
Kavula = of poets (PS); Ghōra – Kavi = terrific poet (AN)
Chitra – Kavi = wonderful poet, and it is a special poetry juglary. (PSN; AN; VY)
Tāra-Kavi = Star among the poets (AN); Diṭṭa – Kavi = Strong poet
Nimaṣha - Kavi (AN) = Capable of composing poems in a very short span of time,
Nūtana – Kavi = New poet (AN); Pulla – Kavi = Shiny poet (KK)
Proudha – Kavi = Matured poet (AN)
Bandha – Kavi = Specialist in the 'Bandha' type of poetry (VV)
Bala – Kavi = Child-poet (AN); Bhaya – Kavi = Fearful (to the opponents) poet (AN)
Madhura – Kavi = Sweet poet (AD); Vārdha – Kavi = Old poet (NN)

Surnames like Kanchu (Brass metal) Ghanṭam (Stylus) (PS), Pyḍi (Golden) Ghanṭala (Stylus) (AN) also exemplify the poetic accomplishments of those particular families.

Pantula

Plural of Marathi pant < Skt. Pandita. A honorific of high ranking officials among the Brahmins.

E.g.: Core parts of the surname with the suffix Pantula.

Pantula (AN; AD; VV). It is individually a surname without any suffix or prefix.

Akka (AD) Pe.N; Ananta (AD) Pe.N; Anna (AD) Pe.N; Kēśava (V) Pe.N

Gunḍa (PSN) Pl.N. Comp.; Gunḍāla (GV); Gunḍa-Vajhula (TG)

Chitti (AD) Pe.N; Parasurāma (AN) Pe.N; Madhunā (AD) Pl.N; Rāmā (VN) Pe.N

Sālwa (MDh) 'Vamsa' Comp. Sālwa (AN).

Peddia

A variant of Pedda–an adjective, meaning Big, great, elder.

E.g.: Core components with the suffix Pedda or Peddi.

Akki (VV) Pl.N; Ani (PS; KN) Pl.N.; Anni (KN) Pe.N; Ellē (VV) Pl.N

Kari (TG) Pl.N. Colour Karri = black ; Gowri (TG) Pe.N ; Chiṭṭi (AD) Pe.N

Chili () Pl.N; Peravana (PSN) Pl.N; Sūri (Vel).

Pragaḍa

(Meaning a Minister, Chief)

Its earlier forms are Peggada (Masculine nominative singular).

Vajjiya Peggaḍa

Peggaḍalu (Masculine nominative plural) ETI, p.200, 8th century.

Peggaḍlu (Masculine nominative) ETI, p.122,1072 AD

Peggeḍal (Masculine nominative) SII, 10,623, 9th /10th century AD.

"The word seems to be a loan from Kannada where-rg-forms are common. The Te. development is pregada instead of pergada. But this normal form is not attested in the material. Pregada occurs only from 1156 AD in the inscriptional dialect of Guntur (See SII 10, 144; 1156 and 10.453; 1282. Cf.Ka. Peggaḍa (Old and inscription), Peggaḍe and heggaḍe (Modern). Some times occurs as a family name." (ETI, P.394).

Except for few exceptions such as Pragaḍa (VN); Rāyani (N) chenna (LN; PSN) and few others which they share with other sub-sects such as Īśvara (GV); ella (GV) all the surnames with the suffix Pragaḍa are owned by the Aruvēla Niyōgi sub-sect of Andhra Brahmans and almost all of them have personal name or place names as the core element as exemplified below.

Akkana; Akkina; Ananta; Anna; Erra; Kanaka; Kāśi; Challa; Chitta; Talla
Durga; Dharaṇi; Pēra; Pēre; Pōta; Bayyana; Bolla; Bōla; Malla; Rāma
Rebba; Lakka ; Vissa ; Ventra; Sarva; Siri ; Hari

Rāju

rāju (masculine nominative singular) King (<Skt. rājan).

EI,27.221-25, 576-600AD
SII,10,606, 600-625AD.AD
EI,27.231-234, 625-650 AD

Normally assumed by the Kshatriya community as a suffix to their personal and family names.

Except in a very few cases as specifically indicated in the below list this surname suffix is also invariably associated with the Aruvēla Niyōgi sub-sect among the Andhra Brahmins. Almost all of them are either personal or place names.

Abba; Achchi; Ādi; Agastya; Agga; Akka; Akki; Allam (AD); Allama (AD)

Amma; Ammi; Amṭa; Ananta; Anisinga; Anka ; Annam; Annama; Appa

Appala (Ps N); Atam; Aytam; Ayyala; Bāchi; Badri; Bakka; Basava ; Bhadri

Bhāskara; Bhaṭ; Bhāva; Bhīma; Bhōga; Bhūpati; Bijji; Biruda; Bomma

Buddha; Buddhi; Byrrāju; Challam; Chamda; Chandra; Chaṭrāju;

Chemma Chenama; Chikka; Dāma; Dāśi (GV); Dēchi; Dēśa; Dēvaḷa; Dhanyam

Donḍam; Dontam; Donti; Drōṇam (Also MDh., GV); Durga – Peḍḍi; Durga (N)

Durgi; Echi (GV); Ellam (also PD); Gādi; Ganga; Gannam; Gavara; Geeta; Ghaṭ

Giri (GV); Gōka; Gōpa (Also PSN); Gōvinda (Also PSN); Gunḍrāju; Jagga; Kāci

Kāḷam; Kāma (Also PSN); Kanaka; Kanchi; Kanṭham; Kasava; Kāśi; Katama;

Keerti; Kēśa; Kēśava; Kēśi; Kēta; Komarrāju (LN); Kōnam; Koppa;

Kunapa (GV); Lachchi; Lakka; Lakkam; Lēkha; Linga; Māchi; Maddi Mādi; M

ādi; Mal; Mallapa; Manchi; Māram; Mudda (Also NN); Mūrti Mutta;

Nāga; Nandi; Nārapa; Neelam; Nimma; Nūka; Pabba; Pāma; Pāpa

Peddi (Also PSN); Pemma; Pēram; Pērrāju; Pinnam; Pōchhi; Pōlam; Pōta

Praha; Pregaḍa; Punnam; Pūrēsanga; Rāchi; Rāma (Also GV); Ranga (GV)

Rudra; Sāgi; Sāmba; Sambhi; Sannidhi (Also Vel.P); Saṭṭi; Seeti; Siddhi

Singa; Singa; Śiva; Sīta; Smi; Sōma; Śrigiri; Sūrapa; Tallam; Tallapa; Tammi

Tāṭi; Timma (Also GV; PSN); Tirumala; Tumma; Vāma; Vandi;

Vāśi (Badagala Kannada); Vēda; Vēgi;Vēma; Vēna; Vissam (Also GV)

Vīram; Yāga; Yati (SV)

Vajhula

Plural of ojja : Teacher, preceptor; Pkt. Upajjhao <Skt. Upādhyāyah.

Often found as a suffix to the surnames of various Brahmin sub-sects. Almost all of principal parts are personal names and occasionally place names. It indicates that certain individuals earned renown as teachers in a family which from then onwards came to be referred with their name constituting the core part of the family name with the suffix Vajhula. In some cases the principal part happened to be a place name indicating that a particular family which originally lived at that place were recognized as teachers.

E.g.:

Abba (AD) Pe.N; Aila (AD; TG) Pe.N; Ananta (AD) Pe.N; Anna (VV; TG) Pe.N

Bhịma (Vel) Pe.N; Bhyrava (VV) Pe.N; Būra (TG) Pl.N; Challa (VV) Pl.N

Chenna (TG) Pe.N; Chiṭṭa (VV; KNV) Pl.N; Dāma (VV) Pe.N; Drōṇa (VV) Pe.N after Pl.N; Durga (KN) Pe.N; Ella (VV) Pe.N; Gādha (KVV) meaning ancient story

Ganga (TG) Pe.N after the river of that name; Gōma (KN) Pe.N; Gōpa (KN) Pe.N

Gōvinda (VV; PSN) Pe.N; Gowra (AN; VV) Pe.N; Gunḍa (TG) Pl.N

Hanumanta (PSN) Pe.N; Jōga (KK) Pe.N; Kārāḍa (AD) Pl.N

Kāśa (KN) Pe.N after Pl.N; Kāśa (VY; TG) Pl.N;

Kāśi (PD;TG;KN) Pe.N after Pl.N; Kṛṣṇa (TG) Pe.N after the river of that name

Lakka (Vel) Pe.N; Māchana (VV) Pe.N; Malla (KN) Pe.N; Mancha (VV) Pl.N

Māra (TG) Pe.N; Nāga (PSN) Pe.N; Nyāsa (TG) Pl.N; Pāla (Vel) Pl.N

Palla (PSN) Pl.N; Pāra (VV) Pe.N; Raghunādha (VN) Pe.N; Raṃa (VV) Pe.N

Ranga (VV) Pe.N ; Rudra (TG) Pe.N ; Singa (KN) Pe.N ; Śishṭa (PD) Title

Sōm (VN) Pe.N; Sōma (VN) Pe.N; Sūra (VN) Pe.N; Talla (VV) Pl.N

Timma ()Pe.N; Tippa (TG; VV) Pe.N; Vallabha (KN) Pe.N; Vishnu (TG) Pe.N

Vissa (KN) Pe.N; Yajña (PSN) signifying a Vedic rite.;

Personal names of the prominent members of a family becoming surnames

Following are some of the examples.

A grand son of *Poṭlapāṭi* Thimmarāju was Ramārāju Rangapparāju (Author of Sāmbōpākhyānam). This change in the surname is due to the fact they belonged to the reign of Rāmarāju, son of Āaraveeṭi Bukkarāju (SAS, IX, p.8 and 42).

Anagham (17th century AD, received the title *Abhinava Danḍi* from Velugōṭi Yāchama Nāyaka. Anagha Amātya obtained for the family several villages and hence he is name assumed importance as the surname of that family (Arudra, X, p.254)

Parasurāma – Pantula Lingamūrthy (18th Century AD) was the author of several works. However, his ancestors were not Telugu people. Some of the Maratha families migrated to the Āndhra dēśa due to some political reasons and settled over here. As one such family belonged to Parasurāma – Pant and hence the surname (SAS XII, p.19).

Ayyalarāju Rāmabhadra was the author of Ramābhyudayam. Regarding his surname there are two opinions: (1) Ayyalarāju (2) Rāya Kavi, whereas the first one denotes a personal name, the second one implies his position as a poet in royal (Rāya - Rāja) Kavi. Both the names could be justified as the originator of the family Ayyalarāju flourished in the court of the Rāyas of Vijayanagar and obtained the tile Rāya kavi (court poet of the Rāya) (ABS Vol. I, p.478)

The first prominent member of the Dōmakonḍa Zamindari in the Medak district, belonging to the Pākanṭi Reddy community, was Kāminēdu and as such the family assumed the surname Kāminēni. Here it must be noted that 'nēni' is a variant of 'nēdu' which generally means a ruler (ASS, p.177). Also, the core part as a personal name "Kāmi" is the colloquial form of "Kāma" – cupid.

Similarly the rulers of 'Chunḍi' in the Nellore district had the same surname as their originator was Kāmi Nayaka (*ibid.* p 538).

Kopparāju Narasimha Kavi (1820-1870) declared in the preface of his Trikūtachala Mahātyam that his family name owes to one of his ancestors by the name Kopparāju (*ibid.* p 334).

Krishna chandra dēva of Jeypore (Odissa), invited one eminent scholar by the name 'Ādi Bhaṭṭa' into his domain wherein was situated the village 'Ajjada' and from then onwards the family is known as the 'Adibhaṭla' (ABS Vol. 3, p.102). Today, it exists as a place name in the Ranga Reddy district.

The well known Harikadha exponent Nārayaṇadās (1864-1945) wished to distinguish his name from the rest of the Āadibhaṭlas and added the prefix Ajjāḍa (a place name) to Ādibhaṭla (*ibid.* p.103). However, as he had no male progeny the surname Ajjāḍa Ādibhaṭla has not gained currency.

Around 1580 A.D. one Sarangu Thammayya functioned as the accountant of the Gōlkoṅḍa (present Hyderabad). The family claimed descent from the semi-mythical character Sārangadhara (SAS Vol.8, p.158). In the latter half of 16th century there existed one Krishna Mantri. The family got the surname Mummaḍi rāju after the name of his grand father (ibid. p.232). It could be generally observed that most of the surnames of the Andhra Brahmin Niyōgi sub-sect has a tendency to end with the suffix Rāju and Pragaḍa. However, Rāju is usually found associated with the surnames of the Andhra Kshthriya communities. For e.g.: Anga Rāju, Amala Rāju, Bala Rāju, Buddha Rāju, Chiṭrāju (Chiṭṭi + rāju), Bhupathi Rāju, Gaṇapathi Rāju, Gade Rāju, Gōka Rāju, Thirumala Rāju, Pinnama Rāju, Tamma Rāju, Rudra Rāju etc.,

Surnames after Professions, Talents, and Titles

Archakam, though in particular this surname is applied in the case of the priests engaged in the worship of Lord Venkateswara at Tirupati the meaning of the term implies ritualistic worship (Archakam) in any temple. It can be surmised as adopted by such families pursuing that particular profession (ABS Vol. I, p.532).

Mention is made up of persons like *Rāyasam* Rāma Chandraiah, *Bokkasam* Bhāskaraiah and *Avasaram* Venkataiah in connection with the preparation for the carnation ceremony of the celebrated South Indian King Śri Krishna dēvarāya (1509-1529). Whereas *Rāyasam* is an office connected with the drafting or writing of the Royal documents (Rāyasam derived from "*Rāyuṭa*" meaning writing). *Bokkasam* (treasury) was a revenue official. Similar Royal functionary is the '*Avasaram*' (need) who is called in to discharge any assigned function demanded by the need based situation. In short, it is a family name denoting a profession (*ibid.* Vol.II, p.38).

Nēbadi Krishna Mantri was one of the courtiers of Kuli Kutubshah (1580-1612 AD.) of Hyderabad. One of his ancestors occupied the posts of 'Nēbati' in the court of Sultan Shah of Beḍada Koṭa. In fact '*Nēbati*' is derivative of "*Nēyabat*" which means an ambassador or resident representative (IAS, Vol. IX, p.251).

Patchakarpūrapu (a variety of Camphor)

Thimmarāju, grand father of Thiruvengaḷa Rāju was the author of 'Chokkanādha Charitara' (16th century). The former has honoured with "Patcha Karpūramu" by Proudha Dēvarāya of Vijayanagar who is impressed by his literary accomplishments. From them onwards it became the surname of that particular family (*ibid.* p.33).

Krishnarāya Bhūṣhana

One Ramarāju, adorned the court of Śrikrishna dēvarāya as an outstanding poet and thus has attained fame as an ornament in his court worthy of praise of Śrikrishna dēvarāya. His progeny adopted that title as a family name (*ibid.*, Vol. X, p.24).

Kaṭṭa

It is commonly believed in ancient times Kari Kala Chola caused a barriage across the river 'Kāvēri'. A family that was engaged in the gigantic construction work has assumed the name 'Kaṭṭa'. Anakaṭṭa is an imperfect Telugu translation for a barriage. (ibid Vol.X, p.185). Baḍagalanaṭi Narasayya (c.1740 AD) author of 'Nimbaja Mahatyam' at the instance of one Thokkaḍam Mannaru Jeṭṭi. A such Thokkaḍam it became their family name (*ibid.* Vol. XII, p.308).

Vāsireddy Sadāsiviah was the ancestor of the zamindars of Amarāvati and Mukthyāla. He accomplished several heroic deeds in the court (service) of Anavēma Reddy and obtained a title 'Vāsi' (outstanding) Reddy. His title has become their family name (ASS, p.39 and 331).

Vyricherla and Sathrucherla

In the Kalingandhra region Kurpam and Mērangi were two important zamindāris. The above are their respective surnames. These are indicative of their prowess against their enemies, resulting in the capture of the latter. The correct form should be Sathru (enemy) Çharla (imprisonment) and Vyri = enemy and Charla = imprisonment (*ibid.* p.352).

Change of Surnames

As the names of the places some times do change due to several reasons, old surnames are also discarded and new surnames were assumed. The following examples demonstrate this phenomena.

Tamarapalli – Pyḍi ghanṭam

Tamarapalli Thimmaiah (c.1575 AD) translated in to Telugu some Sesha Dharmas of Hari Vamsa. One of his ancestor Abba Mantri was honoured by 'Dēvarāya' I (1423 -50 AD) of Vijayanagara with a golden stylus impressed by his poetic talent. From then onwards it became the surname of his progeny (SAS Vol. IX, p.238).

Pydipati – Yēnugu

The original surname of 'gurava' Mantri who was in the court of Chaturbhuja Timma Jagapati (1555-1607AD), the Zamindar of Peddāpuram, was 'Pyḍipāṭi' (a place name). However, around 15th - 16th centuries, his ancestor 'Jalapāla Mantri' obtained an elephant (*Yēnugu*) from the Gajapati's of Kalinga as a reward (*ibid.* Vol.X, p.233 & A.S.S, p.273) There is also an opinion that the reward was in fact made over by the rulers of Peddāpuram themselves (ABS Vol.III, p.1).

Veṇukudurupalli – Diṭṭakavi

Venkataiah was the maternal grand father Yēnugu Pedda Lakshmaṇa Kavi. The former acquired the little Diṭṭakavi (strong in poetry). His son Venukudurupalli Viswanadham named his son after his father. He has as well inherited the title of his grandfather as his surname (*ibid.* SAS, Vol.X, p. 225).

Atmachintala – Chennamarāju

In the family of Atmachintala, (a Place Name) one Chennamarāju (Personal Name) became famous as a minister and from then onwards his personal name became the surname of his descendents. (*ibid.* p.239)

Tarigoppula - Rāyasam – Bōravelli

Tarigoppula Mallanna, (1580-1614 AD) author of Chandrabhānu Charitra was a writer (Rāyasam) in the court of Venkatapathiraya II and his official designation subsequently became their family name. However, since Mallanna's grand sons and great grand sons settled at Bōravilli near Gadwal, that place name has become their family name. (*ibid.* Vol. XI, p. 264)

Dēsirāju –Veeṇa – Nellūri

Venkatāchalam, the youngest son of Dēsirāju Konḍanna served as a commander in the court of Peddavenkatapatirāya. (1630-1642 AD) of Karnataka. Not only he but also his sons Venganna and Ranganna excelled in playing the stringed musical instrument – Veeṇa. And as such their family surname changed into 'Veeṇa' However, Ranganna's eldest son Venkatapathi migrated from Nellore to the court of Abul Hassan of Golkonda. From his time the surname undervent another change as Nellore (ibid. Vol.III, p.147)

Prabhandhānkam – Ratnākaram

The suname of Bhaṭṭu Mūrthy author of Vasucharitra was *Prabhandaankam*. In his line one Gopala Rāju son of Krishnamarāju excelled as a poet and obtained the title 'Ratnākara'. And it has replaced

'Prabhandānkam' which was the original surname (*ibid.* p.188-189 and Vol. p.229).

Pillalamarri – Penumaḷḷa

If any poet dared to declare that goddess Saraswathi is his queen (Vāṇi Nā Rāṇi) that was pillalamarri – Pinavirayya. His younger son Malleswara obtained the village Penumaḷḷa in the 16th century from the Gajapathis of Kalinga. As such the family assumed the surname Penumaḷḷa. (ibid. Vol. XII, p. 258).

Mōdukūri – Grandhavāraṇam – Aḍidam

In the earlier centuries, some of the members of Mōdukūri (a Place name) family used to visit the royal courts with their literary works (*Grandhams*) placed on the back of an elephant (*Varaṇam*). Because of that practice the family name got changed into Grandhavāraṇam. One Nịḷadri in that line excelled not only in poetry but also in warfare. Impressed by his talents one of the Kalinga rulers presented him an 'Aḍidam' (sword). From them it has become their surname (ABS p.141 & ASS, p.411)

Yaḍla – Bommadēvara

The ancestors of the Zamindars of Valluru of the West Godavari– Krishna regions were originally known by the surname Yaḍla (Oxen) by virtue of their cattle wealth. However, when one Nāganna of this family acquired the Zamindari, he adopted the surname 'Bommadēvara' which is a corrupt form of Brahmadēvara as a token of his loyalty towards his former master. (ASS, p. 385-86)

Krishnānēni – Māṇikya Rao

The earlier surname of the Zamindars of Rachauru-Rapalli of the Guntur was Krishnaneni (a personal name). While they were at Telengāṇa which was their former abode Kutubshahi's of Golkonda bestowed on them the title Māṇikya Rao. In fact names like Māṇikya Chandra, Māṇikya Sēna and Māṇikya Dēva were popular among the Jains. The followers of a Jain ascetic Māṇikyaprabhuvu are still there in Telangāṇa (*ibid.* p.360-61).

Rāvela – Maḍiki

Ayyala Mantri (14th Century) originally hailed from Rāveḷḷa village in the Guntur District and as such had the place name as his family name but by the time of his son Singanna, the family shifted to the village Maḍiki in the Godavari region and as such the family name also has changed. (ABS Vol. I, p.477)

Aratla – Mollamūru – Birudurāju

This family originally hailed from Nalgonda district, latter on shifted to Mollamūru. Still later the family came to be known as Birudu (title) Rāju (*ibid.* p.493)

Sāgi – Vathsavāi

According to Rāmavilāsam, Rāmarāju (later half of the 13th century) of Sāgi family shifted to Vathsavāyi village in the Krishna district and from then onwards his line came to be referred by the surname Vathsavāyi (Bharathi, Sept. 1982, p.20 and ASS, p.262).

Jalligaḍala – Kalidinḍi

According to the Kifiyat of Kalidinḍi, the original surname of the rulers of Mogalthuru was Jalligaḍala. Both are after place names (ASS, p.586).

Pālavēkari – Taḍigoḷḷa

Kadaripati, author of "Sukasapthati" referred to his surname as 'Pālavēkari' as well as 'Tāḍigoḷḷa' in the preface as well as in the text of his work. His ancestors in fact mentioned their family name as 'Tāḍigoḷḷa' in the inscriptions.

Literary historians have changed the surnames of poets and authors, for e.g., though the original surnames Jagganna, the compiler of ancient model poems was Rāmāpragaḍa, since he has resided at Pedapāḍu he came to be referred as Pedapāṭi jaggana.

Are Surnames indicative of Caste & Sub-sect Distinctions

It will be interesting to analyse the available data. The two main divisions among the Andhra Brahmins are Vaidiki and Niyōgi. It is generally assumed that while the former mainly concerned themselves with Vedic learning and correlated rituals, the latter involved themselves in the mundane matters (*Laukika*). However, when we check the following representative list, it is revealed in some instances the case is even vice-versa.

Adhikārla (Ve)
Bhaṭrāju (AN)
Bhaṭṭi (Vy)
Chakravartula (AD & Vy)
Karaṇam (AN)
Khaṭāru (GV)
Khazāna (K. Vy)
Kothvala (PN)
Mantri (A.N & Vy)
Manḍaleeka (Vy)
Mahịdhara (Vy)
Nyapathi (Md)
Nyayapati (GV)
Rāṇi (PD)
Rāchamallu (AN)
Radhītara (AD)
Rājula (AD)
Rājyam (PD)
Rāyasam (AN)
Sāmrājyam (GV)
Sēnāpati (V.Vy)
Sēnādhipathyam (Vy)
Ṣhāhukāru (VY)
Suvāṇam (Vy)
Ūrakaraṇam (AN)
Vāhinipati (Ve)

Heggeḍa > Peggeḍa > Preggeḍa

Originally a Kanada office equalent to that of a Minister has become Peggeḍa or Pragaḍa in Telugu with the same or equivalent meaning. Nomally this term is associated as a suffix to some of the Andhra Niyōgi Brahmin families along with their Surnames whose principal enrolment is either a place of personal names.

Agasthayapragaḍa
Akkinapragaḍa
Ananthapragaḍa
Annapragaḍa
Bayyanapragaḍa
Bollāpragaḍa
Challāpragaḍa
Channapragaḍa
Mallāpragaḍa
Mānāpragaḍa
Mantripragaḍa
Mūlāpragaḍa
Pērāpragaḍa
Pōlapragaḍa
Pōthapragaḍa
Rāmāpragaḍa

Chittāpragaḍa
Dharanepragaḍa
Durgāpragaḍa
Eśwarapragaḍa
Haripragaḍa
Kanakāpragaḍa
Kannapragaḍa
Kāśipragaḍa
Kēśapragaḍa
Lakkāpragaḍa
Rebbapragaḍa
Sarvāpragaḍa
Śiripragaḍa
Thallāpragaḍa
Thamāpragaḍa
Tirumalapragaḍa
Ventrapragaḍa
Vissāpragaḍa
Yallāpragada
Yarrāpragaḍa

It could be generally noticed that the surname suffix 'Rāju' is often found associated with the Andhra Niyōgi Brahmin Community. In this case also the core element of the Surnames mostly happens to be either a place or personal name.

Aadirāju
Abbarāju
Agastyarāju
Akkarāju
Akkirāju
Allamrāju
Ammarāju
Ammirāju
Anantharāju
Antharāju
Appalarāju
Apparāju
Ayitharāju
Bāchirāju
Bakkarāju
Basavarāju
Bhadrirāju
Bhavarāju
Bhaṭrāju
Bhimarāju
Dēchirāju
Dēśarāju
Dēśirāju
Dēvaḷarāju
Dhanyamrāju
Dontharāju
Drōṇamrāju
Durgarāju
Gādirāju
Gālirāju
Gangarāju
Gavararāju
Gōparaju
Gōtharāju
Gōvindarāju
Gunḍrāju
Kāḷamrāju
Kāmarāju
Kanchirāju
Kanṭamrāju
Nandirāju
Nāraparāju
Neelamrāju
Pabbarāju
Peddirāju
Pemmarāju
Pōchirāju
Potharāju
Pragaḍarāju
Punnamarāju
Rāchirāju
Rāmarāju
Sāmbirāju
Samnidhirāju
Sarrāju
Sattirāju
Seethamrāju
Siddirāju
Singarāju
Śivarāju

Bhōgarāju
Bijjirāju
Birudurāju
Bommarāju
Buddharāju
Buddhirāju
Challamrāju
Chandrarāju
Chemmarāju
Chennamarāju
Chitrāju
Dāmarāju
Kāśiraju
Kesavarāju
Kolarāju
Kommarāju
Kopparāju
Maadirāju
Māchirāju
Mallaparāju
Malrāju
Manchirāju
Muddarāju
Mutharāju
Tallaparāju
Tāthirāju
Thammarāju
Thimmarāju
Vallabharāju
Vandirāju
Veeramrāju
Vēmarāju
Vēnarāju
Viṭṭamrāju
Yāga-āju

However, that the surnames are not constrained by the caste factor could be demonstrated by the following examples. Here it can be noticed that these surnames of the Brahmins are also held by the other castes and communities in the Andhra Society.

Addēpalli (Kh)
Āchanṭa (Ka)
Adapāṭi (Ka)
Allūri (Kh)
Āthkūri (Ka)
Ayinampūdi (Kh)
Ayyańki (Ka)
Bandāru (Vy)
Behara (Telaga)
Bellamkońd?a (Ka)
Bendapūḍi (Vy)
Bhūpathirāju (Kh)
Boḍḍu (Ka & Vy)
Buddharāju (Kh)
Chāganṭi (Ka)
Chamarthi (Kh & Br)
Chigurupāṭi (Cha)
Chilukūru (Kh)
Chintalapūḍi
Javvādi (Cha)
Jūlūri (Cha)
Jūpūdi (Vy)
Kākāni (Ka)
Kākaraparthi (Kh)
Kākumānu (Cha)
Kalidinḍi (Kh)
Kaḷḷēpalli (Kh)
Kallūri (Ka)
Kancharla (Vy)
Kandula (Vy)
Kānūri (Ka)
Karri (Re)
Kāsi (Cha)
Kaṭāru (Kh)
Kaṭṭamūri (Vy)
Kōdaṭi. (Hari)
Kōdūru (VB)
Kōganṭi. (Ka)
Muppāḷa (Ka)
Muthyāla (Cha)
Nadendla (Ka)
Nārāyaṇam (Vy)
Nērēḷḷa (Vy)
Nimmagaḍḍa (Ka)
Nimmakāyala (Cha)
Panthana (Cha)
Pasumarthi (Vy)
Pendyāla (Ka)
Pentapāṭi (Vy)
Pilli (Ka)
Pirātla (Vy)
Ponnāḍa (Visw)
Ponnūru (Ka)
Pōthula (Cha)
Pragaḍa (Cha)
Pūsapāṭl (Kh)
*Puvvāḍa (Vy)

Chundum (Cha)
Damōdaram (Ha)
Dāsa (Cha)
Dāsaradhi (VB)
Dharaṇikōṭa (Ka)
Divi (Ka)
Elūri (Re)
Garikapāṭi (Kh)
Geddam (Har)
Gōreṇta (Kh)
Goṭṭimukkala (Kh)
Gūdūru (Vys)
Guntūru (Kh)
Jaagarlamūḍi (Ka)
Jampana (Kh)
Kommūri (Vel)
Kōna (Chaturdha)
Koṅḍapalli (Re)
Koṅḍaveeti (Ka)
Koṅdūru (Visw)
Koṭikalapūḍi (Ha)
Kundurthi (Cha)
Kunṭamukkala (Ka)
Kūrāda (VB)
Māganṭi (Ka)
Māmiḍi (Cha)
Mantena (Kh)
Marrāju (Kh)
Mudunūri (Kh)
Muḷḷapūḍi (Vel)
Rāchamallu (Re)
Rājanāla (Ch)
Reddi (Cha)
Rudrārāju (Kh)
Sāgi (Ka)
Ṭanguṭūri (Re)
Taṇuku (Cha & Vy)
Thōṭa (Cha)
Undavalli (Ka)
Uppalapāṭi (Ra)
Uppu (Ka)
Vinukoṅḍa (Cha)
Yuddanapūdi (Ka)

Some Material Objects

Dumpala (Chat), Pachipulusu (Vys), Bellam (Br), Badam (Vys), Nethi (Br), Nuni (Chatu), Ambati (Br & Har), Vithanala (Cha), Kandula (Vys, Re).

Karra (Br), Kaḷḷem (Br), Kuncham (Br),Gangāḷam (Br), Gaḍiyāram (Br), Goḍugula (Br), Pādukala (Br), Maṇugula (Br), Yekula (Deva), Kāgitapu (Ka), Piḍathala (Re), Banḍi (Br, Re), Tāpi (Ka), Sunnam (Br).

Viṣhnu related Surnames

Chakrapāṇi	= Viṣṇu /Kṛṣṇa	Rāghava	= Rāma
Dāmodaram	= Viṣṇu	Raghupathi	= Rāma
Dāsaradhi	= Rāma	Rāmachandruni	= Rāma
Gōvardhana	= Kṛṣṇa	Śridhara	= Viṣṇu
Hari	= Viṣṇu	Śrinivasula	= Viṣṇu
Kamalākara	= Sun	Śripathi	= Viṣṇu
MuraḷI	= Kṛṣṇa	Sudarasanam	= Viṣṇu /Kṛṣṇa
Nārāyaṇa	= Viṣṇu	Varadarājula	= Viṣṇu
Padmanābhuni	= Viṣṇu	Vāsudēva	= Kṛṣṇa

Prabhākara = Sun

Vishnubhaṭla = Viṣṇu

Siva related Surnames

Īswara
Īswarabhaṭla
Īswarapregaḍa
Kāsinādhuni = Lord of Kasi i.e. Śiva
Mallikārjuna
Rudrābhatla
Śankara
Sāmba = Śiva with Aṃba (Uma)
Śiva
Śivala
Śivalenka
Śivarāju
Śivuḍu
Śivva
Umāpathi
Viśwanādha = Lord of Universe

Some other Religions-oriented Surnames

Bēthāḷa
Bhāgavatam
Bhāratam
Bhyri
Darbha
Diwākarla
Diwākaruni
Durga
Dwādasi
Gāyatri
Gōmaṭam
Hanumantha
Jandhyāla
Kanchi
Kāsi
Kōvela
Madwāchāryula
Madwapathi
Mahānkāḷi
Mantrāla
Maruthi
Maṭam
Mōkshagundam
Nandi
Oṃkāra
Paramātmuni
Patri
Pingaḷi
Prayāga
Rāmānujula
Rāmāyaṇam
Rēvaṇa Siddācharya
Salagramam
Sannidhānam
Saraswathi
Saṭagōpam
Śrirangam
Tirumala
Tirupathi
Tulasi
Vāraṇāsi

Related to Nature

Aḍavi	= Forest	Koṅḍa	= Hill
Agnihōtram	= Sacred Fire	Lōkam	= World
Akāsam	= Sky	Parvatam	= Mountain
Brahmānḍam	= Universe	Piḍugula	= Thunder bolt
Cheekati	= Darkness	Prapancham	= World
Gāli	= Wind	Samudram	= Sea
Giri	= Hill		

Hydraulic varieties

Charla	= Water tank	Kolani	= Water tank
Cheruvu	= Water tank	Krishna	= River
Ganga	= River	Nooti	= Well
Gōdāvari	= River		

Flora

Antyākula	= Leaf of	Mallela	= Jasmine Banana tree
Akula	= Leaf	Māmidi	= Mango, Mangifera foetida, Lour
Chengalva	= Lotus (Pūla)	Poola	= Flower
Chinta	= Tamarindus Indica, Linn	Pushpāla	= Flower
Jammi	= Acacia suma, Buck	Rāvi	= Ficus religiosa
Kakumānu	= Pongamia glabra, Vent	Tādi	= Palmyra, Borasus flabellifer, Linn
Kaluvala	= Lotus	Theegala	= Creepers
Kusuma	= Flower	Vangapandu	= Fruit of Vanga, Bringal.
Maṟṟl	= Ficus bengalensis, Linn	Ummetta	= Dhatura genus
Maddi	= Morinda tintoria, Roxb	Vepa	= Margosa, Melia Zadirachta

Maddiseṭṭi	= Here seṭṭi is the suffix	Vusirikala	= Phyllanthus emblica, Linn
Gāra	= Balanites aegyptiaca	Velaga	= Wood Apple, Feronia elephentum, corcca
Cheṛaku	= Sugarcane		

Anatomical

Boḍḍu	= Navel	Mukku	= Nose
Burra	= Head	Pilaka	= Tuft
Geḍḍam	= Chin	Poṭṭa	= Belly
Gōru	= Nail	Śikha	= Tuft
Gunḍu	= Shaven Head		

Ornaments

Bangāru	= Gold	Neelam	= Blue precious stone
Kanṭamaṇi	= Necklace	Patcha	= Precious stone (yellow)
Kanakāla	= Gold	Swarṇa	= Gold
Kāsu	= Coin	Vajrāla	= Diamond
Kidiyāla	= Anklet		

Fauna

Aavula	= Cow	Kēśari	= Lion	Pilli	= Cat
Chepa	= Fish	Kodi	= Cock	Pothula	= Ox
Degala	= Hawk	Kolla	= Cock (pl)	Puli	= Tuger
Dunnapothu	= Ox	Kongala	= Buck	Puligoru	= Nail of Tiger
Elugubanṭi	= Bear	Kundeti	= Rabbit	Theḷḷa	= Scorpio
Enugu	= Elephant	Kurma	= Tortoise	Thuraga	= Horse
Gedela	= Buffelow	Meka	= She Goat	Uḍata	= Squirrel
Gorle	= Goat	Naredla	= OX	Udumula	= A type of Lizard
Gurram	= Horse	Nemali	= Peacock	Yeddu	= Ox

Jerri = A type of snake
Kappala = Frog
Kari = Elephant
Onṭeddu = Ox
Pamula = Snake
Peyyala = Sibbling
Yeḍla = Ox
Yenupothula = Ox

Edibles

Athirasāla = very sweet
Chakkilam = a type of preparation
Chēbiyyam = Rice
Chēmakura = a curry
Chintaginjala = tamarind seeds
Chintakayala = tamarind
Ganti = a variety of rice
Gummaḍi = Cucurbita maxima, Duchsne
Inguva = Hing
Jeelakarra = Spice
Kova = Sweet
Miriyāla = Black pepper
Munji
Nimmakāyala = Nimbu
Nookala =Grounded rice
Pachaḷḷa = Pickel
Pappu = Gram
Pindikura = a curry
Pogāku = Tobacco
Rotti = bread
Sanakkāyala = pea-nuts
Sonṭi = Spice
Thoṭakura = Leafy vegetable
Uppu = Salt
Vāmu = Spice
Vankayala = Bringel Solanummelongena
Vulli = Onion

Auspicious and Inauspicious Indices

Akshintala = sacred rice
Boṭṭu = Tilak
Chithi = Funeral pyre
Deepāla = Lamp
Gandham = Sandal paste
Gorinṭa = a leaf
Guggilam = Dhup material
Jājula = Flower
Javvadi = Perfume
Kalyāṇam = Marriage
Karpurapu = Camphor
Kastūri = Perfume
Kāṭi = Burial ground
Panneru = Perfume
Peetāmbaram= silk cloth
Pramidela= lamp holders
Pretha = Gobbling
Puvvala = Flower
Śrikaram = Auspicious beginning
Vasantha = Spring

Bearing influence of other Regions and Languages

Aare (Maharashtra)	Hōsakōṭa (Karnataka)	Peelkhāna (Urdu)
Amberkhāna (Urdu)	Huggehālli (Karnataka)	Raseedkhāna
Bedadakota (Karnataka)	Kalubarigi (Karnataka)	Sabnavis (Urdu)
Dhārwāḍa (Karnataka)	Katakam (Orissa)	Sambatigalu (Tamil Nadu)
Doodhkhāna (Urdu)	Khanderāyani (Maharashtra)	Shahukar
Fārasi (Urdu)	Kharidehāl (Urdu)	Surābhai (Urdu)
Ganjām (Orissa)	Khazāna (Urdu)	Vaḍādi (Orissa)
Herbā (Urdu)	Mudumbār (Urdu)	Vaḍre (Orissa)
Hejeebu (Urdu)	Navabu (Urdu)	
Hōsadurgam (Karnataka)	Patelkhana (Urdu)	

Eponyms Pertaining Education and Learning

Saraswat Brahmins are one of the Brahmin sects in India. The goddess of learning is known as "Saraswati". Among the Andhra Vydiki Brahmin community, there are surnames like Saraswati. Saraswathula is a surname occuring among the Teleganya and Vēgināṭi Brahmin sub-sects.

Kaḷa is synonym for 'Vidya' or 'Education'. That is why centres of organised education are known as 'Kaḷāśālalu'. Andhra University annually awards the title "Kaḷāprapoorṇa". Among the Velanati Vydiki and Madhwa, one could find surnames like 'Kaḷā' and 'Kaḷānidhi'. In the medieval period centres of learning in Andhra were called as 'Ghaṭika Sthānās'. In an inscription dated Ś1078 – a *Moolaghaṭika Vangmayyam* was mentioned (SII, X 139). Moolaghaṭika Kētana was the author of *Dasakumara Caritra.* Chaduvula in Telugu is a synonym for Vidya. This surname is found among Pradhama Śākha Vydikis. A teacher (*Upādhyāya*) is necessary for imparting any type of education. 'Upādhyāyula' occurs as a surname among almost all the sub-sects of the Andhra Brahmins. 'Vajjala' derived from Sanskrit 'Ojha' also means a teacher. With this suffix one finds nearly 50 Brahmin families throughout Andhra.

Gopala Rao (C 1676 AD) ruler of Anaparthy, acquired proficiency in eight languages and as such was popularly referred to along with that title. However, it has not become a surname.

The '*apabhramsa*' form of "*Akṣhram*" is '*Akkaram*' and it has survived as a surname. 'Script' is a tangible form of '*Bāṣha*' or 'language'. Those who excelled in that technique have become '*Rāyasam*'.

Andhras excelled in Vedic learning and recitation of the Vedas. As a proof of that there are surnames like Vēdam, Vēdarāju, Vēdāntam, Vēdala and Vēdula. There are also surnames like 'Chaturvēdula', Dwivēdi, Rugvēdi, and Sāmavēdam.

Such of the families who could make authentic commentaries on Vedas have become '*Bhāṣyams*'. It is intriguing to know that the surname "Bhāṣhyam" occurs not only among the Brahmins but also among the Kamma and Kāpu communities. 'Aṣhṭakam' is a part of the 'Rigveda'. The family that attained proficiency in it took that surname Aṣhṭkāla. Kappaganthu is a frog hopping special technique in reciting in the Veda and the proficient in it got the surname 'Kappaganthula'. In '*Tharkam*' there are two divisions namely '*Nyayam*' and '*Kānḍam*'. The surnames like 'Kānḍam' and 'Kandibhaṭla' indicate the proficiency of the families bearing that surname, Branches of learning such a Nyaya; Sānkhya, Yōga, Purvamēmāsa, Uttara Mēmāmsa, and Vyśeṣhika constitute the Ṣhaddarshanas. The families who mastered all these acquired the surname "Ṣhaddarshanam". *Vyākaraṇa* or Grammar is essential in classical learning and the experts in it bear the surname Vyākaraṇam.

In general, terms like 'Śāstry' and 'Sūri' are the titles bestowed on learned men. They as such are also found as surnames. Through it is tempting to relate surnames like 'Kadhala', 'Kadha' and 'Gadhavajjula' to the modern form of literature of story telling it is proper to explain them in relation to the proficiency of those families in rendering the ancient '*Gādhās*' or '*Kadhās*' like Rāmāyaṇam, Bhāgavatha, Bhāratha.

Poetry

Perhaps no other Indian language group can boast of such a large quantity of surnames which are potential indices of poetic talents and excellence in its different hues and branches. E.g:

Aghōra Kavi	Kavikonḍala	Nidānakavi
Bālakavi	Kavimukkula	Nimiṣhakavi
Bhandhakavi	Kavirāṇamu	Nutanakavi
Bhayakavi	Kavirāyani	Prouḍha kavi
Birudakavi	Kavitha	Pullakavi
Chayakavi	Kavivarapu	Rāyakavi
Diṭṭakavi	Kavivege	Śrungārakavi
Ghōrakavi	Kavula	Tārakavi
Kavi	Kavulūri	Varthakavi
Kavidhāṭi	Madhurakavi	

Chitra Kavita is a variety of complex composition of poetry. When a son of Kotapalli Rangāchārya, gained expertise in this field of poetry the surname 'Chitrakavi' replaced their original surname. Nearly a century ago one Thurlapāṭi Hanumaiah, became master of poetry and from then onwards the surname Kavirāṭ came in to prevalence. Those who composed poetry, rather at a leisurely pace have become 'Nidāna Kavis' and those who could turnout poetry in minutes have become 'Nimiṣhakavi'. Those who obtained royal patronage name become "Rāyakavis". Those who could obtain titles in general from societies have become 'Birudakavis'.

Oratory

'*Prasangi*' is the one who can speak with authority. 'Prativada Bhayaṃkara' is the one who could outwit the opponents in any debate or argument.

Music

There is a dictum that 'Sāmavēdath Sangeetham' meaning Sāmavēda in its essentiality contains music. Hence, the surname 'Sāmavēdam' and 'Sāmavēdula' alludes to those families proficiency in Vedic recitation. 'Gāndhāram' and 'Niṣhādam' two of the

Sapthaswaras owe their names to the ancient Indian communities Gandharvas and Nişhādas.

(Balantrapu Rajanikantharao, Mana Sangeetha Parinama Charitra, Andhra Pradesh Darshini, Visalandhra Publishing House, Vijayawada, 1976, p.957.)

Kinnera's are one of the ancient tribes of India. Palkurki Somanādha refers to 'Kinnera Veeṇa'. There is a Telugu surname Kinnera. Bharatha's Naṭyaśāstra in its music section mentions 'Āndhri' as one of the eleven misrajāthis. It was an admixture of Gandhāri and Shāṭji. Threfore the inference is that the Andhras were well acquainted with music from the very early period. Such of the families who become experts both in Music and Dance justifiably had the surname 'Bharatam'. 'Sangeetham' as well as its *apabhramsa* form 'singeetham' are found as surnames among the Andhra families.

Singing is an integral part of the music. The surname 'gānāla' and 'pāṭagāni' (*Pāṭa* in Telugu means song) are expressive of the felicity of those families in this realm of musical accomplishment.

'Bayakāḍu' means an expert singer. 'Rāmappayya's' original surname was 'Rāyasam'. He adorned the court of 'Achyuta Dēvarāya' (1529-542) of Vijayanagara and composed Swaramēḷa Kaḷanidhi – a musical treatise and as such his family acquired the surname 'Bayakāram' (Sangraha Andhra Vignana Sarvaswamu Vol.II, p.342-345).

One Venkata Subbaiah (1825-1864) impressed Chatrapathi Shivāji by his musical talent and obtained the title "Swarakāḍu" which has become his family name (Mangipudi Ramalinga Sastry, Andhra Gayakula Charitra, Viswasahitya mandali, Rajahmundry, p.24). Similarly Kondiah of Bandar had the title, 'Swaram' as his surname (Satyavathi, p.106). So is the case with Pallavi Gopalayya (Telugu Samskruthi Vol. II, p.186) and Pallavi Venkatappayya (1860-1935), whose original surname was 'Rājanāla' (*ibid.* p.639). It is interesting to note that Pallavi Gopalayya's son, Krishnaiah acquired a new surname 'Challagāli' (Cool Wind) (Ṣatyavathi, p. 105-106) that too because of the freshness of his singing.

One Subbayya obtained the title "Jhum Jhum Mārutham" (High velocity of wind) a title from the Maharaja of Mysore and that has become his family name. Narassayya, a court musician of Venkatagiri was capable of rendering Keerthanas in all six pitches as such had the title 'Ṣhatkalām'. Seenayya (latter half of 17th century) whose 'Kriti' Śivadeekshaparurālanura, acquired the title 'Ghanam' like Krishna Ayyar who also had a similar title (*ibid.* p.106-509).

In the modern period Venkataramana Dasu (1886-1948), author of 'Veena Rahasya Pranāḷika'; his relative Seshanna (1852-1926) and their ancestors Peddagururāyachāryulu (1794-1822) have all by their expertise in playing the stringed musical instrument Veena had the surname 'Veena'.

The grand father of the Thyagarāja Swamy (1765-1847), the chief among the Carnatic music trinity. Kaḷāhastayya had the surname 'Veena'. The celebrate a South Indian singer and Vaggeyakāra Pacchimiriyam Ādi Appayya's (1730-1820) son Krishnayya by his proficiency in playing Veena had the same surname. So as is the case with Krishnayya, a disciple of Thyagarāja.

Mrudagam is a percussion musical instrument. Vāraṇāsi Ghanṭayya Śāstry (1895-1957) learned this art from Mrudanga Kōdanḍa Rāmayya of Kumbhakonam (T.S., p.198). Maddela is a Telugu equivalent of Mrudangam. Aśwadhāṭi Sreerama Murthy (1876 - 1944) justified his surname by his unparalleled swift in playing that instrument (*ibid.* p.521).

Music is essentially based on 'laya' (rhythm). Garudāchalakavi author of 'Kousalēya Charitra' flourished under the patronage of Giriamma, daughter in law-of Peddasōmanādri (1663-1712) the ruler of Gadwal had the surname 'layagrāhi' (grasper of rhythem) (SAS Vol.XI, p.214-215).

'Nattuva' is a term signifying dancer in Telugu. 'Naṭṭuva' is a dance master as could be inferred from the inscriptional evidence (SII Vol.V, No.1225, Ś 1271 & No.1188, Ś 1172).

Nāchana Sōmanādha in his 'Uttara Hari Vamsa' refers to Kōlāṭamu and Gonḍli – two of the dance forms (Nataraja Ramakrishna –

Natyakala, A.P. Darshini, p.968). Both Kolāṭa and Goṅḍlāla are found among the surnames of Telugus.

'Ōju' means a sculptor. Normally occur as a title at the end of the surnames of artisans communities (K. Eswara Dattu, Inscriptional Glossary, p.55 & 108). In inscriptions, we came across names like Kāśimōju and Pōthōju (SII, Vol.X, No.61, Ś 26 & No.66 Ś 1033). 'Naṭṭavōju' means a dance teacher (SII, Vol.IV, No.663) Ōju is normally found as a surname suffix among the Viswabrahmins.

Folk Arts

'Yakşhgāna' is the earlier form of Bhāgavata Nātya. That form of folk art was practiced by a particular tribe known as 'Jakkula'. It is still, surviving as a surname in the Andhra country. (SAVK Vol.VI, p561). Surnames like 'Jakkamabhaṭla', 'Jakkarāju' are may be indicative of that tradition. In Bhāgavata dance tradition 'Daruvu' is an important component. There is a surname 'Daruvula' which may be indicative of their families expertise in it. Surnames like Akku, Addanki, Guru, Guram all carrying the suffix 'Bhāgvatula' are representive of the mastery over that art form.

Pitchiguntlās are a class of people devoted to the recitation of Puranik stories and Vaṃśa charitras with the accompaniment of 'Dōlu' (Drum). It is surviving as a surname. Puppetry as an art form emanated from the Andhra Desa and spread to the South Asiatic countries. Puppetry is known as Bommalāṭa or Thōlubommalāṭa in Telugu and is still there as surname in Telugu. Byndla or Bavani acquired that name due to the name of the instrument they played known as Bavanika. Pamba, a surname is also due to a particular type of musical instrument. Kāhaḷi, Bākā, Tappeṭa, Thirunāmu, Nowbat, Sannāyi, Gajjela and some other Telugu people in the realm of fine arts like music and dance.

Summation

Tana Pēru ; Talli Pēru
Tānu gāriinchina Tand?ri Pēru;
Tana unna Ūri Pērunu
Vinukaligā Bratukavalayu

- A Telugu poet (Anonymous)

"One has to live worthy of one's own name; the name of his mother, father and place wherein he lives" – thus extolled an anonymous Telugu poet.

To the above obligations – one's own family name Iṅṭi Pēru or Kuṭumba Nāma – has to be necessarily added for that connotes one's roots, lineage, antecedents, and genealogy as an add on value in the social milieu.

Andhras were as ancient as the Aitrēya Bhāhmaṇa (vii 18) and their mother tongue Telugu attained epigraphical poise definitely by the end of the 6th Century C.E. The term 'Kula' which occurred later to the period of the Brāhmaṇās originally denoted 'home' or house of the family. Still later 'Gōtra' denoted the ancestral family from which its members traced their descent. In this order of social identity and in their cosmogonic antecedents 'Inṭi Pēru' (eponym) gained currency from the late ancient through early medieval periods and attained chrysalis and crescendo by the advent of the modern period in the Andhra country and its history. The present enquiry is aimed at tracing its evolution and multi dimensional hues along with personal names (Anthroponomics) which partake a major share of them.

Traversing

Their member

The list appears to be bourneless; their sheer immensity without any alpha and omega leaves one agape and rictus with its potential to assume an encyclopedic and compendiumic size. An effort is made to constellate them at a modest level.

Their Nature

Place names and personal names appears to be Arcturus and Belphegor in the conopy of onomastics. Their presence cannot be diminutioned and descryed and have to be pursued with a diligent discerning and diapason, as each one of them is a disparate entity though at the outset they may appear to be dissonant. They are not eidolon and far from causing ennui needing ensconce, their effulgence attracts the elite as well as the commonality.

Though it is not an arcane subject, as such, it nevertheless prerequisite an astuce and assuagic approach and the contrivance of an architectonic perseverance. The ambit of the work is perceptible but an aesthesis requires an avid and an aesthetic concern an adapt handling. To delve into the inventory of surnames / personal names which are not circumscribed and appears like an argosy and to arraign them requires the contivence of an artificer without indulging in any daedal and daubling. Without loosing oneself in the labyrinth and hieroglyph with all the kinetic ken one has to tackle them without subscribing to a credo. Some of them are blazon and bardic. Some are bent to belie. Some are amicable. Some are acrid and adamant not at any ones beck and behest. While some try to put on blinkers and make the researcher baulk. Some of them are like canticles and dulcets. Some of them are beleagueral with biazarreric interpretation besetted as they are with battened assumptions. Simplessed they i.e., almost require a thaumaturgy – wonder worker.

Aspirations

The present work seeks to evolve the socio-cultural impulses and compulsions that varies as the centuries ago by affecting the psyche of the people in adopting new norms and forms in the name giving process – whether personal or family. The main purpose remained as suggested by the very title – to formulate a Dictionary containing the data in systematic and standardized formulae. Thus, a fresh if not an altogether new angle of approach towards constructing the late ancient and early mediaeval history of the Andhra Country as reflected in the family and personal names – the former being mostly consisting of place names and personal names to a very large extent. In fine, to present a new perspective in unveiling the social history at a personally perceptible formulation.

Actuality

In certain reality all the set objects - which of course necessarily assumed new ranges and dimensions along with the flow of the progress of work – are addressed in a systematic approach thereby enabling the realization of the desired results in a practically positive and purposeful manner. To score the goals in accordance with the sanctioned parameters of an objective research, the prerequisites i.e., the epigraphical sources are exhaustively explored. The perseverant efforts yielded a multi-dimensional data that has been thoroughly marshaled whereby it yielded promosing features to embellish the core material into a tangible form i.e., that of a Dictionary of Eponyms most of which were also anthroponomic in content and variety.

Utility

The vision and mission or the outreach of any project – whether in pure or applied sciences or in soft sciences like the humanities in general and history in particular should be to aesthetically, educatively and purposefully positive to meet the aspirations of the stakeholders i.e., the society. A work like this is likely to generate academic inquisitiveness not only among the serious research addicts but also satisfy the curiosity of the commonality. That the researcher believes has been faithfully accomplished to the extent possible thereby justifying the sanctimoniousness of any academic endeavor. The Dictionary is so designed not only to meet the occasional curiosity of those who seeks to know about their 'roots' and 'routes' but also as a standard ready recokner to relume and ignitiate further advanced and problem oriented research in the subject.

Point D' Appui

In summation, the author notes in a sense of insatiation that in this chiaroscuro account there are certain chinks, crysts and chasms in manuitae. The punctilio remains that the outreach is sempiternal and the present work is simplessed.

DICTIONARY

A

Abbā – ravula
Pe.N Abba-tūru, Dharwar region, Karnataka
(of Abba - rāvu family) EI, V, p.247

Abba – rāju
Pe.N
Abba = Father;
rāju – Suffix; See above
AN; Kh; Abbi-rāju – IVR IV, No.185, ś 1543; SII, XVI, 158, 1547 AD

Abbā – vajhula
Abbā – Pe.N;
Vajhula – suffix; See above
AD

Abbāram (Abba – varam)
Pl.
NAN

Abbūri (Abba-vūri)
Pl.N; Abb ūru, Sattenapalli Tq., Guntur Dt.
AN; VV; ARE, 1933 : 250

Abhańga – rāvu
Abhańga = That which has no destruction or obstruction, rāvu-suffix
Pe. N indicative of heroism or chivalry

Abhra – peddi
Pe.N
Velnāṭi; Abracimtala Pl.N. IVR, IV, No.30, ś 1334
May be the head (peddi) of the village such as Abhra – pūḍi

Abhra – pūḍi
Pl.N
Abhra = Mica – a mineral

Achchi – rāju
Pe.N
Achchi, stumped form of Achyuta, i.e., Viṣṇu
rāju – suffix AN

Achytuni
Pe.N
AchyutaAchyuta = one of the 24 incarnations of Viṣṇu and Kṛṣṇa. Immovable; firm; solid; imperishable; never failing
AN; This family was referred to in 'Palnati Vira Charitra'.

Achyutana
Achyuta+Anna
Pe.N
Achyuta
Compare Achyutuni (of Achyuta); Anna (elder brother)

Aḍapa < Aḍapam
An employee in the royal court who used to carry the 'tāmbula' for the king.
Niyōgi; Ka Pl. N. Aḍapamuḍi – Sullurpet Tq., Nellore Dt. SII, XVI, 281,1572AD

Aḍaparti
Pl. N (Aḍa-parti)
AN; NN

Aḍavi / Aḍivi
Pl. N, Forest; Bapatla Tq., Guntur Dt.
AN

Aḍavi – Divve
Aḍavi = forest
Divve = Dēśi term for Deepam (light)
N

Aḍavikolanu
Aḍavi + Kolanu
Pl. N; Tenali Tq., Guntur Dt.; Tadepalligudem Tq., West Godavari District

Aḍavi = Forest
Kolanu = water tank
AN; SII, X, 81, ś 1041

Aḍavula dēvi
Pl.N; Repalle Tq. Guntur Dt.
Aḍavula < Aḍavi (Forest); Dēvi = Island
Kaṇva

Aḍḍa-gedda
Pl.N; Aḍḍa = obstructing; Geḍḍa = a small rivulet
AN

Aḍḍala
Pl.N
VY, Br.; ISGO, 15, ś 1380

Addaṃki
Pl.N; once capital of the Reddy Kings, Addanki Tq., Prakasam Dt.
VY, AN, AD , M.Dh & SV; SII,VI, 248, ś 1437; EI; 19; 273

Addaṃki. Bhāgavatula
Addaṃki – Pl. N
Bhāgavatula = proficiency in rendering Bhagavatam (an art form)
SV

Aḍḍavaram (Aḍḍa-varam)
Pl.N
V.N.

Aḍḍē –palli
VY; VN; Kh; Pl. N. Repalle & Guntur Tq.

Addū-luri
Pl.N
GV

Adhikārla
Title indicative of authority or office
VN

Aḍigoppula / Aḍigopula
Pl.N.; Planad Tq., Guntur Dt.

Aḍitham
Adjuctive meaning educated; possessed; remembered.
Vy

Aḍusu + milli
Pl.N; Bapatla Tq. Guntur Dt.
Aḍusu = Marshy land; Milli = Place name suffix
VV & TG

Agastya – rāju
Pl.N; 'Agastyēsvaram, Mallēsvaram, Kolhapur Tq., Mahabūbnagar Dt.'
Agastya is regarded as the first teacher of science to the Dravidian tribes in South India and is believed to have been immortalized as the star canopus; also another name for Siva. (Maneka. p7)
AN; ARE, Hyderabad, 1966; 249.

Agata-varam
Pl.N
Kaṇwa

Agga-rāju
Pl.N
Agga < Agni (Fire) ; Raju - suffix
AN

Aghōra – kavi
Title
Aghōra = Not terrible ; Kavi = poet
AN

Adharāpurapu
Pl.N
M.Dh

Aghōranāthuni (Aghōra-nāthuni)
Pe.N; Aghōratnātha + ni (of)
Aghora is another name for Śiva. Not terrible. A worshipper of Śiva and Durga.
D

Agnihōtram
Title (Religious)
Agnihōtram = Generally means fire.
Ahavaniya, Dakshināgni and Garhapatya are regarded as Tretagnis. Those who offer oblations religiously are called Nityāgnihōtris and those who observe this rite as per convenience are called Kāmyagnihōtris.
SV, Vy, Vel.

Agrahāram
Pl.N; Pulivendula Tq., Cuddapah Dt., Anantapur Tq's, Anantapur Dt.
Denotes a land grant normally made over to the Brahmins; also sometimes made over even to the Vaisya and other communities.
vel.

Ahōbala
Pl.N
Place name Ahōbalam. Allagadda Tq., Kurnool Dt. Jammalamadugu Tq.; Cuddapah Dt. Also another name for the deity Narasimha, whose strength (balam) was awe-inspiring marked exclamation (Ahō).
VN; ARE, Hyderabad 66; 37

Ainam-pūdi
Pl.N; Divi Tq., Krishna Dt., Ayanavolu, Vinukonda Tq., Guntur Dt., SII, 504, s1235, IVT, IV, 409, ś 1480
AN; 'Ainavōli' – SII, IV, 709, ś 1480

Ainā-pantula
Pl.N; Pantula – suffix
D

Ainā-parti
Pl.N; For all Place Names with prefix Aina might have derived from

the above
Ainavōlu
Pr.N

Aina-peddi
Pl.N
Peddi – Suffix
V

** Aināpurapu**
Pl.N
Pr.N

Ainā-vajhula
Pl.N
Vajjhula – suffix
V

Aitam-rāju
Pe.N; Pl. N Aitam pudi, Tanuku Tq. W.G. Dt.
AN; IAP Mahabubnagar, Vo. II, No.43, ś 1275.

Aitā-vajhula (Aita = Goddess Parvati)
Pe.N
TG & AD

Ajāta
Title
With no enemy; with no equal adversary
M

Ajjaḍa
Pl.N; Bobbili Tq. Vizianagaram Dt.
AD; PD

Ajjarapu
Pl.N
AN

Amḍela
Anklet,
SII, XIV, 255, 1562 AD

A ṃduvilla
Pl.N
Br. Gōtra; Kāśyapa; ISGO, 15, ś 1380

Ananta-raju
Pe.N
Kh
SII, XIV,252,1561AD

Annangeri
Pe.N
Br. Gōtra; Bhāradvāja
ISGO,15, ś 1380

Anumpalli
Pl.N; Gutti Tq., Anantapur Dt.
AN

Appale-bhatla
Pe.N
Br. Gōtra; Sānḍilya
ISGO, 15. ś 1380

Aripirāla
Pl.N
KK & M.Dh

Avachi
Pl.N; Near Kanch, TN
Srinadha (15th C) dedicated this 'Haravilasam' to Avachi Tippayya Setti.

Avalengi
Pl.N
Pālakonḍa Tq., Śrikakulam Dt. Mukhalingam Inscriptions, ś 1048

Avasarāla
Employment
AN; GV
SII, XVI, 36,147 AD; ibid, 79, 1525 AD

A

Akhandaṃ
Title; Perpetual sacred lamp; without division
Vel; PN

Akaḷamkaṃ
Title; unblemished
SV

Akka – bhattula
Battula plural of Batti – or Vikruti of Sanskrit, Bhakti (devotion).

Akkā – pantula
Pe.N; Akka, now generally used as a feminine from – elder sister
AD; Pantula < Panth < Pandit

Akka – rāju
Pe.N; Akka usually elder sister but also means father as Appa, while again also means sister.
AN; SII, X. 712, ś 1520.

Akkana – pragaḍa
Pe.N; Akka + Aṇṇa, both referring to elder relations. Anna = elder brother
AN; Pragaḍa < Kannada Heggaḍa meaning as Minister, or one who is in the royal service.

Akkana (Akka + Anna)
Pe.N: See above.
NN

Akkena – palli
Pl.N; Another form of Akkana (above)
GV; AN

Akkena – Pragaḍa
Pe. N; See above
See Akkana – Pragaḍa
AN

Akkenēni
Pe.NAkke; (See above)
Neni < Nayaka = Chief

Akki – Peddi
Pe.N; Akki, another form of 'Akka' (see above)
VV; Peddi – elderly – an honorific

Akki – rāju
Pe.N; I (See above)
AN; IAP, Nalgonda II, No,77, ś 1404.

Akki – reḍḍy
Pl. N;
Eluru Tq., West Godavari Dt.

Akkina – palli
Pl. N; Akinapalli, Asifabad Tq., Adilabad Dt.
KK

Akku – Bhāgavatula
Pe.N; Akku < Akka (see above)
AD; Bhāgavatula, pertaining to recitation of Bhāgavatam dealing with the divinity of Viṣṇu or Kṛṣṇa

Akṣhaya
Title; unending
D

Akṣhimtala/Akṣhatala
Title; Auspicious sacred rice
PN; one Akṣhatala Tirumala –bhṭṭa who caused the steps to Mallikarjuna swamy temple at Vijayawada; SII, IV, 793, ś 1511

Alamalakala
Pl. N
PS.

Allāḍa – bhaṭla
Pl.N; Allada, Śrikakulam Tq., & Dt. ; SII, XVI, 77, 1525 AD

Allāḍi
Pl.N
TG; PD

Allam – rāju, Allama – rāju, SII, XVI, 330, 1634 AD
Pe.N; Pl .N. Allamūru, Nandyala Tq., Kurnool Dt.AN;
AD ; SII, X, 528 ś 1241

Allam-seṭṭi
Allam = ginger
In that sense can be expected among the Seṭṭi (merchant) community. But here it also occurs among Vyḍiki Brahmins. So also the eponym Allama-seṭṭi found among the Velnāṭi Brahmins.

Allasāni; SII, XVI, 68, 1519 AD
Pe.N; Alasāni – ibid, 65, 66, 15118 AD; Krishnarāya
NN ; IVR, IV, No.117, ś 1440
The surname of Peddana, the 'Āndhra Kavitā Pitāmaha'
All-mūḍi
Pl.N
AN

Allu
Vaisya, Ka, IAP, Nalgonda I. No. 97 ś 1228

Allūri
Pl.N; Alluru – Ongole Tq; Prakasam Dt. NDI, Ongole : 7-10.
AN; Kh; Nandigama Tq, Krishna Dt. Koilakuntla Tq, Kurnool Dt.

Alūri/Alūru
Pl.N; Anantaputam, Prakasam, Srikakulam Distircts; Ballari Dt. Karnataka, Kaikalur Tq, Krishna Dt. Nandigama Tq, Krishna Dt.

Alva-konḍa
Pl.N; Alukuri Rayachur Dt, Karnataka
NN; Mallikharjuna Sastry (1871-1917) Pundit and Author.

Amalāpuram
Pl. N; Amalapuram Tq, East Godavari Dt.
VV: CITD, 4:36

Amalūri
Pl.N
TG

Amaḷḷadinne
Pl. N Tadipatri Tq, Anantapur Dt.

Amana – manchi
Pe.
NVV

Amarām
Pl.N; Rajam, Palakonda Tq's, Srikakulam Dt.
Vel

Amara-nāyani
Pe.N
SII, XIV, 256, 1463AD

Amaravādi (Amara = Undying; Vādi = Argumentater)
Title
SV; TG

Amarēsam
Pe. N
Amba(ṭi)dipūḍi
Pl. N; Sattenapalli Tq, Guntur Dt, Ambati < Ambali = rice gruel.
VV

Amgajāla
Pl.N
IVR, IV. No.30 ś 1334

Amirapu
Pl. N
AN

Amka-rāju
Pe. N
AN

Amma (mi) rāju
Pe.N
AN

Ammana – bhaṭla
Pe.
NVV

Ammanabrōlu – a territorial administrative division during the medieval period
Pl.N; Ammanabrōlu, Ongole Tq, Prakasam Dt; Ramannapeta Tq, Nalgonda Dt.
AN; IVR, IV No.304, ś 1467; NI, Ongole 146, ś 1433.; SII, VI, 248, ś 1437; VI, 19, ś 1468.

Ammanūri
Pl.N; Arkonam Tq, Tamilnadu

Ampē-rāyani
Pe.N
Bada Kannada

Amruta – Vākkula
Title
PS.N

Amta-rāju
Pe.N; Pl.N; Anantarajupeta, Pulivendula & Rajanpet Tq's, Cuddapah Dt.
AN

Amtarvēdi
Pl.N; Rozole Tq, E.G. Dt.
SV

Aṃbā-dāsu
Pe.N; Amba = Goddess Pārvati; Dāsu = Servant
Pl.N; Aṃbavaram, Cuddapah Tq. & Dt., Aṃbalam, Jammulamadugu Tq. & Cuddapah Dt.
PN

Aṃbāla
Pe.N.
Br.
IAP. Warangal. 110 ś 1386; CTi. IV, No. 50, ś 1386

Aṃdavōlu
Pl.N
TG

Aṃdra
Pl.N; Vizianagaram Dt.

Aṃdugula
Pl. N
AN; Baḍagala Kannaḍa; IAP Cuddapah, II, 165, ś 1466

Aṃdukūri
Pl. N
PN

Aṃgalūri
Pl.N; Gudivada Tq, Krishna Dt.; Arigaturu,Gudivada Tq; Krishna Dt. EI,5:126
SV; EI, Vol. No.16, No.8; Karimnagar Dt, IAP, Karimnagar; 29

Aṃgara
Pl.N; Ramachandrapuram Tq, East Godavari Dt.
KN; KKV; M.Dh; VY; AN

Aṃki-rēvula
Pl.N
NN; AN

Aṃadavilli
Pl.N
TG

Aṃdalūri
Pl.N; Bhimavaram Tq, W.G. Dt.
Br.

Aṃdugala
Pl.N; IVR, IV, 280 ś 1468

Aṃgaḍi
Pl N.; Retail shop, Aṃgallu, Kalahasti Tq, Chitoor Dt.

Anagāni
Pl.N

Anaghu
Title; Sinless
AN

Anaṃ – bhatla
Pe.N
AN; Vel

Anaṃgi
Pl.N; Ongole Tq, Prakasam Dt.
VY

Ananta – bhaṭla; Ananta = Ādiśēṣha
Pe.N; Pl.N; Ananta-bhaṭla Khandrika, Kandulur Tq, Prakasam Dt.
TG

Ananta – nēni
Pl.N

Ananta – pantulu
Pe.N
AD

Ananta – pregaḍa
Pe.N
AN

Ananta – rāju (la)
Pe.N
AN

Ananta-deekshitulu
Pe.N
M

Anantagiri
Pl.N; Palnadu Tq, Guntur Dt, (with a fort); Vikrabad Tq, Rangareddy Dt,

There are other places with this name in Andhra Pradesh.
TG ; SII X, 565, ś 1391.

Anantarāmulu
Pe. N
Kan

Anantarapu
<Anantaram= a later family; can also be a shortened form of the place name Anantapuram.
TG; PN

Anantātmakula
Title; metaphysical
GV

Ananta-vajula
Pe.N; Vajhula - Upadhyaya
D; A.D ; CTI, IV, No. 50, ś 1386; IAP Warangal, 110, ś 1386

Anaparti
Pl.N; Ramachandrapuram Tq, E.G. Dt.
TG; AN

Anappinḍi
Edible; a variety of rice preparation
PA; AD

Anāsavarapu
Pl.N
GV

Ande
Anklet

Animarla
Pl.N; Animela , IVR, IV, 324, ś 1471
AD

Anipeddi
Pe.N; Annepeddi, IAP, Nalgonda, I, 82, AD 1279.
Ps; KN: SII, X, 402, ś 1186; X, 569, ś 1319; EP An; V, p127, No.19. ś 1346

Anisinga-rāju
Pe. N; Ani- singha = Lion in the battle-field on earth.
AN; raju – suffix

Aniyanka
Title; prowess in the battle field
AN

Anna – dēvara
Pe.N
LN; TG

Anna – dēvula
Pe.N

Anna – vajula
Pe.N
TG; VY; AD

Annadāna – bhaṭla
Title; Food charity (Annadānam)
AN; Batla – suffix

Annadānamu
Title; Charity of food
AN; Kan; SII, X, 577, ś 1332

Annama – mantri
Pe. N
AN; Kh

Annama rāju
Pe.N
(Anna + Amma)

Annam-rāju
Pe. N; Annemarāju Vịraya Bōyinḍu, IVR, IV, No.255, ś 1466
AN

Annapa(ma)rāju
Pe.N
AN

Annā-pantula
Pe.N
AD

Anna-pregaḍa
Pe.N; Anna (elder brother), Pregaḍa - Minister
AN

Annārapu
Pl.N
AN; Vel. Niyogi

Annasamudram
Pl.N
GV

Annavaram
Pl.N; Annavaram in the East Godavari Dt, is famous as the abode of Satyanarāyaṇa Swamy.
Vel. Niyōgi; However, there are several other places with the same name elsewhere in Andhra for example 2 in Krishna and 3 in Guntur Dt.

Annavarapu
Pl.N; see above
AN; KN; Vel.; ISGO, 63, ś 1422.

Anne
Anna = brother
Br.; SII, V, 1231.

Annemu
Pl.N

Annēparti
Pl. N
TG

Anni – peddi
Pe. N
KN

Antyākula
Leaves of the Banana tree

Anumakoṇḍa
Pl.N; Warangal Tq, & Dt, IAP, Warangal, No. 24
Br.

Anumanchipalli
Pl.N; Jaggayapeta Tq, Krishna Dt.
SV; SII, X, 259, ś 1134, Chāvali Anni-manchi appears to have been connected with the name of the place.

Anumarlapūḍi
Pl.N
Ps.N

Anumpalli
Pl.N; Gutti Tq, Anantapur Dt, IVR IV, 552, ś 1548
AN

Anumula
Pl.N; Anumula – koṇḍa, Kanigiri Tq, Prakasam Dt.
TG

Anumula – palli
Pl.N
GV

Appa – rāju
Pe.N; Pl.N; Appa raju palle, Cuddapah Tq, & Dt.
Ps. N

Appa Dwedula (Appa+Dwivēdi)
Pe.N + Title; mastery over two Vedas
VY; KN; 'Appaya - dvivēdula' – ISGO, 15, ś 1380

Appāji (Appa + Ji) honorific suffix
Pe.N; The dear name of the famous minister of Krishnadēva Rāya of Vijayanagara dynasty – Timmarasu.
Vel.N: Appāji pēṭa – Guntur Tq, Anantapur Dt.

Appala
Pe.N
VN, TG, KN

Appale
M.Dh.

Appaḷḷa Chakravartula
Appana (Appa + Anna)
Pe.N; The deity at Śimhachalam (Visakhapatnam Dt) is also reverentially referred to as Appanna
KN

Appanna – bhaṭla
Pe.N
NV

Appanna – Dēvara
Pe. N; Appanna – see above
TG; Dēvara = deity.

Apparavu
Pe.N; Pl.N; Apparao Palle, Kamalapuram Tq, Cuddapah Dt. Tadepalligudem Tq.
W.G. Dt.

Appikaṭla
Pl.N; ·Bapatla Tq, Guntur Dt,. Also in Krishna Dt.
Vel.N; SII, VI, 125, ś 1094

Arava – palli
Pl.N (Arava another name for Tamil); Repalle Tq, Guntur Dt.
TG

Archakaṃ
Vy.; Profession worshipping
Pl.N; Archarapuram, Parlakimidi Tq, Odissa.

Arigela
Pl.N; Vayalped Tq, Chittoor Dt.

Aripirāla
Pl.N; Gundivada Tq, Krishna Dt.
KK & M.Dh

Arisānapalamu
Pl.N
SV

Arja
Pl.N; Arja – revula is very earlier name for Nizampatnam.
Pl.N; Parlakimidi Tq, Odissa

Arumbāka
Pl.N; Repalle Tq, Guntur Dt.; Sullur pet Tq, Nellore Dt.

Aśvarōmula
Br.
Gōtra: Kauśika; ISGO, 15 ś 1380

Atirasāla
Title; Very sweetend
VY

Attalūri
Pl.N; Sattenapalli Tq, Guntur Dt.
AN

Attavilli
Pl.N
VY

Attili
Pl.N; Tanaku Tq, West Godavari.
VY; AN; Reddy; SII, IV, 728, ś 1152; SII V, 27, ś 1319; X, 510, ś 1237

Attōṭa
Pl.N; Tenali Tq, Guntur Dt.
Ps.

Attūru
Pl.N; Siddhavatam Tq, Cuddapah Dt., Narasaraopeta, Guntur Dt.
Kamma; IVR, IV, 320 ś 1472.

Avadhānula
Title; Avadhānam a literary feat is especial to Telugu people. Ganerally denotes Vedic learning with concentration.
TG; AD;VN

Avalengi
Pl.N; Palakonda Tq, Srikakulam Dt.

Avasarāla
Profession; employment; 'Avasaram' is an office in the royal court to attend to the immediate needs.
AN; IAP Cuddapah, II, 51, ś 1399.

Avudūru
Pl.N; Agudūru, Pulivendula Tq, Cuddapah Dt.
NN; IAP Cuddapah, II, 167ś 1466.

Avutupalli
Pl.N
AN

Avvā
Pe.N
AN

Avvāri
Pl.N
TG

Ayāchitula
Title meaning un-soliciting
Vel.

Ayalūri
Pl.N
SV

Ayanavarapu
Pl. N;
Ayanāpuram, Amalapuram Tq, E.G. Dt.; Ayanavilli, Amalapuram Tq, E.G. dt
TG

Ayyadāvara
Pe.N
AN

Ayyagāri
Masculine respectable; Pl.N., Ayyavāripalle, Gutty Tq, Anantapur Dt.
AN; PD; Ayyagārlapalle, Kalyanadurgam Tq, Anantapur Dt.

Ayyala rāju
Pe. N
AN

Ayyalasōmayājula
Title
PD

Ayyalavarapu
Pl.N
AN

Ayyaṃki
Pl.N; Divi Tq, Krishna Dt.
AN; PD

Ayyapa rāju
Pe.N, Pl.N; Ayyaparāju pālem, Gudur Tq.

Ayyapa (Ayya+Appa)
Pe. N
KN

Ā

Āchaḷḷa
Pl. N
PD

Āchanṭa
Pl.N; Āchanṭa - pura, Narasapur Tq.; E.G. Dt.
VV; NN; AN, Eg, 23:61

Āchārya – bhaṭla
Honorific Adjective; Āchārya = Teacher; bhaṭla – suffix
VN

Ādhyātma – bhaṭṭrau
Title indicative of mastery over matters divine.
SV

Ādi
Adjective; beginning
KKV

Ādi – bhaṭla
Pl.N; Ranga Reddy District. Can also be a Title meaning the original scholar.
PD

Ādi – mūrtula
Adjective
Niyōgi

Ādi – thāṇā
Professional
Ādi = beginning ; Thāṇā = An office
Niyōgi

Ādikāndam
Ādi = beginning; Kānḍam = part of Rāmāyaṇa, like Parva in Mahābhārata

May be indicative of the families mastery over recitation or interpretation of that work.
NN

Ādimadhyam

Ādi-puḍI
Pl.N; Bapatla Tq. Guntur Dt.
AN & Vel

Ādi-rāju
Pe.N
AN; PD

Ādirāla
Pl.N
TG

Ādi-Vajhula
Ādi (Supra) ; Vajhula – suffix; Title meaning original teacher
PD

Ādukūri
Pl.N
AN & TG

Ādūri
Pl.N; Repalle Tq, Guntur Dt.
SV; AN; SII, X, 278, ś 1153; EI, 19:151

Ādurti
Pl.N
Ps.N

Ākārapu
Pl.N. Ākāram, Nalgonda Tq. E.G. Dt.
Kan; Ps; SII, Nalgonda, I, No.143 un-dated.

Ākeḷḷa
Pl. N
VV; AN; Krishnamurty (1930-1993) Intellectual

Ākoṇḍl
Pl.N
AD

Āku – lūri
Pl.N
Niyōgi & GV

Āku – maḷḷa
Pl.N; Koilakuntla Tq.; Kurnool Dt.
AD; IVR, IV, No 244, ś 1466

Ākunūri
Pl.N; Gannavaram Tq., Krishna Dt. Ākunūru, Janagaon Ta, Warangal Dt.; &
GV; ISGO, 15, ś 1380; IAP, Warangal ; 3

Ākurāti
Pl.N;

Āla – pāḍu
Pl.N; Tenali Tq, Guntur Dt.; Kaikalur Tq, Krishna Dt.
AN

Āla – parru / paṭṭu
Pl.N
Kan

Ālamu
Pl.N
Br.
IAP, Warangal 110, ś 1386; CTI, IV, No.50 ś 1386.

Ālamuri
Pl.N
A.N; IVR, IV, 323, ś 1472.

Ālamūru
Pl.N; Anantapur Tq., Guntur Dt.; Gōtra : Kaundinya
AN; Ālamūru – ISGO, 15, ś 1380; SII, XVI, 174, 1550 AD

Ālapāṭl
Pl.N; Ālapāḍu, Tenali Tq, Guntur Dt.; Inscription of Pedakōmaṭi Vēmā

Reddy
VV ; EI, XI, p.316, ś 1335

Ālēru
Pl.N
PN; IAP Mahabūbnagar Vol. II, No.11, ś 1194.

Ālēṭl
Pl.N
Kan; same as above

Āḷḷa – mūḍi
Pl.N
Vel; AN

Āḷḷa – pūḍi
Pl.N
D

Ālu – kūru
Pl.N
AD

Ālūru
Pl.N; Ālūru, Tadiparti Tq, Anantapur Dt.
AN; MV

Āṃaṃcherla
Pl.N; Nellore Tq & Dt.
AN

Āmudālapalli
Ps.N; Ganavaram, Bandar Tq's, Krishna Dt.
AN; EI, XXXII

Ānaṃ
Pl.N

Ānaṃdula
Pl.N
Br. Gōtra; Harita
ISGO, 15, ś 1380

Ānanda rāju
Pe. N
AN

Ānanda rao
Pe.N; Pl.N Ānandarao pēṭa, Anantapur Tq. & Dt.
Ps.N

Āndra
Pl.N
Ps.N

Āṇepu
From Aṇiyam
Pl. N.

Āniviḷḷa
Pl.N
V; AD

Ānūru
Pl.N
AN

Ārādhyula
Title (religious)
Ps.N, DD; GV; SII, IV, 699, ś 1468

Āraṭla
Pl.N
AD

Āravilli
Pl.N; Tanuku, West Godavari Dt.
SV; EI, VII, VII, No.25

Āre
Pl.N; denoting Maharastrian influence; Kalahasti Tq. Chittor Dt.
KKV; PD

Āremanḍa
Pl.N; Bapatla Tq, Guntur Dt.
D

Ārikapalli
Pl.N
AN

Ārukapalli
Pl.N
Ps.N

Āryasōmayājula
Title
PD

Ātmakūri
Pl.N; Ātmakuru Tq, Kurnool Dt; Anantapur Tq & Dt, Ramannapeta Tq, Nalgonda Dt.
AN; Ātukūru IVR, IV, No.67, ś 1428.

Ātmūri
Pl.N
GV

Ātrēya
Pe.N
AN

Ātrēyapurapu
Pl.N; Kakinada Tq, E.G Dt.
AN

Ātukūri
Pl.N; Gani-Ātukūru, Gannavaram Tq, Krishna Dt. IA, 9; 102
AN; IAP Karimnnagar Dt., Tq, s 888

Āuṭupalli
Pl.N.
AN

Āvantsa
Pl.N; 'Avancha', Mahabubnagar Tq, & Dt.
TG; GV; IAP Cuddapah Dt, III 115, ś 1584

Āvulapalli
Pl.N; Puganur division, Chittoor Dt.
N; SII, X, 504, ś 1235

Āvunūru
Pl.N
AN

Āyalavarapu
Pl.N
AN

Āyalūri
Pl.N
SA

Āyapiḷḷa
Pe.N
AD

Āyupiḷḷa
Pe. N
AD

B

Bachchu
Merchant, though normally connotes vaiśya affiliation, this occurring as an eponym in the context of the 'Golkonḍa vyāpāris' (merchants) appears to be appropriate
GV

Bachchu – palli
Pl.N; Kalyanadurg Tq, Anantapur Dt.
GV

Bachellapāṭl
Pl.N
AN

Bāchi – manchi
Pe.N; Bāchi – affectionate corruption of 'Bhāskara' (Sun) ; manchi - suffix
TG

Bāchi – rāju
Pe.N; see above
AN; IAP Cuddapah, II, 171 ś 1466

Bāchina
Pe.N; Bāchina derived from Bhāskara (Sun)
Kn

Bādampūḍl
Pl.N; Tadepalligudem Tq, West Godavari Dt.
SA

Baddepūḍl
Pl.N; Kandukuru Tq, Prakasam Dt.
AN

Baḍigaṇḍlapāṭl
Pl.N
GV

Badvēti
Pl.N; Baddevōlu, Nellore Tq, Dt.
AN

Bahujanapalli
Pe.N
DV

Baicha – rāju
Pe. N
Kh; SII, XVI, 149, 1546 AD

Bakka-rāju
Pe.N
AN

Bāla = young child
Pe.N
KN

Bāla – kavi
Pe.N + Title
Young poet
AN

Balabadhra – pātruni
Pe.N ; Pl.N; Balabadhra puram, Peddapuram Tq, E. G. Dt.; Balabadhra rājapuram, Chipurupalli Tq, Vizianagaram Dt.
Balabadhra, Pe. N; Pātruni = patra : a title during the period of the Sūryavamsi Gajapathi's of Orissa.
AN

Bālāntrapu
Pl.N; 'Bālantram' Ramachandra puram Tq. E.G. Dt.
AN

Balēmarti
Pl.N
AN

Balijēpalli
Pl.N; Sattanapalli Tq, Guntur Dt. ; compare : Balijapalli, Chittor Tq, Dt.
The suffix of the Pl.N 'Balija' (a caste) is derived from vanija (merchant or trader).
VV; Ei, XXVII, p 274-5.

Balivāḍa
Pl.N; Srikakulam Dt.
VN

Ballamūḍi
Pl.N; Bandlamudi, Ongole Tq, Prkasam Dt.
VV; PD; VV;AD

Ballapalli
Pl.N
AD

Ballāri
Pl.N; Ballāri now in Karnataka
AN

Bammera
Pl.N; Bammarige, Nalgonda Tq & Dt.
AN; KIAP, Nalgonda, 42

Banḍa
Hydraulic; a water source, Bissomcuttack Agency, Odissa
AN

Banḍāru
Treasury; Office ; Pl.N; Banḍārupalli, Guntur Tq. & Dt. ; Banḍāruvari - palle, Chitoor Tq & Dt; Banḍārupalli, Kalahasti division, Chittor Dt.
AN; VV; VN; SII, V, 1214, ś 1231

Banḍi
Cart; Pl.N ; Bandivaripalli, Chandragiri Tq, Chittoor Dt.
PD; TG

Bangāri
Pe.N; Bangaru = Gold.
Kan

Bangāru – gāri of Bangāru
P.N

Bankupalle
Pl.N
AD

Banṭumilli
Pl.N; Amalapuram Tq, E.G Dt; Bandar Tq, Krishna Dt.; Gajapatinagram Tq, Vizianagarm Dt.
NN

Bāpaṭla – Bhāva paṭṭana, Bhāva paṭṭu; Bapatla Tq, Guntur Dt.
Pl.N
AN; Ps.N; SII, VI, 143, 165, 169, ś 1058, ś 1204, ś 1089.

Barri
She-buffalo
PD

Bāru
Pl.N; in Maharashtra
Vel.

Bārvādi
Pl.N
TG

Basava – rāju
Pe.N
AN; SII, V, 117, un-dated.

Bāṣhyam
Explanation of metaphysical treatises.
VY; SII, V, 1164, ś 1569, ibid 1203, ś 1688.

Battalapalle
Pl.N; Battulapalle, Chittor Dt; Dharmavaram Tq, Hindupur Tq, Anantapur Dt.
AN

Battenapāṭi
Pl.N
Ps.N

Bayya
Pl.N; Bayyavaram, Darasi Dt, Prakasam Dt, Anakapalle Tq, Visakhapatnam Dt.
VV

Bayyana-Pragaḍa
Pe.N; Pl. N; Bayyanapalle, Hosur Tq, Tamilnadu
AN

Beḍadakōṭa
Pl.N; Bidar, Karnataka
M.Dh

Beḍadavōlu
Pl.N; Beḍadūru, Jammalamadugu Tq, Cuddapah Dt.
AN; IVR, IV 316, ś 1471

Behara
Title; Profession meaning merchant; also see introduction
AN; Ps.N; Telagas

Bejawāḍa
Pl.N; Krishna Dt, Now, Vijayawāḍa
Re; SII, IV, 1717, ś 1072; ISGO, 15, ś 1380

Bellam
Eatable ; Bellam = Jaggery, Pl. N; Bellam, Anakapalli Tq, Visakhapatnam Dt.
KN

Bellaṃkoṅḍa
Pl.N; Sattenapalli Tq, Guntur Dt.TG;
AN; KN ; Ps.N; SII, VI, 248, ś 1437

Beluguppa
Pl.N; Kalyanadurgam Tq, Anantapur Dt.; Bele in Kannada means agriculture produce
AN; Guppa is Pl. N suffix

Bērapūḍi
Pl.N; Tuni Tq. E.G. Dt
AN; Ps.N; EI, V, p70-74, ś 1024

Benne – kaṃṭi
Pl.N;
Br; IVR, IV, No.206, ś 1456

Bennūru
Pl.N; Bennavōlu, Vīravalli Tq, Visakhapatnam Dt
KK

Bētana-bhotḷa
Pe.N
Vel.; ISGO, 15, ś 1380

Bētapūḍi
Pl.N; Bhimavaram Tq, West Godavari
AN; Ps.N.; Ps.N ; IVR, IV, 272, ś 1468

Bētavōlu
Pl.N ; Gudivada Tq, Krishna Dt.

Bhadhram
Safety; see below
VY

Bhadri – rāju
Pe.N; Pl.N; 'Bhadri' in Parlakimidi Tq, Odissa; 'Bhadripalli' in Produtturu Tq, Cuddapah Dt.
Ps. N; Kan ; IAP, Mahabubnagar, Vol. II, No.18, ś 1220.

Bhāgavatam
Religious work; Also a dance form.
VY

Bhāgavatula (of Bhāgavatam)
see Bhāghavatam Ps.N;
TG; VV; KN; AD; SII, XVI, 281, 1572 AD; Gōtra : Kapi, IS40, 15, ś 1380

Bhāghavata
See Bhāgavatam
TG; SII, VI, 1052, ś 1272

Bhairava bhaṭla
Pe. N
AD; TG; SII, V, 26, ś 1334.

Bhairava bhoṭla
Pe.N
AS; EP.An. II, p.90, The Changadu Grant of Immadi Narasimha

Bhajana – palli
Pl.N.;
Br.; IAP, Cuddapah, III, 112, ś 1476; IVR, IV, No.405, ś 1479

Bhaṃdāru
Office,
Br.; ISGO, 15 ś 1380

Bhamiḍi
Pl.NVV;
VN

Bhamiḍimarri
Pl.N
TG

Bhamiḍimukkula
Pl.N
TG

Bhaṃiḍipalli
Pl.N
KN

Bhaṃiḍipāṭi
Pl.N
VV

Bhanda-kavi
Title ; A variety of poetic talent
AN

Bhāratula
Itihasa
TG

Bhāratam
Itihasa
AN

Bhartipūḍi
Pl.N
AN

Bhāṣhyakārula
Pe.N; Bhāṣhyakāra is another name for the celebrated Vaiṣhnava pontiff Rāmānuja
VY

Bhāskara – rāju
Pe.N;
AN; Gōtra : Kutsa; ISGO, 15, ś 1380.

Bhāskara-rāju
Pe.N; Pl.N; Bhaskarapuram, Udayagiri Tq, Nellore Dt.
AN

Bhāskaruni
Pe.N; see above
NN

Bhāskra – bhaṭla
Pe.N; see above
TG; SII, V, 100, ś 1456 AD; ISGO, 16, 1458 AD

Bhaṭla Penumarti
Pl.N
AN

Bhaṭ - rāju
Profession
AN

Bhaṭṭa
Title; Learned man
VY

Bhāṭṭam
Title: Eradication in certain part of the Veda
VN

Bhaṭṭāri
Title
KN

Bhaṭṭāru
Title
Ps.N; VY

Bhaṭṭiprōlu
Pl.N; Repalle Tq, Guntur Dt.
AN; VV; SII, IV, 1154, ś 1060

Bhavāni bhaṭla
Pe.NKN;
KK

Bhava rāju
Pe.N
AD; SII, VI, 147, ś 1078; ibid, 145, ś 1214.

Bhaya-kavi
Title: (Bhaya = fear) Kavi = poet
AN

Bhētana bhaṭla
Pe.N
VV

Bhima (mana) vajhala
Pe.N
Ps.N

Bhịma rāju
Pe.N
AN

Bhịmasōla
Bhịma = big; Sōla = a unit of measurement
AD

Bhịmavarapu
Pl.N; Chalukya Bhịmavaram, near Samarlakota, East Godavari Dt.
GV; AN

Bhōga – rāju
Pe.N; Pl.N; Bhōgāpuram, E.G; Visakhapatnam Dt's.
AN; IAP, Medak, 137, ś 1233.

Bhōgānagaramu
Pl.N
M.Dh

Bhōgavarapu
Pl.N
GV

Bhrugubanḍa
Pl.N; Sattenapalle Tq, Guntur Dt.

Bhuddhavarapu
Pl.N
AN

Bhujabalapaṭnam
Pl.N
SV

Bhūpati rāju
Pe.N; Pl.N; Bhūpati – pālem, Viravalli Tq, Visakhapatnam Dt. Bhū + pati = Lord of the earth; Rāju = suffix, signifying ruling class
AN & Khs

Bhūtanādhuni
Pe.N
Br.; Gōtra :Goutama; ISGO, 15, ś 1380 ; IVR, IV, No.210, ś 1536AD, SII, XVI, 155, 1546AD.

Bhuvanagiri
Pl.N; Bhuvanagiri Tq,
TG; IAP, Warangal Dt, 18, 1108AD

Bhyrava Vajula
Pe.N; Bhyravapaṭnam, Bhadrachalam Division, Khammam Dt, Kaikaluru Tq, Krishna Dt.
VV; IAP Warangal, 110, ś 1386.

Bijji rāju
Pe.N; Bijji < Bijaya < Vijaya
AN

Bikkavilli
Pl.NVel.,
VV

Bikkavōlu
Pl.N; Ramachandrapuram Tq, E.G dt.
VY; SII, V, No. 48, ś 1372; No.49, ś 1380.

Biṛakāyala
Vegetable
KKV

Biruda-rāju
Title; Birudu means title ; IVR, IV, No. 19, ś 1318.
AN; Kh; SII, XVI, 16, 1396 A.D; IAP Cuddapah II, 28, ś 1318.

Birudu
Title; Birudu means title
TG

Bitraguṇṭa
Pl.N; Kandukuru Tq, Prakasam Dt, Kavali Tq, Nellore Dt.
Ps.N; 'Biṭṭagumṭa' – ISGO, 15, ś 1380

Bobbiḷḷapāṭi
Pl.N; Nandigama Tq, Krishna Dt.
AN

Bochchimanchi
Pl.N
TG

Bochchupalli
Pl.N
AN

Bōḍapāṭi
Pl.N
AN; SII, V,104, ś 1345; IAP Warangal, 51, Kakatiya Ganapati deva.

Bōḍasakurti
Pl.N; 'Bōḍasakurti' – Amalapuram Tq, E.G. Dt.
Ps. N

Boddanapalli
Pl.N; Boddainapalli, Nagaram Tq, Mahabubnagar Dt.
AN

Boḍḍapāṭi
Pl.N ; Boḍḍapāṭadu, Srikakulam Tq & Dt.; Parlakimidi Tq, Odissa. (Inscriptions of Vajrahasta III, Eastern Ganga) Tenali Tq, Guntur Dt. Bejawada Tq, Krishna Dt., Viravalli Tq, Visakhapatnam Dt.
AN; VV

Boḍḍu
Physical feature; Naval
GV & Vy

Boḍḍucherla
Pl.N; Bḍḍucerlu, IVR, IV, No.213, ś 1458.
AN; TG

Boḍḍupalli
Pl.N
TG; GV

Bōḍi
Clean shaven. Pl. N; Bōḍāvāripalle, Kalahasti Division, Chittoor Dt, M.Dh, Ka; IVR, IV, No.171, un-dated; SII, XVI, 88, of the times of Krishnadēvarāya

Boggavarapu
Pl.N
AN; GV; KK; SII, X, 577, ś 1332.

Bokka

Geographical; hole. Can be a shortened form of 'Bokkasam' (treasury) considering the name demeaning there appears to be on attempt to change the name as 'Brahmānḍaṃ' (awe-inspiring - world).
VV

Bokkasam

Treasury
SII, XVI, 46, 1510AD, IVR, IV, 58, ś 1415 = 1493 AD

Bōla pragaḍa

Pe.N
AN

Bolla-prgaḍa

Pe.N ; Pl.N; Bollapalli, Vinukonda Tq, Guntur Dt, Bollavaram, Kurnool Tq & Dt.
Ps. N

Bollavarapu

Pl.N; Hamlet of Proddaturu, Tq, Cuddapah Dt.,
GV; IAP, Cuddapah Dt, III, 93, ś 1643, IVR, IV, No. 232, ś 1465.

Bommakanṭi

Pl.N; IAP, Nalgonda II, No.32, ś 1130, Ep. An. II, p79. The Krāku Grant of Harihara II, 1376 AD.
AN; SII, XVI, 54, 1516 AD; IAP Karimnagar Dt., 30, ś 1157.

Bommalūri

Pl.N; Gudivada Tq, Nuzivid Tq, Krishna Dt.
Ps.N

Bomma rāju

Pe.N; Bommarājupalle, Puganur division, Chittoor Dt; Vinukonda Tq, Guntur Dt.AN;
Ps.N

Bommavarapu

Pl.N; Bommavaram – Atmakur Tq, Nellore Dt; Rajampet Tq, Cuddapah Dt.
Ps.N; IAP, Cuddapah III, 205, ś 1557.

Bommiḍi
Pl.N; Tadepalligudem, West Godavari Dt.
AD

Bommi-reḍḍi-palli
Pe.N; Bomma, a corrupt form of Brahma.
AN; Bommireḍḍi – SII, XVI, 75, 1523AD; Pl.N; Kanigiri Tq, Prakasam Dt.

Bōnala
Pl.N
TG

Bōnamu
Bhōjanamu = food; IVR, IV, 190, ś 1454

Bōni
Pl.N; Bheeminipatnam Tq, Visakhapatnam Dt.
AD; 'Brōni' SII, X, No.724, un-dated.

Bontā
Veg. Vydiki ; Adjective; Large ; Big.
Pl.N; Bontāvaripalli, Kanigiri Tq, Prakasam Dt.

Bontala
IAP, Mahabūbnagar, Vol. II, No,11 ś 1194.

Bōruvelli
Pl.N; IAp, Mahabūbnagar, Vol. 1, No.114, 1107 AD.

Boṭṭu
An auspicious mark on forehead like Tilak.
VN.V

Bōyinapalli
Pl.N; Boyinampalli, Kurnool Dt; IVR, IV, No.7, ś 1292.
GV

Brahma-jōsyula
Pe.NV; TG; IVR, IV, No.282, ś 1468 = 1546 AD. SII, XVI, 155, 1546 AD.

Brahmāṇḍaṃ
Physical world. Also an appreciative remark.
AN; Ps.N; VV

Brahmapuri
Pl.N ; 'Gōkaṇa Brahmapuri' IAP, Nalgonda, 44, Western Chālukya.
Ps. N ; IAP, Mahabūbnagar, I, 131, 1127 AD.

Brahmēsewarapu
Pl.N see above.
KK

Brundāvanam
Pl.N ; Puranically the garden of Rādha-Krishna. Sacred basil has also the other name Brundāvanam particularly revered by the Śri Vaiṣhnavās. However Pl.N also prevails in for example, Tekkali Tq, Śrikakulam Dt; Darsi Tq, Kanigiri Tq, Prakasam Dt ; SV ; VN

Buchcherla
Pl.N ; Buchcha = small; Cherla = Cheruvu = Tank
AN

Būda – rāju
Pe.N ; Būda-vāda, Badavel Tq, Cuddapah Dt; Prakasam Dt.
AN

Buḍaṃpāṭi
Pl.N ; Budampadu, Guntur Tq & Dt.
VV

Buddha varapu
Pl.N; Gannavaram Tq, Krishna Dt.
AN

Buddha-rāju
Pe.N ; The prefix may be related Buddhavaram (Gannavaram Tq, Krishna Dt). Which in turn reveals Buddhist affiliation.
AN

Buddhi-rāju
Pe.N; 'Buddhi' basically means food. It can also be related to

'Buddha'.
LN

Buddu
Pe.N ; May be a derivative from Bhuddha.
Vel.P

Bugga
Hydrononic; a water source
KN

Buggōpādhyulu
Pl.N + Employment; Upādhaya = teacher
KN

Bulusu
Leafy Vegetable; Pl. N; Bulusu – pādu; Bulusu – mūdi.
AN

Bulusulapālem
Pl.N; see Bulusu (above)
AN

Būrāḍa
Pl.N ; Rajam Tq, Palakonda Tq, Srikakulam Dt
AD

Buraṃ Bhāghavatula
Title
KN

Būrgula
Pl.N; 'Būrugula' Kambham Tq, Prakasam Dt; Būrugulapalle – North Arcot Dt, T.N.
KN

Burrā
Physical & Mental ; Burra = Head; here indicative of either the size or qualities.AN; VN; Pl.N, Burrāvāri Gollalavalasa, Chipurupalli Tq, Vizianagaram Dt.
Burrāvāri Agrahāram, Vizianagaram Tq.

Burugugaṇḍla Kamdāḷai
Pl.N ; 'Buruvugadda' – ISGO, 15, ś 1380
SV; 'Burugugeḍḍa' in Mahabūbnagar Dt, Huzurnagar Tq, Nalgonda Dt.

Būrugupalli
Pl.N ; Chodavaram division, East Godavari Dt.
M.Dh; TG; IAP, Nalgonda, II, 1082 AD.

Būssāra bhaṭla
Pe. N
VN.V

Byravarapu
Pl.N
AN

Byrrāju
Pe.N
AN

C

Cakkarāla
Pl. N
TD

Ceṃgolani
Pe.N
Br.; Gōtra : Kouśika; ISGO, 15, ś 1380

Ceranapeddi
Pe.N
Br.; Gōtra : Haritasa; ISGO, 15, ś 1380

Cētakūri
Pe.N
Br.; Gōtra : Kāśyapa; ISGO, 15, ś 1380

Chaṃḍuru-bhoṭla
Pe.N ; 'Chandu paṭla' – Bhuvanagiri Tq, Nalgonda Dt. Chandrupatla – Tiruvur division, Krishna Dt.
Ps.N

Chāḍa
Pl. N
TG; KNV

Chadaluvāḍa
Pl.N; Cadalavāḍa, Ongole Tq, Prakasam Dt.; Tenali Tq, GunturDt; Bhadrachalam Tq, Khammam Dt.
AN; Pg.N; Pu.D; AN; IVR, IV, 425, ś 1481

Chaduvula
Titl ; Chaduvu = study; learning reading.
Pg.N

Chāganṭi
Pl.N; Chagallu, Tadipatri Tq, Anantapur Dt, SII,VI,139, ś 945, Camgollu, Kandukuru Tq, Nellore Dt.
LN ; NI, Kandukur (78) of the time of Achyutadevaraya of Vijayanagara

Chāganṭipāṭi
Pl.N
SA

Chakkilaṃ
An eatable variety
AN

Chakrāla
Pl.N
TG

Chakrapāṇi
Pe.N; Another name for Viṣṇu and Kṛṣṇa
GV

Chennupāṭi
Pl.N; Chennupāḍu – Alampuram Tq, Mahabubnagar Dt, Khammam
Chakrāvadhānula
Title; Chakra+Avadhāni
KN

Chakravartula
Title: Emperor
AD; VY ; IVR, IV, No. 237, ś 1466.

Chalamchyāla
Pl. N; Chalamchala, Kandukuru Tq, Prakasam Dt.
AN; NI Kandukur (5)

Chalapāka
Pl. N
AN

Chalivēnḍra
Pl. N; A place where food and water are offered.

Ps; Chalivendula – Hindupur Tq, Anantapur Dt; 'Chalipandiri' SII, Vi, 622, ś 1120

Challa
Pl.N; (cool; butter-milk) Challagaraga – Karimnagar Dt, Chaııavaripalle, Puganur Tq, Chittoor Dt. ; SII, X, No.504, ś 1235.
VV; Ps.; ISGO, 15, ś 1380.

Challā Vajula
Pl.N + title
VV; Vel.

Challam rāju
Pe.N
AN

Challamūḍi
Pl.N
AD

Challapalli
Pl.N
AN; VV

Challapiḷḷa
After the name of the deity- Viṣṇu.
AD

Challā-pragaḍa
Pe.N
AN

Chāmarla
Pl.N
VY; SII, V, 1202, ś 1036.

Chāmarti
Pl.N
AN; AD; VV; SII, V, 1212, ś 1132; ibid, 1221, ś 1731.

Chaṃdarāju
Pe. N
AN; TG

Chaṃdarāla
Pl. N
AN

Chaṃdrā bhaṭla
Pe. N; Pl.N 'Chandrapattāna' – Chandrupatāla, Bhuvanagiri Tq, Nalgonda Dt, IAP, Nalgonda, I, No.43.
TG; KN

Chaṃdramōuḷi
Pe.N; Another name for Śiva
AN; SA

Chaṃḍūri
Pl. N; Chanduru, Puganur division, Chittoor Dt.; Ongole Tq, Prakasam Dt.
TG; Ps.N ; NDI, Ongole, 28-A.

Chāmi – rāju
Pe.N – Chāmi – rāju Erraya Pregaḍa
Niyōgi
IAP, Nalgonda, I, No.98, lines 7-8, ś 1233.

Chandragiri
Pl. N ; Chandragiri Tq, Chittoor Dt.
TG ; SII, IX, Part -2, No.429, ś 1327.

Chandrapāṭi
Pl. N
AN

Chandra rāju
Pe. N
AN

Chandurti
Pl. N
TG

Chappili
Pl. N
M ; IAP Cuddapah Dt, III, No.9, ś 1812.

Charigoṇḍa
Pl. N ; Kalvakurti Tq, Mahabūbnagar.
AN

Charla
(Hydrononic; an abbrivated form of cheruvu- water tank). Pl.N; Bhadrachalam Division, Khammam Dt.
AD

Chatrāju
Pe. N
AN

Chatrāti
Pl. N; Chatrayi, Tiruvur division, Krishna Dt.
AN

Chaṭṭi
Pl.N, Ps.N, MDh.; Chat+t+ipuram ; SII, X, 173 ś 1072.

Chaturvēdula
Title indicating proficiency in the four Vedas.
TG

Chavalapalli
Pl. N
GV

Chavalapūḍi
Pl. N
AN

Chāvali
Pl. N; Tenali Tq, Guntur Dt, IVR, IV, No.469, ś 1489.
AN; VV; S; SA; 'Cavali' – ISGO, 11, ś 1377; SII,X, No.373, ś 1182.

Chaya-kavi
Title pertaining to poetry.
AN

Chēbiyyamu
Food item; a variety of rice.
VV

Chēbrōlu
Pl. N; Bapatla Tq, Guntur Dt, Pitapuram Tq, East Godavari Dt.
Vel.P; SII, IV, No.102, ś 1006. EI, V, No.10, ś 1024.

Chechu
Name of a tribe
AN

Cheteḷḷa
Pl. N
VV

Cheemakurti
Pl. N; Ongole Tq, Prakasam Dt. 'Cēmakurti' IVR, IV, No.21, ś 1322.
AN; TG

Cheemalakonḍa
Pl. NVV;
TG

Cheemalamarri
Pl. N
AN

Cheemalapāṭi
Pl. N; Cheemala – pāḍu, Bejawada Tq, Krishna Dt.
VV

Chējerla
Pl. N; Narasaraopeta Tq, Guntur Dt, IVR, IV, No.107, ś 1440.
AN

Chēkūri
Pl. N; Chēkūri – pāḍu, Ongole Tq, Prakasam Dt.; SII, X, 405, ś 1187.
Ps. N

Chelamacherla
Pl. N
VY

Chellūru
Pl. NAN;
VV

Chēmakūra
Vegetable
Ps

Chēmbōlu
Pl. N
VV

Chemiṭiganṭi
Pl. N
VV

Chemjerla
Pl. N ; Chējerla, Ongole Tq, Prakasam Dt.
AN

Chemmakāyala
Pl. N
KKV

Chemma rāju
Pe.N
AN

Chemuḍupāṭi
Pl. NVV; ISGO, 63, ś 1422.

Chengalva
Flora ; lotus; Pl.N.; Changalvapuram – Agrāharam, Tiruttani Division, Tamilnadu.
AN

Chenna
Pe. N; Chennavaram, Anantapur Tq, Dt.
V; Vy; SII, V, 1231

Chevuḍupāṭi
Pl. N ; a type of soil.
VV

Chēvūri
Pl. NAN ;
GV

Cheyyūru
Pl. N; Amalapuram Tq, East Godavari Dt.
VV

Chigurupāṭi
Pl. N; Sattenpalli Tq, Guntur Dt.
VV

Chịkaṭi
Pl.N ; SII, VI, ś 1118

Chikka-rāju
Pe. N ; Pl. N; Chikka – varam, Gannavaram Tq, East Godavari Dt.
AN ; IVR, IV, 256, ś 1466.

Chilaka
Pl. N; (Chikka = Parret) ; Chilakalūru, Chodavaram Division, East Godavari Dt.
AN

Chilakalapūḍi
Pl. N; Bandar Tq, Krishna Dt.
AN

Chilakamarri
Pl. N
SV

Chilakamarti
Pl. N
AD

Chilakapāṭi
Pl. N; Chilakapāḍu, Chodavaram division, East Godavari Dt.
AN

Chilama – rāju
Pe.N. ; IAP, Nalgonda I, No.110, ś 1287
Niyōgi

Chillā
See chilli (below)
Vel.

Chillari
Pl. N; Chillara, Alampur Tq, Mehabūbnagar Dt.
AN ; TI : 20.

Chillarige
Pl. N
M.Dh.

Chilli
Pl. N; Chili – Narasannapeta Tq, Srikakulam Dt.
PD ; EI, 4: 185.

Chilukuri
Pl. N; Murtujanagar
Tq, Nalgonda Dt. – IAP, Nalgonda I, 68, ś 1167, Bejawada Tq, Krishna Dt.
Vel; AN; M.Dh.; CTI, IV, No.6, 1067 AD & No.10, 1096AD; SII, VI, 187,
Kulōtunga – Chōḍa Ry. 9; IAP Medak, 79, No.1086 AD.

Chiṃchināḍa
Pl. N ; Narasaraopeta Tq, West Godavari Dt.
VV

Chimmapūḍi
Pl. N
AN

Chiṃtagingala
Flora
VV

Chiṃtaguṇṭa
Pl. N; Kolhapur
Tq, Mahabūbnagar Dt.; Kalahasti Division, Chittor Dt, Venkatagiri Tq, Nellore Dt.
TG ; SII, X, 528, ś 1241.

Chiṃtakirinda
Pl. N
VV

Chiṃtakuṇṭa
Pl. N; Markapuram
Tq, Prakasam Dt, Sirvel
Tq, Kurnool Dt.NN ; IVR, IV, 217, ś 1460.

Chiṃtala
Pl.N ; IAP, Cuddapah III, 84, ś 1800.
Br.

Chiṃtalacheruvu
Pl. N ; Vinukonda Tq, Guntur Dt. ; Sirivel Tq, Kurnool Dt.
AN; AD

Chiṃtapallli
Pl. N ; A very common name for example in Visakhapatnam, Guntur Dt, etc.,
Sattenapalli & Palnad Tq, Guntur Dt; Kakinada Tq, East Godavari Dt.
VV; AN ; IVR, IV, 272, ś 1468; SII X, 291, ś 1162; X, 493, ś 1226; IV, 1281.

Chiṃtam
Pl.N; Chiṃta, Podili Tq, Prakasam Dt.
AN.

Chiṃtapeṇṭa
Pl. N
AN

Chiṃtapēṭa
Pl. N
AN

China – muktēvi
Pl. N ; Bejawāḍa Tq, Krishna Dt.
AN

Chinnavasuvula
Pl. N
Ps. N

Chintalapalli
Pl. N; Kambam Tq, Kurnool Dt.
V

Chintalapāṭi
Pl. N; Chintala – pāḍu, Nandigāma Tq, Krishna Dt., Kanigiri Tq, Prakasam Dt.
VV; AN; SI90, 15, ś 1380.

Chintalapūḍi
Pl. N; Mahabūbnagar Tq, & Dt,; Ellavaram Division, East Godavari Dt, Parsi division, Nellore Dt.
AN; GV ; SII, X, 283, ś 1157.

Chintalūri
Pl. N ; Rāmachandrāpuram Tq, East Godavari Dt.
AN; SII, VI, Times of Kulottungachoda.

Chintāmaṇi-bhaṭla
Pl.N + Title ; Chintāmaṇi, Ballari Dt, Karnataka
M.Dh. ; Chintāmaṇipuram; Hyderabad Tq, CTI, IV, No.21, C.V.51 = 1126 AD

Chintāmaṇi,
Tekkali Tq, Śrikakulam Dt.
Chintāmaṇi is also mean a wishfulfiling stone; A mantra; A Buddhist text; A form of Yōga; light blue colour; a touch stone.

Chirāla
Pl. N ; Chirala Tq, Prakasam Dt, E.G. 24:137.
AN

Chirapuri
Pl. N
Vel.

Chirrāvūri
Pl. N; Guntur Tq & Dt.
Vel. ; SII, IV, 710; ś 1483.

Chiruku-milli
Pl. NT
G

Chirumavōlu
Pl. N
AN

Chiruveḷḷa
Pl. N; Chiruveḷḷa – gunta, Nuzivid Tq, Krishna Dt; Chiruveḷḷa, Khandrika,
Atmakur Tq, Nellore Dt.
Ps.N

Citatūri
Pl.N ; IVR, IV, 211, ś 1458.

Chitra-kavi
Title ; (Chitra = new; wonderful; Kavi = poet)
Ps.N; VY; AN

Chitrapu
Pl.N ; Chitram, Gundivada Tq, Krishna Dt.
AN

Chiṭṭa
Title ; Pertaining to book-keeping
VV

Chiṭṭalūri
Pl.N ; SII, IV, 1077, ś 1085.
Br. ;

Chiṭṭam
Pl. N; Chityala, Dhone Tq, Kurnool Dt.
TG

Chiṭṭa-pragaḍa
Profession see Chiṭṭa (above)
AN

Chiṭṭāvajula
Pl. N. Profession
VV; KNV ; ISGO, 15, ś 1380.

Chiṭṭela
Pl.N
Ka ; SII, XVI, 252, 1561AD

Chiṭṭeḷḷa
Pl. N; Chittela, Nandigāma Tq, Krishna Dt, Tiruvur division, Krishna Dt.
PD

Chiṭṭi
Small
VV

Chiṭṭi pantula
Pe. N
AD

Chiṭṭai peddi
Pe. N
AD

Chiṭṭumūri
Pl. N Pg.
N

Chittūru
Pl. N; Chiṭṭoor Tq & Dt.Pg.
N

Chivukula
Pl. N
VV

Chōbēru
Pl. N; Tuni Tq, East Godavari ; Guntur Dt.
PD

Chōḍavarapu
Pl. N; This Pl.N frequently occurs due to the Chōḷa hegemony over the Andhra region. Chōḍavaram Tq, Visakhapatnam Dt & E.G Dt, etc. Kāḷahasti division, Chittoor Dt.
AN; VV ; SII, VI, 860, 1283.

Chollēṭi
Pl. N ;
V

Choppakaṭla
Pl. N
KNV

Choppalli
Pl. N; Bhadrachalam Tq, East Godavari Dt.
PD

Choppelli
Pl. N ; same as above
AN

Choragudi
Pl. N; Gudivada Tq, Krishna Dt.
AN

Chotneru
Pl. N
PD

Chukkabhatla
Pe. N
KN

Chunderu
Pl. N
AN

Chundi
Pl. N; Kandukuru Tq, Prakasam Dt.
AN; NI Kondukur (20)

Chunduri
Pl. N
VV ; SII X, 499, ś 1188

Chuttagunta
Pl. N
Yag

Cimta
Pl. N
VV; Pg. N; Pg.V

D

Daggupāṭi
Pl.N; Daggupāḍu, Bapatla Tq, Guntur Dt.
Ps. Niyogi; Ka ; SII, XVI, 231, 1558 AD

Daggupalli
Pl.N; Daggumilli, Gudivada Tq, Krishna Dt.
AN Drujjavarm inscription of Anavēma.

Daitā
Divine
TG

Dākūri
Pl.N; Medak Tq & Dt.
Ps.N; IAP, Medak ; 4

Dāliparti
Pl.N
AN

Dāma – rāju
Pe.N; Pl.N ; Damagaṭla – agrahāram.
AN; IVR, IV, 509, ś 1503.

Dāmalūri
Pl.N; Dāmulūru, Bejawada Tq, Krishna Dt.
Ps.N; SII, VI, 221, ś 1148; ibid, IV, 681, ś 1065.

Dāmasāni
Pe.N
TG

Dāmā-vajhulu
Pe.N
VV

Daṃdyāla
Pl.N
Vel.P; SII, X, 504, ś 1235

Dāmerla
Pl.N
Ps.N; GV

Daṃguḍu
Title; well grounded, may be in learning.
VV

Dammālapāṭl
Pl.N; Dammālapāḍu, Sattenapalli Tq, Guntur Dt.
AN; ARE, 1933: 268.

Dammēṭi
Pl.NK
N

Dāmōdara
Pe.N;
Br.; Gōtra : Kouśika; ISGO, 15, ś 1380.

Dāmōjivarapu
Pl.N

M.Dh

Daṃturti
Pl.N
TG

Dandaṃ-rāju
Pe.N
AN

Danḍi
Pl.N; Sumptuous; may also be a place name
VV

Danḍi-bhaṭla
Pe.N
VV

Danḍiguṇṭa
Pl.N; Kovur Tq, Nellore Dt.
Pu.D

Danṭu
Flora variety
VV; TG

Dańtulūri
Pl.N
Kh.

Darivēmula
Pl.N; Palnad Tq, Guntur Dt,
TG; SII, X, 526, ś 1241.

Darmi; correctly 'Dharmi'
Title; righteous person
AN

Darśni
Audience
Ep.An.VI, p98, No.30, ś 1513.

Darvēpalli
Pl.N
GV

Daśa-grandhā-la
Literacy; ten books
N

Dāsi- rāju
Pe.N
GV

Dasika
Numerical; Ten
'Dasi' is an officer over ten villages

Dāsaraadhi
Pe.N; Another name Lord Rāma
VY

Dasträju
Office or bsiness; Dastram = a bundle of papers; pawn brokerage
M.Dh

Däsu
Occurs as a suffix with some other core elements
Dasu = Servant, mainly devotional

Däṭla
Pl.N
Kh.; SII, X, 435, ś 1197

Davēji
Pe.N
KN

Dävulüri
Pl.N; Davuṭüru, Tenali Tq, Guntur Dt; SII, X, No. 112, ś 1065
AN; ISGO, 63, ś 1422; EI.8:146.

Dēci-rāju
Pe.N
AN

Deekshitulu
Title (Religious & Scholastic); Pl.N; Dịkşhatula Agrahara,
Viravalli Tq, Visakhapatnam Dt.
KN

Deepala
Pl.N; Deepam = light of a lamp.
TG

Deńdukūri
Pl.N
VV

Deńdulūru
Pl.N; Deṃdalūru – Eluru Tq, W.G Dt,; Chodavaram division, E.G Dt.
VV; Vel.P; IVR, IV, No.239, ś 1466.

Dēś -bhaṭla
Pe.N
Praganti

Dēśa-rāju
Pe.N
AN; GV; Ps.N

Dēśi rāju; (compare Dēśa-rāju. In both cases Dēśa = Country)
Pe.N
AN

Dēvagiri
Pl.N (Modern Doulatābad once capital of Yadava dynasty)
TG; EI, 20: 23-F

Dēvaguḍi
Pl.N; 'Dēviguḍi', Jammalamadugu Tq, Cuddapah Dt.,
Ps.N;

Dēvaguptapu
Pl.N; Dēvaguptam, Amalapuram Tq, East Godavari Dt.
AN

Dēvaḷa-rāju
Pe.N; Dēvaḷam = temple.
Pl.N. Dēvala – cheruvu, Hindupur Tq, Anantapur Dt.
AN; IVR, IV, No.129, ś 1442.

Dēvaḷḷa
Pl.N
TG

Dēval rāju
Pe.N
Ps.N; SII, VI, 232.

Dēvam-bhaṭḷa
Pe.N
Ps.N

Dēvanakoṇḍa
Pl.N; Pattikoṇḍa Tq, Kurnool Dt.
TG

Dēvara-bhaṭla
Pe.N (After Dēvara = God; King). Pl.N. Dēvara - Koṇḍa. Divi Tq, Krishna Dt.
Ps. N

Dēvarakoṅḍa
Pl.N; Dēvarakoṅḍa Tq, Nalgonda Dt, Vayalpod Tq, Chittor Dt.
T.G; M.Dh; VV; IVR, IV, No. 164, ś 1450.

Dēvarā-palli
Pl.N; Sirisilla Tq, Karimnagar Dt,; Amalapuram Tq, E.G.Dt.; Bejawada Tq,
Krishna Dt.
Ps.N; SII, X, No.504, ś 1235.

Dēvarsu; (Dēva + Arsu)
Pe.N; Dēva = God; Arsu = King in Kannada
KK

Dēvi
Pl.N
VY

Dēvulapalli
Pl.N; Kāmavarapu kōta Tq, West Godavari Dt.
KK; Vel

Dhanukoṅḍa
Pl.N
Ps.N; AN; SV; SII, XVI, 130, 1544 AD.

Dhanwāḍa
Pl.N; A variation of Dhārwāḍa. See below.
M.Dh

Dhanyaṃ - rāju
Pe.N
AN

Dharaṇidevula
Title; Means Bhusūra = Brahmana
AN

Dharaṇikōṭa
Pl.N; Well known Archeological site in Guntur Dt.
VV

Dharaṇi-pregaḍa
Employment; see above
AN

Dharbha
Pl.N; Dharbhāvāri Khandrika, Chittor Dt, Darba-gudem, Pithapuram Tq, E.G.Dt.
Religious; sacred twigs.
VV

Dharbha-muḷḷa
Religious; sacred twigs
VV

Dharmāji
Pe.N; Pl.N; Dharmāji-Gudem, Kāmavarapu kōṭa Tq, West Godavari Dt.
M. Dh

Dharmāla
Pl.N
Ps. N

Dharmāpuram
Pl.N; 'Dharmapuri' – Ongole Tq, Prakasam Dt.
AN; EI, 9, 49.

Dharmavaram
Pl.N; Dharmavaram Tq, Anantapur D.; Nidadavolu Tq, W.G. Dt.
An; VY

Dharwāḍa
Pl.N; in Karnataka; Chodavaram division, East Godavari Dt.
M.Dh

Dhavala
Pl.N
PD

Dhēnukoṅḍa
Pl.N; Dōnakoṅḍa, Darsi Tq; Prakasam Dt, IVR, IV, No.25, ś 1328.
AN

Dhēram
May be from Dera = Tent Army camp
VV

Dhilli
Pl.N; Correctly Delhi, Capital city of India
VV; M. Dh

Dhūḷi
Pl.N
VV

Dhūḷipāṭi
Pl.N
VV; ISGO, 15, ś 1380.

Dhūḷipāla
Pl.N; Sattenapalle Tq, Guntur Dt.
AN; MER, 1932-30, No.269, ś 1679.

Dhumḷrāvu
Pe.N
M.Dh

Dhūrjāṭl
Pe.N; Pl.N; Dhūrjāṭi Ammapālem, Venkatagiri Division, Nellore Dt, Another name of Lord Śiva; Sporting mighty locks of hair.
PNN; AN; SII, V, 113, ś 1338.

Digumarti
Pl.N; Digumamu, Narasapuram Tq, W.G Dt.
Ps.N; IA, 13:23.

Digavalli
Pl.N; Nuzvidu Tq, Krishna Dt.
AN

Diṃtyāla / Diṃityāla
Pl.N
VV

Dinavahi
Office; Dina = daily ; Vahi = account
AN; 'Dinvai', IVR, IV, No.129, ś 1442.

Diṅgara – bhaṭlaru
Religious
Diṅgari = Śiṣhya; disciple or student
VY

Diṅgaru
Religious;
Diṅgiri = śiṣhya; disciple or student
VY

Diṭṭa-kavi
Title; Diṭṭa = strong ; Kavi = poet A
N; SV; SII, VI, 233.

Divākarla
Pe.N; Divākara = Sun; Divākara śarman, E.P. An. III, p.21.
VV; SII, X, 9, ś 983.

Divākarla-bhaṭla
Pe.N; See Divakara V; Gotra: Kasyapa. ISGO, 15, ś 1380.

Divākaruni
Pe.N; See Divākara
V

Divi
Pl.N; Divi = Island ; Divi Tq, Krishna Dt.
VY; SII, IV, 952, un-dated; EI, 3 : 8277.

Divili / Dimili

Pl.N; Situated in Sarvasiddhi Tq, Visakhapatnam district, it is the original abode of a Brahmin sub-sect – Dimili Brahmins. There is another 'Dimila' in Parlakimidi Tq, Orissa.

Doḍḍa

Title. Big; mighty. Pl. N. Doḍḍavaram, Ongole Tq, Prakasam Dt.
VV

Doḍḍa sōmāyajula

Title
Sōmayājula = Performer of sōma sacrifice
Vel.

Doḍḍipaṭla

Pl.N; Narasapur Tq, West Godavari Dt.
AN

Dokka

Anatomical; stomach
PD

Dōmankūci

Pe.N
Br.; IAP Nalgonda, II, 40, ś 1167.

Doṃtaṃ – rāju / Donta – rāju

Pe.N; Dońta – varma. Tadepalligudem Tq, West Godavari Dt.
GV

Dońḍapāṭi

Pl.N; 'Dońḍapāṭa' Muzfurnagar Tq, Nalgonda Dt. SII, X, 241, ś 1107, Donḍapāḍu, Narasaraopeta Tq, Guntur Dt. Gudivada Tq, Krishna Dt.
Vel.; SII, V, 34, ś 1356; IAP Cuddapah, III, 125, 44-dated.

Dōnepāmula

Pl.N
Ps.N

Dōnēpūḍi
Pl.N; Tenali Tq, Guntur Dt.
VV; EI, 3; 8277.

Dōnūru
Pl.N
AN

Dood-khāna
Pl.N or employment
Dood = milk (in Hindi)
Khana = Place (in Hindi)
KKV

Dōranāla
Pl.N; Alampur Tq, Kurnool Dt.
TG; SII, X, 504, ś 1235.

Dōrbala
Title; mighty prowess
TG

Dowlatābāda
Pl.N; (modern Dowlatābād)
M.Dh; GV

Drōna
Flora; In Telugu 'Tummi' tree; Pl.N; Drōṇāchalam, Kurnool Dt, Pe.N. Droṇā śarman,. EP.An III, p.22, 10th Century AD.
TG; SII, X, 174, ś 1092.

Drōṇa – bhaṭla
Pe.N
Br.; SII, IV, 1096, ś 1079.

Drōṇā vajula
Pl.N; Drōnādi, Drōnādula, Narasaraopeta Tq, Guntur Dt.
VV; SII, X, 137, ś 1077.

Drōnaṃ rāju
Pe.N
AN; M. Dh; GV

Dūbaguṇṭa
Pl.N; Atmakur Tq, Nellore Dt; Kanigiri Tq, Prakasam Dt.
AN; SII, X, 528, ś 1241

Duḍḍu
From Doḍḍa = mighty; big. Here Duḍḍu means a strong wooden staff
PD; AD

Duḍḍukūri
Pl.N; Niḍadavōlu Tq, West Godavari Dt.
Bada Kannada Niyōgi

Duggirāla
Pl.N; Tendi Tq, Guntur Dt.
AN; VV; SII, IV, 709, ś 1480; X, No. 96, ś 1056.

Duḷḷa
Pl.N; Rajahmundry Tq, East Godavari Dt.
Ps.N; Ka; SII, IV, 105.

Dunnapōṭu
Animal; he- buffalo, the one employed for the purpose of tilling (Dunna) the soil in preparation for agriculture.
PD

Dūpāṭl
Pl.N; Markapuram Tq, Kurnool Dt., IVR, IV, 344, ś 1474
Vy; SII, XVI, 164, 1547 AD; EP. An VI, p 98, ś 1513.

Duragāla
Pl.N
AN

Durbhā
Pl.N
TG

Durbhāka
Pl.N
M

Durbhākula
Pl.N; Durbhākulavāri – Khandrika, Kandukur Tq, Prakasam Dt.
TG

Durga
Pe.N; Durga = Goddess Parvati
AN

Durgaṃ
Pl.N; Durgaṃ = Fort. Anantapur Tq. & Dt.
TG; SII, XVII, 330, 1643 AD.

Durgā-pregaḍa
Pe.N; = Goddess Parvati
AN

Durga-rāju
Pe.N; Durgaṃ = Fort
N

Durgarāju peddirāju
Pe.N
AN

Durgā-Vajhala
Pe.N
KN

Durgavarapu
Pl.N; Gudur Tq, Nellore Dt.
Ps.N

Durgi
Pl.N; Palnad Tq, Guntur Dt.
TG; N; IVR, IV, No.121 ś 1440

Durgi-rāju
Pe.N
AN

Durisēṭī
Pl.N
GV

Dūrvāsula
Pe.N; (one of the Saptariṣhis Durvāsa)
VV; ISGO, 15, ś 1380.

Dūsi
Pl.N
VN. Pl.N
AN.V

Duvvūri
Pl.N; Kovur Tq, Nellore Dt.; IVR, IV, No. 333, ś 1473.
VV; Reddy; SII, XVI, 6, 1382 AD; SAP Cuddapah, II, 16, ś 1304.

Dwādaśi
'Tithi'- Name of a day in Hindu calendar; also number twelve.
TG; VV

Dwāraka
Pl.N
VV

Dwarakā
Pl.N; Bearing the influence of Dwaraka in Gujarat. Dwarakāpuram, Tiruttani division, Tamilnadu, Kāḷahasti division, Chittoor Dt.
VY

Dwarakā
Bhamidipāṭi
Pl.N;
Vel.

Dwevēdi
Master of the two Vedas
AD; Nārāyaṇa – dvivēdula, Gōtra : Bhāradvāja, ISGO, 15, ś 1380.

Dwi-bāṣhyam
Title; Dwi = two; Bhāṣyam = Commentary on scriptures.; Also proficiency in two languages (Dwibāṣhi < Dubāsi)
AD; TG

E

Eḍapāṭi
Pl.N
AN

Eddu
Ox
PD

Ekkirāla
Pl.N
SV

Elakūci
Pl.N
V

Elamanchili
Pl.N; Elamamci, may be connected with Telugu 'elamu' – shiny, splendid.
Ps; SII, VI, 705, ś 1313; ETI, p. 246

Ella – Jōsyula
Pl. N. + Profession (Jyotisha)
VV

Ella – pantula
Pe.N
VV

Ella – pragaḍa
Pe.N + Office
AN; GV

Ella – vajhula
Pl.N + Profession (Teacher) Pl. N. Ellavajhula palle, Venkatagiri Division, Nellore Dt.
VV

Ellakara
Pl.N
SV

Ellaṃ – rāju
Pe.N
AN

Ellamanda
Pl.N
AN

Ellambhoṭla
Pl.N
TG

Ellē – peddi
Pl.N + title (elder)
VV

EluganṭI
Pl.N.
Ps.

Enamaciṃtala
Pl.N;
Jammulamadugu Tq, Kadapa Dt.

Erra
Colour Red
Br.; CP of AP, Vol. I, p.102, 1293 AD

Erra – pragaḍa
Pe.N; SII, X, 73, ś 1037

Erraguṇṭla
Pl.N; Cumbum Tq, Kurnool Dt
VV; IAP, Kadapa III, 129, ś 1650

Erraguntlapāṭī
Pl.N; Sattenapalli Tq, Guntur Dt.
Ps.N; SII, VI, No.229

Erramilli
Pl.N
AN; TG; Ps.N

Erranūri
Pl.N
VV

Ē

Ēchi – rāju
Pe. N
GV

Ēchūri
Pl. N
VV

Ēḍida
Pl.N
VV; AN

ĒḍugunḍlapāṭI
Pl. N
PS

Ēḍunūtala
Pl. N
PS

Ēkā
Single; Unique.
AN

Ēleswarapu
Pl.N; Nalgonda Dt.
VV

Ēluripāṭi
Pl.N
VV; SV

Ēnugu
Elephant
AN; IVR, ś 407 1479

Ēnugudhāti
Title
SV

Ēnugupalli
Pl.N
PS

Ēchūri
Pl.N
AN

G

Gabbiṭa
Pl.N
TG; VV; CTI, IV.No. 37, Line 38, ś 1223; IAP, Nalgonda I, 95, Line 17, ś 1223.

Gabbupalli
Pl.N
AN

Gaḍḍaṃ
VV; Ps.N; Re; Gaḍḍaṃ Amili Reddy, SII, XVI, 30, 1643 AD, Gaḍḍeṃvāri – palle IAP, Cuddapah, II, 172, ś 172.

Gaḍḍamaṇugu
Pl.N
AN

Gāde
Grannery, Pl. N; see below.
AN; SV

Gādēpalli
Pl.N; Gāde – pūidi, Bandar Tq, Krishna Dt.
TG; AN

Gādhā-vajhala
Title ; Gādha = story
KNV

Gādhi-rāju
See Gadi-raju
AN; but the gotra is different; 'Gadhi – varma' – SII, IV, 949, ś 1693.

Gādi
A structure where in 'Dhanyam' (rice) is stored
AN; GV

Gāḍicherla
Pl.N; Gāḍicheruvu, Bhuvanagiri Tq, Nalgonda Dt.
Ps.N; KIAP, Nalgonda ; 50.

Gāḍi-rāju
Pe.N; Gāḍhi<Gādhēya, another name for sage Viśvāmitra
AN

Gaḍi- śāstrula
Title; Gaḍi (Supra); Śāstrula = of śāstra ; Learning
V

Gaḍiyāram
Measurement of time; Clock
VV; M; (same as Ghaḍiyāram); KK

Gādubhaṭla
Pe.N
TG

Gajarāmpalle
Pl.N after Pe.N; Gutti Tq, Anantapur Dt.
AN; IVR, IV, No. 245, ś 1466.

Gajavalli
Pl.N; Gazvel Tq, Medak Dt, A.P.
KKV; IAP, Medak, 51, ś 994; No.161, un-dated.

Gājulapalli
Pl.N
Ps.N

Gāli
Wind, one of the panca bhūtas; Gālivāripalli, Vayalpad Tq, Chittoor Dt.
AN; KN

Gaṃdra koṭa
Pl.N; Gandram, Bandar Tq, Krishna Dt.
TG

Gaṃga
KN; Hydronomic; Ganges, river, (Skt. Ganga); SII. IV, 1007, 1065CE.
Potable water is also generally called as Ganga.

Gaṃgādharabhaṭla
Pe.N
Gamgadhara = Śiva; Bhatla – suffix, title

Gaṃgālaṃ
A title of vessel in which water is stored.
VV

Gaṃgapaṭṭaṇapu
Pl.N
VS

Gaṃga rāju
Pe.N
AN

Gaṃga-Vajhula
Pl.N + profession
TG

Gaṃgavaram
Pl.N; Darsi Tq, Nellore Dt.
Ps.N; NI, Darsi (25), ś 1176.

Gāṃgēyula
Pe.N; Gāngēya = Bhishma
KN

Gaṃpa
Basket
AN

Gaṇapati bhaṭla
Pe.N
KN

Gaṇapavarapu
Pl.N; Earlier known as Padminipuram, Bapatla Tq,; Narasaraopet Tq, Guntur Dt.; Bhimavaram Tq, West Godavari Dt.
NN; TG; SII, X, 157, ś 1087.

Ganḍavarapu
Pl.N; Kovur Tq; Nellore Dt.
AD; NDI, Nellore : 19

Gandhaṃ
Sandal wood paste, Pl.N; Gandha-nūru, Ellavaram division, East Godavari Dt.,
Gandhavaram, Bhimunipatnam Tq, Visakhapatnam Dt.
Ps. N

Gandhasiri
Pl.N; see above
Ps.N; Re ; SII, VI, 93, 1163 AD; ibid, IV, 790, ś 1112.

Ganḍi-dāsu
Gadi = Fort, boarder; threshold ; dasu = servant; attendant
Ps.N

Gańḍikōṭa
Pl.N; Gańḍikōṭa – sima – a territorial division

VV; TG; M.Dh; AN; IAP, Cuddapah Dt, III, 128, ś 1179.

Gandūri
Pl.N
AN; VV

Gangavarapu
Pl.N; Gangavaram – Vinukonda Tq, Krishna Dt, SII, X, 465, ś 1212;
Gangavaram in Kamalapuram Tq, Cuddapah Dt, CAD
AN; IAP, Cuddapah, I. No.141, ś 1179.

Gangiseṭṭi
Pe.N;
Balija; IAP, Medak, 139, ś 1241.

Gangupāṭi
Pl.N
AN

Ganigipūḍi
Pl.N
Ps. N

Ganjām

Pl.N; Pedda & Chinna Ganjām – Bapatla Tq, Guntur Dt.

VY; SII, VI, 606, ś 1057.

Gannaṃ – rāju

Pe.N; Gannam < Kannam< Kanha <Krsna

AN; GV

Gannavarapu

Pl.N; Gannavaram – Narasaraopet, Guntur Dt, Huzur Nagar Tq, Nalgonda Dt.

AN; PD; VV; IAP, Nalgonda, I, No. 64, ś 1135.

Ganṭi

Pl.N; Razolu Tq, East Godavari Dt.

Ganṭi plates of puruṣhōttama Dēva, Ś 1411 = C.E 1489, (ISGO, No.53)

PD; Ka; SII, XVI, 39, 1498 AD; ibid, IV, 664, ś 1060.

Ganṭi – Mahāpātruni

Pl.N + Title ; Mahapatra = a high ranking minister under the suryavamsi Gajapatis of Orissa.

KKV; KK; ISGO, 53, ś 1411

Ganukōṭa

Pl.N

V

Gārgēyapuram

Pl.N

V

Garikapāṭi

Pl.N; Garikepāḍu, Bapatla Tq, Guntur Dt.

TG

Garikavalasa

Pl.N

VNV

Garimeḷḷa
Pl.N
Vel.; AN

Garivēmula
Pl.N
GV

Gārladinne
Pl.N; Podili Tq, Prakasam Dt.; Anantapur Tq & Dt.
AN; IVR, IV, No.131, ś 1443.

Gārlapāṭi
Pl.N; Gāralapāḍu – Guntur Tq & Dt – SII, X, 391, un-dated. Gārapāḍu, Nuzivid Tq, Krishna Dt, EI, 18 : 34677, Podili Tq, Nellore Dt, NI, Podili, 33, 1547-48 AD.
Ps.N; SII, X, 391, un-dated.

Gārlapūḍi
Pl.N
AN

Garnēpūḍi
Pl.N
AN

Garwēpalli
Pl.N
GV

Gaṭṭupalli
Pl.N; Kavali Tq, Nellore Dt.
AN; TG; IVR, IV, No.49, ś 1363.

Gavaravarapu
Pl.N; 'Gavaravaram', Bhadrachalam Tq, Khamam Dt.
AN

Gavarrāju
(Gavara+ rạju)

Pe.N; see above.
AN

Gāyatri
The sacred mantra Gāyatri
TG

Geḍḍamaḍugula
Pl.N
KK

Geḍḍem
Pl.N; Gaḍḍaṃvāripalle, Chandragiri Tq, Chittoor Dt.
KK

Ghaḍi- śāsala
Correctly Ghaṭaśāsula, EP. An. IV, pp 95-96, ś 1141.
Śāsala may be a corruption of Śāstrala (of Śāstras).
KK; SII, IV, 667, ś 1054.

Ghaḍiyāram
Same as Gaḍiyāram; clock
KK; SII, V, 10, ś 1326.

Ghanam
Large; big.; Also a sampradāya in Carnatic music
VY

Ghaṅṭa
Bell. Pl.N; Gantavāri Kuppu, Tirttuni Tq, Tamilnadu.
AN; Ka.

Ghaṅṭala
Bell
KK

Ghaṅṭasāla
Pl.N; Divi Tq, Krishna Dt.
Vel.P; AN ; SII, IV, 713, ś 1146; ibid, X, 84, ś 1047.

Ghaṭạm
Pot; a musical percussion instrument
TG

Ghaṭrāju
Pe.N
Ps. N

Ghattēpalli
Pl.N
Ar

Ghaṭṭi
Strong
V

Ghaṭṭu
Pl.N; Madanapalli Tq, Chittor Dt.
Ps.N

Ghaṭṭupalli
Pl.N
TG; AN

Ghōra –Kavi
Title
Ghōra = fearful; Kavi = poet
AN

Giḍugu
Pl.N
AN

Giri
Mountain, Pl.N; Giri-vāri –pālem, Chipurupalli Tq, Vizianagaram Dt.
KK

Girrāju
(Giri + rāju)
Pe.N
GV

Gobbūri
Pl.N; Gobbūru, Anakapalli Tq, Visakhapatnam Dt.; Gobbuvāri palli, Rajampeta
Tq, Cuddapah Dt.; IAP Cuddapah, III, 170, un-dated.
TG; Kh; SII, XVI, 169, 1548 AD; ibid, 182, 1552 AD.

Gōḍa
Animal, if it is a corruption of Ghoḍa = horse
VNV

Godāvari
Well known river in Andhra. Pl.N; Godāvari-puram, Tekkali Tq., Srikakulam Dt.
Ps.N; VNV

Goḍavarti
Pl. N; Goḍa-varru, Guntur Tq, Tenali Tq, Guntur Dt.
VV; VY; SII, IV, 709, ś 1480; ISGO, No.15, ś 1380.

Goḍlavalli
Pl.N
TG

Goḍugula
Goḍugu = Umbrella. Pl.N; Goḍugu-rāyi, Ellavaram division, East Godavari Dt.
TG
Once upon a time, it was a privilege conferred by the rulers as a mark of respect or recognition. Chatramu = Goḍugu

Gōgula
Flora
Ps.N

Gōgulapāṭi
Pl.N; Eluru Tq, West Godavari Dt., Narasaraopeta, Guntur Dt.
AN; PsIf Gōgula, the core element, is a corruption of 'Yōgula' (of Yōgi = mendicant) the suffix pāṭi should be pāḍu indicating totally that it was a Buddhist or Jain settlement.; SII, X, 565, ś 1317.

Gōka rāju
Pe.N; Pl.N Gōka – rāju palle, Nandigama Tq, Krishna Dt.
AN

Gōkulānanda
Pe.N; Another name of Kṛṣṇa, the delight of Gōkukla
AD

Gōli
Pl.N; Palnad Tq, Guntur Dt.
TG

Gollakōṭa
Pl.N
TG; KNV; CTI, IV, No.28, 1217 AD.

Goḷḷamūḍi
Pl.N; Nandigama Tq, Krishna Dt.
AN, Kan; SII, IV, 702, ś 1440

Gollanapalli
Pl.N
AN

Gollapalli
Pl.N
VV

Gollāpinni
Pl.N
V

Gollaprōlu
Pl.N; Pithapuram Tq, East Godavari District.; Ancient name Kolliprolu.
AN; EI, V, pp70-74, ś 1024.

Gollapūḍi
Pl.N; Bejawada Tq, Krishna Dt.; EI, 23:163; NDI, Atmakur, 24.
AN; VV; ISGO, 15, ś 1380

Gollūri
Pl.N; Gollakōṭa – Warangal Dt.
GV; IAP, Warangal : 91

Gōma-Vajhala
Pe.N
KN

Gonḍyāla
Pl.N
TG

Gōneḷḷa
Pl.N
VV

Gongūru
Pl.N
Pe.D

Gontēṭi
Pl.N
AN

Gōnukoṅḍa
Pl.N
TG

Gōpā-Jōsyula
Pe.N
Ps. N

Gōpāla-bhaṭla
Pe.N
Vel.; 'Gōpāluni' – IAP, Nalgonda II, 115, un-dated.

Gōpalam
Pe.N; Another name of Krṣna
SV

Gōpāluni
Pe. N of Gōpāla. See above.
AN; SII, VI, 120, ś 1197.

Gōpa rāju
Pe.N; Pl.N; Gōpavaram, Prodduturu Tq, Cuddapah Dt. IVR, IV, 195, ś 1455
Ps.N; AN; SII, X, 773, ś 1619.

Gōpā-Vajhala
Pe.N; See above for Pl.N.
KN

Gōpịnādhamu
Pe.N; Gōpịnādhapaṭnam – Tadepalligudem Tq, W.G Dt., Gopinadhapatnam, IAP, Cuddapah, II, 112, ś 1448.
VV; SII, V, 1248, ś 1393; X, 577, ś 1332.

Gopiṇaṃbāla
Pe.N
VY

Gōrinṭa
Pl.N; Gōranṭla – Guntur Tq & Dt, EI, 12:62; Gōranṭla, Hindupur Tq, Anantapur Dt. IVR, IV, 143, ś 1446.
KN; SII, VI, 1036, ś 1305; ibid. IV, 709, ś 1480.

Gōrti
Pl.N
VV; ISGO, 15, ś 1380.

Gōrugantula
Talent ; Like 'Kappagantula' It is a variety of intonation of the Veda
VV

Gōsala
Pl.N; Cow - pen
VV

Gōtēṭi
Pl.N
Ps; SII, V, 166, ś 1548.

Goṭṭipāṭi
Pl.N; Narasaraopet Tq, Guntur Dt., Goṭṭipātivāri palle, Chandragiri Tq, Chittor Dt.
N; SII, VI, 622, ś 1120; X, 504, ś 1235.

Goṭṭumukkala
KKV; SV; VY; Kh.; Nandigama Tq, Krishna Dt. 'Goṭṭumukkala' EP. An. VI, p97, No.13, ś 1513.

Gōvāḍa
Pl.N; Repalle Tq, Tenali Tq, Guntur Dt.
N; SII, VI, 972, ś 1305.

Gōvardhanam
Pl.N; 'Gōvardhana – puram' Parlakimidi tq, Odissa, Gōvardhana – Giri, Dhone
Tq, Kurnool Dt.
VY

Gōvindalūru
Pl.N; Gōvindapuram, Rajam Tq, Srikakulam.
VV

Gōvinda rājula
Pe.N; 'Gōvinda Vaṃsa' – SII, VI, 184
PSN; AN

Gōvinda-Vajhula
Pe.N
Ps.N; VNV

Gōvindu
Pe.N; Another name for Krishna.
GV; VV

Gōwḍu
Pl.N; related to Gowda country
KNV

Gōwra vajhla
Pe.N
AN; VV

Gōwripeddi
Pe.N
TG

Gōwta rāju
Pe.N
AN

Gubba – rāju
Pe.N; IVR, IV. No. 185, ś 1543.
Br.

Gūḍa
Pl.N; Suffix
Vel; TG; VV

Guḍāla
Pl.N; Amalapuram Tq, East Godavari Dt.
TG

Guḍavāḍa
Pl.N; Guḍavāḍa correctly Guḍivāḍa. Nalgonda Tq, & Dt. and in Krishna Dt.

Guḍimeḍa
Pl.N
AN

Guḍimaḷḷa
Pl.N;
LN

Guḍimeḷḷa
Pl.N; Guḍimeḷḷa – lanka, Razolu Tq, East Godavari Dt.
SV

Guḍimeṭla
Pl.N; Nandigama Tq, Krishna Dt.
VV

Guḍipalli
Pl.N; Guḍimelapāḍu, Ongole Tq, Prakasam Dt.
TG

Guḍipāṭi
Pl.N; Darsi Tq, Prakasam Dt. SII, X, 473, ś 1214. ; Guḍipādu – Produturu Tq, Cuddapah Dt.
NN; TG; Ps.N ; SII, VI, 599, ś 1162; X, 473, ś 1214.

Guḍipuḍi
Pl.N; Sattenapalli & Bapatla Tq, Guntur Dt.
KK; AN; SII, VI, 608, ś 1069, ibid, IV, 699, ś 1468.

Gūḍu
Pl.N; Shelter
TG

Guḍulūru
Pl.N
AN

Guḍumāni
Pe.N
TG

Gūdūru
Pl.N; Gūdūru Tq, Nellore Dt.;
AN; TG; KN; SA; SII, X, 504, ś 1235.

Gūḷikallu
Pl.N
AN

Guḷḷapalli
Pl.N; Gunḍlapalli, Huzurnagar Tq, Nalgonda Dt.
VV

Gumma
Pl.N; Gummasamudram, Kāḷahasti Division, Chittoor Dt. 'Gumma Pundi'
AD; EI, 5 : 142.

Gummaḍi
Pl.N; Gumuḍam, Chipurupalli Tq, Vizianagaram Dt.

Gummadūri
Pl.N; Rajempeta Tq, Cuddapah Dt.
GV; SII, IV, 778, ś 1087.

Gummalūru
Pl.N; Bhimavaram Tq, West Godavari Dt.; Elamanchili Tq, Visakhapatnam Dt.
VNV; JAHRS, 5 - i : 57

Gumma rāju
Pe.N
AN

Gummidala
Pl.N
KKV

Guṅḍa
Pl.N
Ps.N; IAP Cuddapah Dt, III, No.21, ś 1789.

Guṅḍāla
Pl.N; Done Tq, Kurnool Dt; A.P.; Bhadrachalam Tq, Khammam Dt.
GV; SII, XVI, 268, 1569 AD; IAP, Mahabūbnagar, II, 26, ś 1186.

Guṅḍā pantula
Pe.N
Ps.N

Guṅḍā vajhala
Pe.N
TG

Guṅḍēpalli
Pl.N; Tadepalligudem Tq, West Godavari Dt.
AN

Guṅdepūḍi
Pl.N; Gondepūḍi, Gudivada Tq, Krishna Dt.
V

Guṅḍimeḍa
Pl.N; Guntur Tq & Dt.
AN; SII, VI, 128, ś 1071.

Gunḍla
Pl.N
Ps.N

Guṅḍlakunṭa
Pl.N
Ps.N

Guṅḍlapuri
Pl.N
TG

Guṅḍlavallēṭi
Pl.N
AN

Gundrāju (Gunḍu + rāju)
Pe.N
AN

Guṅdrāṭi
Pl.N
GV

Guṅḍu
Pl.N; Guṅḍuvāri – Guḍem, Bhadrachalem Tq, Khammam Dt.
TG; KK

Guṅḍugolana
Pl.N; Eluru Tq, West Godavari Dt.
VV

Guṅḍumaḷḷa
Pl.N
GV

Guntrēpu
Pl.N
AN

Guṅṭupalli
Pl.N; Near Kāmavarapukōṭa, Eluru Tq, West Godavari Dt; Bejawada Tq, Krishna Dt., Buddhist site. 2nd Century. BC
Ps.N; N

Guntūri / Guntūru
Pl.N; Head-quarters of a district in Andhra Pradesh.
AN; SII, VI, 228, ś 1119, SII, X, No.293, ś 1163; 299, ś 1165.

Guṅugutūri
Pl.N
AN

Guṅupāṭi
Pl.N
AN

Guṅupūdi
Pl.N ; one of the five Aramas in Andhradesa, Bhimavaram Tq, West Godavari Dt.
VV

Guraḍlapūdi
Pl.N
TG

Gurajāḍa
Pl.N; Gannavaram Tq, Krishna Dt.
AN

Gurajāla
Pl.N; Guruzāla, Paland Tq, Guntur Dt. ARE; 1930 : 879;
AN; IAP Cuddapah, III, 169, un-dated.

Gurajapalli
Pl.N
IVR, IV, 132, ś 1442.

Gurijala
Pl.N
Vaisya; IVR,IV, No.30, ś 1334.

Gurla
Pl.N
VN

Gurramkoṇḍa
Pl.N; Vayalpad Tq, Chittoor Dt; Venkatagiri Division, Nellore Dt.
M.Dh.

Gurrappaḍiya
Pl.N; Kandukur Tq, Nellore Dt.
Ps.N

Gurubhāgavatula
Title
KN

Gurudanti
Title; Guru = Teacher; Danti = elephant
TG

Guruzāḍa
Same as Gurajada.; But the gōtra is different
AN

Gūṭāla
Pl. N; Polavaram division, East Godavari Dt.
VV

Guṭṭi-bhāskara
Pl.N + Pe.N; Guṭṭikoṅḍa – Polnad Tq, Guntur Dt; Gutti Tq, Anantapur Dt.
V

Guṭṭina
Pl.N
TG

H

Haddanūri
Pl. N
GV

Halambaram
Pl. N
M. Dh.

Haṃdrēnki
Pl.N
Br.; SII, VI, 227, 1548 A.D.

Hanumantha- Vajhula
Pe. N ; Pl. N ; Hanumantha – puram, Śrikākulam Tq & Dt.; Guḍivāḍa Tq, Krishna Dt.
Hanumān, heavy jawed; son of Vāyu, the Mārutha God of wind.

Hari
Pe. N; Pl. N ; Harivāṇam, Sirugupta Tq, Ballāry Dt, Karnataka.
TG; Vel ; Haripuram Parlākimiḍi Tq, Odissa.
Hari, another name for Viṣṇu. ISGO, 15, ś 1380

Hari-dēvara
Pe. N; Pl. N; see above
Vel.

Hari-dēvula
Pe. N Pl. N; see above
Vel

Harihara – nādhuni
Pe. N after Viṣṇu and Śiva
Br.; SII XVI, 199, 1554 AD

Hari-pregaḍa
Pe. N Pl. N; see above
AN

Hēmanci bhaṭla
Pe. N
Vel

Hērba
Pl. N
M

Hōsadurgam
Pl. N; Near Hampi, Karnataka State. Sewell, Forgotten Empire pp. 292-299
VY; N. Venkataramanayya, Kampili and Vijayanagara, p. 2-3.

Hōsakōta
Pl. N ; Hārinahalli & Hōspeta Tq's, Bellary Dt. Karnataka
V

Hōta
Hōta = performer of a Yajña; well versed in Rg. Vēda
Vel.; Pl.N; Hōtavaram in Amanabrōlu Sīma – Guntur Dt.; EI,VIII, ś 1441

Huggēhaḷḷi
Pl. N
GV

Hunḍi
A heap of rice; the box in the temple where the devotees deposit their monetary or other offerings.
M.Dh

I

Ichchāpurapu
Pl. N ; Sompeta Tq, Srikakulam Dt.
TG

Iḍuputūri
Pl.N KKV

Ilapakurti
Pl.N; Narasannapeta & Tadepallem Tq's, West Godavari Dt.
AN; AS

Iṃdavarapu
Pl. N
Indur is the earlier name for Nizamabad.

Iṃdrakanṭi (Indrakanṭi)
Pl.N
TG; KK ; IAP Mahabubnagar, Vol. I, 167, ś 1094.

Iṃdu(pa)rti
Pl.N
GV

Iṃdukūri (Indukūri)
Pl. N
Kh ; IVR, 574, of the time of Venkatapatiraya – I, Vijayanagara.

Iṃdurti
Pl.N
AN ; KK

Iṃdutūri (Induturi)
Pl. N.
Br.; EP. An. IV, p.105, ś 1213.

Iṃguḍiga
Pl. N
KKV

Iṃguva
Pl. N
Vel.; ISGO, 15, ś 1380

Iṃkollu
Pl.N; Bapatla Tq, Guntur Dt.
VN; IVR, IV, 29, ś 1334

Iṃṭūri (Inṭūri)
Pl.N; Tenali Tq, Guntur Dt. Inṭūr
ETI, p.231

Inamanameḷḷuru
Pl.N.; Ongole Tq, Prakasam Dt.
AN

Inapakutika
Title
VV

Inuganṭi
Pl.N;
SV; VI, 228; ś.1119; X, 188, ś 1095.

Inumeḷḷa
Pl.N; Vinukonda Tq, Guntur Dt.
AN; SII, VI, 598, ś 1085

Ippaganṭa
Pl.N ; Kondukur Tq, Prakasam Dt.
AN

Ippili
Pl.N;
Srikakulam Tq & Dt.
Vy; SII, V, 1088, ś 1057.

Iragavarapu
Pl.N; Tadepalligudem Tq, West Godavari Dt.
AN

Iruganṭi
Pl.N
SV

Iruku
Pl.N
PD

Iruvanṭi
Pl.N
M.Dh

Isakapalli
Pl.N ; Narasaraopet, Guntur Dt; Rajampet Tq, Cuddapah Dt,; AD1284
TG ; SII, X, 537; un-dated.

Iṭikirāla
Pl.N
Vel.

Iṭukala
Pl.N ; Itikyala, Koilakuntla Tq, Kurnool Dt; IAP, Medak 112, un-dated (Kakatiya period)
VV

Ivatūri
Pl.N AN ;
IAP, Nalgonda, II,32, ś 1130

Iyuṇṇi
Pl.N
SV

Ī

Īchalūru
Pl. N
AN

Īdara
Pl.; Nuzvid division, Krishna Dt.; Darsi Tq, Prakasam Dt.
A.N

Īdūḍi
Pl. N; Īdudi, Parlakimidi Tq, Orissa
AN

Īdupagullu
Pl. N; Bezawada Tq, Krishna Dt.
AN

Īdūrūi
Pl. N; Idūru, Tadepalligudem Tq, West Godavari Dt., Nellore Tq & Dt.
AN

Īmani / Īvani
Pl. N; Tenāli Tq, Guntur Dt.
VV

Īraṃki
Pl. N
VV

Īśwara
Pe. N; Another name for Śiva
AN

Īśwara – bhatḷa
Pe. N
KK

Īśwara – pragaḍa
Pe. N
AN; GV

J

Jadąvilli
Pl. N Bapatla Tq, Guntur Dt.
V CP of AP, I, p 22-23.

Jaladaṃki
Pl.N; Kavali Tq, Nellore Dt.
AN; ISGO, 72, ś 1443.

Jinnūri
Pl.N; Narasāpuram Tq, West Godavari Dt.
Ps.N

Jōsyula
Title: Expert in astrology
AN; Ar; Ps.N; TG; VV ; SII, VI, 666, ś 1359.

Julākaluva
Pl.N; Anantapur Tq & Dt.
AN

Jāḍani
Pl. N
V

Jāgarlamūḍi
Pl. N; Tenali, Bapatla Tq's, Guntu: Dt.
TG

Jāgarlapūḍi
Pl. N;
VV; Jagarlapuṃdi – Gōtra : Bharadvāja – ISGO, 15, ś 1380

Jagga-rāju
Pe.N; Jagga, after Lord Jagannadha of Puri.
AN Pl. N. Jagga – raju – palle, Kalahasti division, Chittoor Dt.

Jaggu bhaṭla
Pe. N; Jagga (see above)
VV

Jājala
Pl. N
TG

Jakkana bhaṭla
Pe. N Pl.N. Jakkam -- Ceruvu, Penugonda Tq, Anantapur Dt.
KK; SII, IV, 1748, ś 1121; X, No.177, ś 1093.

Jakkana palli
Pl. N
AN; SII, IV, 748. ś 1121; IAP Nalgonda, II, No.48, ś 1182.

Jalapāla
Pl. N
AN; Jalapāla can also indicate a certain type of hair-style.

Jalasūtram
Title; Expert in hydrology or water mechanics.
VV

Jallēpalli
Pl.N Khammam Dt.
KN Baattle of Jallipalli ś 1283

Jallipalli
Pl. N
VV

Jambuladinne
Pl. N; Anantapur Tq & Dt.; Sirvel Tq, Kurnool Dt.
AN

Jammalamaḍaka
Pl.N; Kanigiri Tq, Prakasam Dt.
VV

Jammi
Pl. N; Flora jammi = Sami. Jammikuṇṭa – Huzurābad Tq, Karimnagar Dt, IAP, Karimnagar, No.9 ; Jammipalli – Sattenapalli Tq, Guntur Dt., SII, X, 265, ś 1142.
M. Dh

Jaṃpa
Pl.N;
Br.; SII, V, 1231 Srikurmam Inscription.

Jaṃpana
Pl. N; Jampani, Tenali Tq, Guntur Dt.
VV; Kh ; SII, XVI, 130, 1554 AD.

Jaṃpani
Pl.N; Tenali Tq, Guntur Dt., SII, X, 365, ś 1181.
SV; IVR, IV, 237, ś 1466.

Jānamaddi
Pl. N
V

Janamanci
Pe. N
TG

Jānapāṭi
Pl.N; Palnad Tq, Guntur Dt.
VV

Janaswāmi
Pe. N
VV; ISGO, 15, ś 1380.

Jańdhyāla
Sacred thread
TG; VV

Jańgālapalli
Pl. N
AN

Jannamubhōṭla
Pe. N; Jannamu, a Vikruti of Yajña
TG

Jarugumilli
Pl. N
VV

Jaṭaprōlu
Pl. N
TG

Jaṭāvallabhula
Title ; May not be after Jaṭāchōḍa bhịma, a ruler; can be from 'Jaṭa', a tradition in the rendition of Veda.
KN

Javvadi
Pl. N; Javvāji, Kangudi division, North Arcot Dt, Tamil Nadu.
Ps.N

Jayanti; Jayanti, Nandigāma Tq, Krishna Dt.
Title ; Victory or Pl. N ; Jayantipura; IAP, Nalgonda, I, No.42, C.V. 50.
VV; SII X, 274, ś 1152.

Jeediganṭī
Pl. N; Jịdikallu, Jangaon Tq, Warangal Dt.A N; KKV; IAP, Warangal, No.57.

Jeediguṇṭa
Pl. N
KK

Jeevanige
Pl. N
M.Dh.

Jiḍḍu
Oily
VV

Jiguru
Sticky Paste
TG

Jillēḷḷa
Pl. N ; Produturu Tq, Cuddapah Dt.; Siruvella Tq, Kurnool Dt, SII, XIV, 256, 143 AD.
KKV; Ps.N; TG ; IAP Cuddapah Dt. III, 96, ś 1539.

Jillēḷḷamūḍi
Pl. N; Kandukuru Tq, Prakasam Dt; Bapatla Tq, Guntur Dt.
AN

Jnambākam
Pl. N
AN

Jōga vajhula
Pe. N
KK

Jonna bhaṭla
Pe. N
TG; VV

Jonnāḍa
Pl. N
VV

Jonnalagaḍḍa
Pl. N; Sattenapalli Tq; Guntur Dt.; Nandigāma Tq, Krishna Dt
AN; VV; SII, IV, 709, ś 1480; X, 529, ś 1241; ISGO, 15, ś 1380.

Jonnavittula
Pl. N
VV

Joppini
Pl. N; SVR, IV, 164, ś 1450.

Jōsya bhaṭla
Title; expert in astrology
TG; SII, VI, 622, ś 1120.

Jūlēru
Pl. N
M.Dh

Jūlūri
Pl. N
M.Dh; VV ; IAP Cuddapah II, 27 (of the times of Proudhadevaraya of Vijayanagar)

Jūpalli
Pl. N; Udayagiri Tq, Nellore Dt., IVR, IV, 146, ś 1446.

Jūpūḍi
Pl. N; Sattenapalli Tq, Guntur Dt.
AN; SII, X, 509, ś 1236.

Juttiga
Pl. N; Tanuku Tq, West Godavari Dt.
AN

Jūtūri
Pl.N; Penugonda Tq, Anantapur Dt. SII, XVI, 248, 1560 AD.
Kh.

Jyōtivantula
Title : Jyoti = light or after the village Jōti ; Siddhavatam Tq, Cuddapah Dt., A.P.
GV; IAP, Cuddapah, I, No. 133, ś 1169.

K

Kāci bhaṭla
Pe. N
VV; 'Kanci Adikāri' – SII, IV, 815, ś 1472

Kāci rāju
Pe. N
A.N; Kancirāju , IVR IV, No. 369, ś 1477

Kaḍakuduru
Pl. N; Kaḍava kuduru, Çhirala Tq, Prakasam Dt. ; EI, 15: 253.

Kaḍala , Correctly Kaḍali
Hydronymic; Sea ; Razolu Tq, East Godavari Dt.
A.N ; Gotra: Kāśyapa; ISGO, ś 1380. Gōtra : Kaunḍinya.

Kaḍamala – Cherla
P. N
Br.; IAP Warangal, 110, ś 1386.

Kādaṃbari
Title; Study of the world of the same name by poet Harsha
AN

Kadapa
Pl. N
Head Quarters town of the district of the same name spelled until recently as Cuddapah
SV SII, XVI, 130, 1544 AD; EI, 28 : 67. ; IVR, IV, No.108, ś 1439.

Kadha
Story such as of Rāmayaṇa
A.N

Kaḍimēḷ'
Pl. N
Pg.N

Kaḍiyāla
Pl. N; Kaḍiyam = Anklet
VV

Kaikāla
Pl.N

Kaiva
Pl. N
V

Kaivāram
Employment; hearlder or praise chanter in Royal Courts.
TG; Pl. N; Kaivāramu – Kōta, Chintamani Tq, Kōlar Manḍalam, Karnataka state,
SII, X, No.402, ś 1186

Kāja
Pl. N; Krañja', Narasāpur Tq, West Godavari Dt.
Br.; Krañga – SII, IV, 699, ś 1468, ibid, 709, ś 1191, SII, V, 106; X 534, ś 246.

Kākāni
Pl.N; Kākāni, Narasaraopeta Tq, Guntur Dt.; Kakandivada earlier form – ETI, P.R 69, 732 AD
Ps.N; VV ; SII, X, 271, , ś 1145

Kākara
Pl. N
A.D

Kākaraparṭi
Pl. N; Tanuku Tq, West Godavari Dt.
A.D

Kākarāla
Pl. N
A.D; SII, VI, 70, , ś 1312.

Kākarla
Pl. N; Cumbum Tq, Kurnool Tq; Podili Tq., Prakasam Dt.
KN; A.N

Kākarlamūḍi
Pl. N ; Bandar Tq., Krishna Dt.
Ps. N

Kāki
Pl.N ;
IVR, IV, 264 , ś 1467.

Kākirala
Pl. N
Ps. N

Kākulapāṭi
Pl. N; Divi Tq, Krishna Dt.
A.N; SV

Kākuḷavarapu
Pl. N
M.Dh

Kākumānu
Pl.N; Bapatla Tq, Guntur Dt.; Ep. An. III, p.16 ; ARE, Hyderabad, 65 c p-5
A.N; The kakumranu Grant of Chalukya Bhima I, 10th Century A. D.,

Kākunūri
Pl. N; Nagaram Tq, Mahabūbnagar Dt.; Nandyal Tq.,
Pg.N; V; IVR, IV, No. 164, ś 1450.; SII, X, 528, ś 1241.

Kākuṭūri
Pl.N; Kāvali Tq, Nellore Dt.
Pg.N

Kalabarige
Pl.N; Gulbarga, Karnataka State.
KK; A.N ; ISGO, 61, 15th Century A.D; SII. X, 729.

Kāladhāri
Pe. N
AS

Kalaga
Pl. N
VV

Kāḷahasti
Pl.N; Chittoor Dt.

Kalakaḍeme
Pl. N
V

Kālam cheṭṭi
Pe.N
V
Normally the suffix 'Cheṭṭi' is found associated with the Vaiśya names and surnames in the variant 'Seṭṭi'.

Kāḷaṃ rāju
Pe.N; Pl. N; K āḷaṃ rāju-pēṭa, Gajapathinagaram Tq, Vizianagaram Dt.
A.N

Kālanādha bhaṭla
Pe. N
A.N; T.G; KNV

Kaḷānidhi
Title; Preserver of learning or art. See Kala
M.Dh

Kalasapūḍi
Pl. N
A.N

Kalavacherla
Pl.N; Rāmachandrāpuram Tq, East Godavari Dt.
A.N; SII, VI, No. 957, ś 1219.

Kalavaganṭi
Pl.N
A.N

Kalavaguṇṭa
Pl. N
A.N

Kalava kōlanu
Pl.N
TG; CTI, IV, No. ś 1386, IAP Warangal, 110, ś 1386.

Kalavala
of Lotuses
GV

Kalavala palli
Pl.N ; Savasiddi Tq, Visakhapatnam Dt; Podili Tq, Prakasam Dt.
V; SII, VI, 667, ś 1344.

Kalavalapu
Related to Lotus (Kalava)
A.N

Kalavapūḍi
Pl.N; Gudivada Tq, Krishna Dt.
SV SII, IV, 699, ś 1468.

Kali bhaṭla
Pe N
VV

Kalidiṅḍi
Pl.N; Kaikalur Tq, Krishna Dt.
A.N; Kh ; ETI, p.267; EI, 29: 62.

Kaligoṭla
Pl.N; 'Kallugotla' – Kalugotla, Nandikotkur Tq, Kurnool Dt.
A.N; SII, 9 – i ; 124; IMP, Kurnool, 443.

Kalikivāyi
Pl. N ; Kandukur Tq, Prakasam Dt.
SV

Kalikodime
Pl. N
KN

Kāḷipaṭnam
Pl.N; Narasapuram Tq, West Godavari Dt.
A.N

Kāḷḷa
Pl.N; Bhimavaram Tq, West Godavari Dt.
TG

Kāḷḷaguṇṭa
Pl. N
VY

Kāḷḷakūri
Pl.N; Bhimavaram Tq, West Godavari Dt.
A.N; SV

Kaḷḷemu
Horse strap
TG

Kaḷḷēpalli
Pl.N; Pedda Kaḷḷēpalli; Machilipatnam Tq, Krishna Dt., SII,VI, No.79, ś 1718 ;
Kaḷḷēpalli, Srikakulam Dt; Śrungavarapu Kōṭa Tq, Vizianagaram Dt.
Vel. P; Badagala Karana Kamma Vaidiki; Uṭkaḷa Gowḍa Pūjāri

Kāḷḷūri
Pl.N; Hindupur Tq, Anantapur Dt., Guntur Tq & DT., Ellavaram Division, East Godavari Dt;
GV; A.N; SV; Vel. ; IAP Cuddapah – III, 151, ś 1724. IVR, IV, No. 477, un-added; EI, 31:129.

Kāḷūri
Pl. N
M.Dh

Kalvacherla
Pl.N; Sultanabad Tq, Karimnagar Dt.
A.N

Kalyāṇaṃ
Auspicious
SII, XVI, 214, 1516 AD.

Kāmana
Pe. N
Re; SII, XVI, 330, 1643 A.D.

Kāmanūri
Pl.N
N.N

Kāma rāju
Pe.N
Ps.N; A.N ; ETI, p. 272, AD1018.

Kāmarāju geḍḍa
Pl. N
A.N

Kāmarasu (Kāma + Arasu)
Pe.N; IVR, IV, No.71 ś 1430
V; LN; SII, XVI, 257, 1563 AD ; IAP Cuddapah III, 130 undated; II, 63, ś 1430.

Kāmariṣi
Pe. N
A.N

Kāma samudram
Pl.N; IVR, IV, No.237; ś 1466.
SV; SII, XVI, 130, 1544 AD; IAP Cuddapah III, 180, ś 1645; II, 6, ś 1272

Kamalākara
Pe. N; A mass of lotuses; Another name for sun
KK

Kāmāvantula (Correctly Kāmā pantula)
Pe. N
A.D; VNV

Kāmavarapukōṭa
Pl.N; Eluru Tq, West Godavari Dt.
A.D

Kaṃbāladinne
Pl.N; Hindupur Tq, Anantapur Dt.
Pg.N

Kaṃbhaṃ
Pl.N; IVR, IV, 221, ś 1462.

Kaṃbhaṃpāṭi
Pl.N; Sattenapalli Tq, Guntur Dt.
VV ; Kaṃbhaṃpāḍu, Markapuram Tq, , SII, i.204; Palnadu Tq, Guntur Dt, SII, X, 666, ś 1033.

Kām bhaṭla
Pe. N
VNV

Kaṃcharla
Pl.N; Kaṃacherla, Vinukonda Tq, Guntur Dt.
Ps.N; IVR IV, No.237, ś 1466.

Kaṃdaḍy
Pl. N
SV

Kaṃdāḷa
Pl.ND;
SV

Kaṃdarāḍa
Pl.N
M.Dh

Kāṃdrēgula
Pl.N; Kakinada, Peddapuram Tqs; East Godavari Dt.
KKV

Kaṃdu
Pl. N
A.N

Kaṃdūri
Pl.N; Kandukuri-vari-Agraharam, Ongole Tq, Prakasam Dt.
SV; VV; ISGO, 15, ś 1380.

Kaṃkanṭi
Pl. N
A.N

Kamma
Thatch
Also a name of caste Kamma
VV

Kaṃtēpalli
Pl.N; Nellore Tq & Dt
Ps.N

Kaṃtēṭi
Pl.N ; Guntur Tq, Guntur Dt.
VV; Vel.P; Salamkalyana Nandivarma, II, Kanteru Inscription,EI, 18: 57

Kaṅadā
Pl.N
N.N

Kānādi bhaṭla
Pe.N; The core element kanadi may be related to the earlier referred Kanada
TG

Kanaka bhaṭla
Pe. N
TG

Kanakadaṅḍi
Holder of a golden staff
TG

Kanakāla
Pl. N
AN; VV

Kanakā pragaḍa
Pe. N
A.N

Kanaka rāju
Pe. N
A.N

Kānala
Pl.N; Nandyala Tq, Kurnool Dt.
N.N

Kańcaṃ
Plate made with Cańchu metal; IVR, IV, 239 ś 1466.

Kānchanapalle
Pl. N
GV

Kanchu-ghańṭala
A mark of recognition, Kanch = brass metal, Ghanta = bell
Ps.N

Kānci
Pl.N 'Kāñchipuram', Kanigiri Tq, Prakasam Dt.
AD; AN; IAP Nalgonda II, No.41, ś 1171

Kańci bhoṭla
Pe. N
VV

Kańcinādhamu
Pe. N
D

Kanci – rāju
Pe.N;
SII, XVII, 105, 1533AD.

Kandā
Food;
VV

Kaṅdāḷa
Pl.N; SII, XVI, 127, 1542 AD; X, 577, ś 1332.
Di. SV

Kaṅdikaṭṭa
Food item
Ps.N

Kaṅdikoṇḍa
Pl. N
A.N; KNV

Kaṅdikuppa
Pl. N; Amalapuram Tq, East Godavari Dt.
K.N

Kaṅdimaḷḷa
Pl. N
A.N

Kaṅdarpa
Pe.N: SII, V, 1231; SII X, 402 ś 1186; Srikurmam Inscription.
TG; IAP, Mahabūbnagar Vol.II, No.5, ś 1154.

Kaṅdrakōṭa
Pl. N
SV; SII, X, 395, ś 1183.

Kaṅdula
Pl. N
VV

Kaṅdūri
Pl.N; Kanduri; Kandr (a) bulrush
Br.; ETI, p.279, SII, X,420, ś 1190; Ep. An. IV, pp.56-57.

Kaṅdukūri
Pg. N; VV; LN; AN; M.Dh.
Pl.N ; Nellore Dt, Devarakonda Tq, Nalgonda Dt, IAP, Nalgonda I, No,100, ś 1232
ETI, p.259, AD 848.; Kandukuru Tq, Prakasam Dt.

Kaṅkipāṭi
Pl.N; Kankipadu, Gannavaram Bejawada Tq, Krishna Dt.
A.N; EI, 17:328

Kaṅṭi
Pl.N;
Br.; SII, VI, 743, ś 1350.

Kannēkaṅṭi
Pl.N; 'Kanekallu' – Miryalaguda Tq, Nalgonda Dt,; Kanekallu, Rayadurga Tq,
Anantapur St, E.G.; 4:212
TG; IAP, Nalgonda I, No.77, AD1265.

Kannēpalli
Pl. N
VV; K.N

Kānugurti
Pl.N; Kanukurtavaripalle, Chandragiri Tq, Chittoor Dt, Kanugurti, Mahabubnagar Dt, on the border of AP and Karnataka.
M.Dh

Kānukolanu
Pl. N
A.N

Kānukollu
Pl.N; Gudivada Tq, Krishna Dt.
A.N

Kanumaḷḷa
Pl. N
TG

Kanumarla
Pl.N; Gudivada Tq, Krishna Dt.
VV; EI, XXV, p.137, 146, ś 1260.

Kānuparti
Pl.N; Kanuparru – Narasaraopet Tq, Guntur Dt, EI, 31:77, Kanuparti,

Ongole Tq, Prakasam Dt, SII, VI, 606, ś 105; Addomki Tq, Prakasam Dt: Rapur Tq, Nellore Dt.
A.N; TG ; IVR, IV, No. 42, ś 1348; IVR, IV, No.558, ś 1558.

Kaṇupūri
Pl. N
Pg.N

Kānūri
Pl.N; Tanuku Tq, West Godavari Dt; Bonda Tq, Krishna Dt.
A.N; VV; EI, 35 :149.

Kaṇva
Pe.N
Br.; ISGO, 15, ś 1380..

Kaṇvapuri
Pl. N
Pg.N

Kāpagaṇḍi
Pl. N
TG

Kāpavarapu
Pl.N; Kāpavaram, Bhadrachalam Division, Peddapuram Tq, East Godavari Dt.
A.N; TG

Kapila
Cow; An instrument for lifting water from a water source
A.N; Ka; Also the name of a Rishi – SII, IV, 796, ś 1348.

Kapilavāyi
Pl. N
TG; KN

Kapisthalaṃ
Pl. N
SV

Kappagantu
A tradition of reciting Veda like a frog
PG.N

Kappagaṅtula
Title
A style of recitation of Veda like a Kappa (Frog) gentu (Jump)
Ps.N; VV

Kara
Pl.N; Bandar Tq, Krishna Dt.
A.N

Kāraṃchēṭi
Pl.N; Bapatla, Guntur Dt.
VV; SII, IV, 228, ś 1119

Karaṇamu < Skt. Karaṇah
Employment; Village accountant. ETI,p.264, 8th Century AD
A.N; IAP, Mahabubnagar Vol.II, No.15, ś 1202.

Karavadi
Pl.N; Ongole Tq, Prakasam Dt.
A.N; SII, XVI, 286, 1575 AD.

Kārḍa vajhula
Pl.N; Karada, Bobbili Tq, Vizianagaram Dt.
A.D

Kareḍla
Oxyzen (redla) Here 'Ka' stands for the colour-black
VV

Kāreṃpūḍi
Pl.N; Palnaḍu Tq, Guntur Dt.
GV; SII, X, 402, ś 1186; X, 134, ś 1076.

Kari
Elephant
Ps.; SII, X, 1231, Eastern Ganga Anangabhima

Kari peddi
Pe. N
TG

Karlapālem
Pl.N; Bapatla Tq, Guntur Dt.
Ps.N

Karlapūḍi
Pl.N; Gudur Tq, Nellore Dt.
Ps.N; IVT, IV, No. 272, ś 1468.

Karnuūtala
Pl.N; Guntur Tq, & Dt.
Ps.N; SII, X, 571, ś 1326.

Karra
Stick; Pl.N. Karra – vari- sthavaram, Tanuku Tq, West Godavari Dt.
PD

Karri
Black
PD; VV

Kārūcoḷa
Pl.N; Narasaraopet Tq, Guntur Dt.
Ps.N

Kārumanci
Pl.N; Vinukonda Tq, Guntur Dt; Pattikonda Tq, Kurnool Dt.
A.N

Karumūri
Pl.N
A.N

Kāsalanāṭi
Pl.N; Kasalanati – khandrika ; Raipur Tq, Nellore Dt.
By itself it is the name of a Brahmin Subsect
V

Kāsara
Pl. N
TG

Kāsarabāda
Pl.N; Nandigama Tq, Krishna Dt.
A.N

Kāsarabāja
Pl.N; Correctly 'Kasarabada' (see above)
A.N

Kāsaram
Pl. N
AK

Kasava rāju
Pe. N
A.N

Kāsavarapu
Pl.N
A.N

Kāśa vajhala
Pl. N
TG; VV ; KN

Kāśi
Pl.N; Benaras PD; KN; SV

Kāśi bhatla
Pe.N
PD; VV; TG; Ps. N; VNV

Kāśichainula
Pe. N
KN

Kāśinādhuni
Pe. N; after Śiva, lord of Kāśi
Ar. N

Kāśi pragada
Pe.N
A.N

Kāśi rāju
Pe.N
A.N

Kāśi somayājula
Pe.N
DD

Kāśi vajhula
Pe.N
PD; TG; KN

Kastūri
A kind of perfume: scent
A.N; KKV

Kāsukhēla
Pl. N
KKV

Kāsula
Pl. N or Kasu = Coin (Monetary)
YS

Kāsulameesula
See Kasu
Ps. N

Kaṭa
Title. Skt. Kaḷa = Vidya ; Art
VV

Kaṭanagaḍḍa
Br.
Gōtra: Ātrēyasa; ISGO, 15, ś 1380

Kaṭakam
Pl. N

Capital of Odissa during the medieval period.
KN; TG; Vel.

Kāṭe palli
Pl. N
TG

Kāṭhāru
Sword
GV

Kāti
Pl.N; burial ground
A.N; Ps.N; VNV

Kāṭimēṭi
Pl.N
TD

Kātrapāṭi
Pl.N
A.N

Kāṭrāvula palli
Pl.N; Peddapuram Tq, East Godavari Dt.
A.N

Kāṭrāyi
Pl.N
Ps.N

Kaṭṭa
Pl.N; in the sense of Anicut or barrage
TG; IVR, IV, No. 117, ś 1440.

Kaṭṭamūri
Pl.N; Peddapuram Tq, East Godavari Dṭ, Sattenapalli Tq, Guntur Dt.
VV; A.N

Kaṭṭekōla
A weapon made up of wood
A.N

Katti
Sword ; SII, XVI, 70, 1521 AD.

Kaṭṭu
Pl.N
K.N

Kaṭṭumūḍi
Pl.N
A.N

Kaṭṭumūri
Pl.N
sA.N

Kātugaṅṭi
Pl.N
GV

Kātūri
Pl.N; Kalahasti division, Chittoor Dt.
A.N

Kāvali
Pl.N; Kavali Tq, Nellore Dt.
A.N; NI, Kavali (50), ś 1558.

Kāvalipāṭi
Pl.N
A.N

Kāvalivarapu
Pl.N
A.N

Kavi
Title
Poet
N

Kavi dhāti
Title Forceful poet
SD

Kavi koṅḍala
Title
A mountain among the poets
PS

Kavi mukkula
Title pertaining to poetry
KNK
Pl.N
KNV

Kavi purapu
Pl.N; Tanuku Tq, West Godavari Dt; Bandar Tq, Krishna Dt.
A.N

Kavi-rāṇamu
Title pertaining to majesty in poetry
VNV

Kavi-rāyani
A raja or raya among the poets, Pl N.; Kavirayani-valasa, Bobbili Tq, Vizianagaram Dt
VNV

Kavita
Title
Poetry
V

Kavivige
Title - poetry
M.Dh.

Kavula
Kavula kuntla – Markapur Tq, Prakasam Dt.
PS; SII. IX – i; 204.

Kavulūri
Pl.N
A.N; Ps.N ; IAP, Cuddapah, III, 89, ś 1662.

Kāvūri
Pl.N; Narasaraopeta Tq, Guntur Dt.
A.N; VV SII, IV, 916, Undated ; X, 122, ś 1075.

Kavva
Pl. N
SV

Keerti rāju
Pe. N
A.N

Kēśa rāju
Pe. N
AN

Kēśānapalli
Pl.N Razole Tq, East Godavari Dt.
A.N; IVR, IV, 242, ś 1466.

Kēśānupalli
Pl.N; Narasaraopet Tq, Guntur Dt.
A.N

Kēśā pragaḍa
Pe. N, Pl. N ; All the Pl. N with the prefix ' Kēśā ' ought to have been derived from place names like Kēśāva – patna, Bhadrachalam division, East Godavari Dist.
A.N

Kēsari
Title, if it means Siṃha (Lion)
Pe.N after Narasiṃha, the 4th Avatara (incranation) of Viṣṇu
KKV

Kēśāva bhaṭla
Pe. N; Pl.N ; Kēśā – bhaṭla – Khandrika, Podili Tq, Prakasam Dt.
V; SII, XVI, 288, 1576AD.

Kēśāva pantula
Pe. N
V

Kēśāva rāju
Pe. N
A.N

Kēśa varapu
Pl. N
A.N

Kēśi rāju
Pe. NA.N; Kēśi rāja preggaḍe –IAP, Nalgonda, II, No.20, C.V.50 = AD1125.

Kētamukkala
Pl.N
VV

Kēta rāju
Pe. N; Pl.N, Ketarajapalle, Razolu Tq, East Godavari Dt.
Ps.N

Kētavarapu
Pl.N; Sattenapalli Tq, Guntur Dt ; Eluru Tq, West Godavari Dt.
TG; SII, VI, 248, ś 1437

Kētu
Reddy
IAP, Nalgonda, I. No.94, ś 1222

Keytēpalli
Pl.N
VV

Khamampāṭi
Pl.N
Vel.

Khambhammeṭṭu
Pl.N
AN

Khanḍāḷam
Pl.N
M.Dh.

Khanḍavalli
Pl.N ; Tanuku Tq, W. G Dt, Kamadavalli (Gotra; Bhāradvāju) ISGO, 15, ś 1380.
AN; SV; KN; VV ; SII, VI,210 ś 1090.

Khandērāvu / Khadērāyani
Pe.N
Ps. N

Khandrika
A unit of cultivable land. Pl.N. Razolu Tq, East Godavari Dt, Tanuku Tq, W.G Dt.
VN

Khanṭaṃ rāju
Pe.N
Ps.N; SII, IV, 709, ś 1480

Khāsukhēla
Employment
GV

Khāsunavisu
Employment
Ps

Khāzana
Treasury
KKV

Kiḍāṃbi/Kiḷāṃbi
Pl.N; Kimidi in Odissa , EI, IV, No.45.
SV

Kochcherlakōṭa
Pl.N; Kochcherla, Vinukonda Tq, Guntur ; IVR, IV, 147, ś1474
A.N; SII, V, 117, un-dated.

Kōḍaganṭi
Pl.N
VV

Koḍagaṭṭu
Pl. N
GV

Kodaṃanchili
Pl.N; Narasapur Tq, West Godavari Dt.
Vel.P

Koḍamarti
Pl. N
VNV

Kōdāṭi
Pl.N
GV

Koḍavanṭi
Pl.N
Vel.

Koḍavaṭiganṭi
Pl. N
Vel.

Kōḍi
Pl.N
Ps. N

Kōḍicherla
Pl.N
AN

Koḍimala
Pl.N
Ps.N

Kōḍuganṭi
Pl.N
TG

Koḍukula
Koduku is correctly 'Kolukula', Markapuram, Tq, Prakasam Dt.
PD; VV

Kōḍūri
Pl.N; Mahabūbnagar Tq & Dt; Markapuram Tq, Prakasam Dt, Guntur Tq &Dt SII, C, 509, ś1236.
AN; TG; Ps. N; SV ; Kōdūru – Kamdapuram Tq, Cuddapah Bhuvanagiri Tq,
Nalgonda Dt, SII, VI, 118, ś 1203 ; IAP, Cuddapah Dt. No,7, ś 1825.

Kōganṭi
Pl.N; Sattenapalli Tq, Guntur Dt.
M.Dh.

Kōganṭipālepu
Pl.N
Ps.N

Kōlapalli
Pl.N
KN

Kokkirigaḍḍa
Pl. N
K.N

Kokkonḍa
Pl.N ; in Gazvel Tq; Medak Dt. A.P.
A.N; M.Dh. IAP, Medak, 53, ś 995.

Kōlāchalam
Pl.N
TG

Kolachina
Pl.N
TG

Kōlaganṭi
Pl.N
AD

Kolakalūri
Pl.N. Kolaṃkalūru, Tenali Tq, Guntur Dt. SII, X, 297, ś 1240; 158, ś 1087.

Kōlagaṭla
Pl.N; Atmakur Tq, Nellore Dt. ; SII, X, 422 ś 1191

Kōlaguṭla
Palnad Tq, Guntur Dt. ś 1519, MER, 1929-30 No.88

Kōlakula
Pl.N; Ps. N

Kōlanka
Pl.N; Kakinda Tq, East Godavari Dt.
Hydronymic; water tank
AN

Kolanu
Pl.N; same as Kolani – ETI, p.289, 915-25 AD ; Kolleru lake in West Godavari Dt.
VV; SII, V, 181, ś 1115

Kōlapalli
Pl.N
KN

Kōlapaṭi
Pl.N
Br.; IAP, Nalgonda II, No.11, ś 1020.

Kolavāsi
Pe. N
AN

Kōlavennu
Pl.N; Vijayawada Tq, Krishna Dt.
AN SII, X, 352, ś 117; 317, ś 1170 (Kōlaventi)

Kolipāka
Pl.N; Kolanupaka, Bhuvanagiri Tq, Nalgonda Dt.
AN ; IAP, Nalgonda, II, No.3, ś 978.

Kolipākam
Pl.N
GV; Kollipākke, IAP, Nalgonda, II, No.7, 1082 AD

Kolla
Pl.N; Kolla –pūdi – Nellore Dt.
VV; NDI, Nellore : 106.

Kollaparti
Pl.N
AN

Kolli
Pl.N; Kollivāri – Gudem, Eluru Tq, West Godavari Dt.
VV; Kollipāra, Tenali Tq, Guntur Dt. EI, 8:238.; E.A, 3:3

Kollimarla
Pl.N; Bapatla Tq, Guntur Dt.
AN

Kollūri
Pl.N; Kollūru – Repalli Tq, Guntur Dt. EI, t,: 142
AD; KK; VV; PD ; SII, VI, 129, ś1067; X No.95, ś 1055.

Kōmali
Pl.N; Repalle Tq, Guntur Dt.
VV; EI, 19; 259

Kōmāndūri
Pl.N
SV

Komaragiri
Pl.N after Pe.N; Amalapuram Tq, East Godavari Dt.
The name of one of the Reddy Kings.
NN; SII, V, 30, ś 1335

Komaravōlu
Pl.N; Markapur Tq, Prakasam Dt., SII, IX, 9 - I ; 204.
AN; SII, Vi, 961, ś 1322.

Komarōsi
Pl.N; 'Kommaresmi' SII, V, No.61.
VV

Komarrāju
Pe.N; Pl.N. Kommana (Kumarapuram) Pithapuram Tq, East Godavari Dt.
LN; SII, X, 274, ś 1152 ; EI, 18:60 ; SII, V 90, ś 1099.

Koṃdapalle
Pl.N
Br.; ISGO, 15, ś 1380.

Kommājōsyula
Pe.N
KN

Kommālapaṭi
Pl.N; Kommala-pādu, Narasaraopeta Tq, Guntur Dt.
P.S

Kommaḷḷapalli
Pl.N
AS

Kommana
Pl.N; Kurmanna palli
Br.; SII, VI, 238, ś 1077.

Kommana peddi
Pe.N
Ps.N

Komma rāju
Pe.N
AN; GV; Ps.N

Kommini
Pl.N
Vel.

Kommu
Horn
TG; VV

Kommūri
Pl.N; Bapatla Tq.; Guntur Dt.; SII, X, No.738 un-dated ; IAP Cuddapah III;
M.Dh; AN; ISGO, 78, 16th Century AD; IVR, IV, No.105, ś 1438

Koṃpalli
Pl. N
A.N; KK; SV ; EP. Am IV, pp 97-98, ś 1141.

Kompella
Pl.N
VV

Kompena
Pl.N; Kompera
VV; JAHRS, 20:84

Kōna
Pl.N; Corner; Kōna – sīma between Amalapuram and Rajol Tq, East Godavari Dt,
The land between Gowtami and Vasishta, branches of Godavari river, Bandar Tq,

Krishna District
AN ; EI, IV, p. 83, ś 1117.

Koṇakanchi
Pl.N; Nandigama Tq, Krishna Dt.
K.N

Konakonḍla
Pl.N; Gootly Tq, Anantapur Dt.
SII 9-1 :136.

Konam bhaṭṭa
Pe.N
KK

Konam rāju
Pe.N
GV

Koṇḍa
Oronymic = mountain
A.N; Ps.N ; IAP, Cuddapah Dt.,
III, 86, un-dated.

Koṇḍā josyula
Pe.N
TG

Koṇḍamaḍugu
Pl.N ; Palanad Tq, Guntur Dt.
A.N; SII, X, No.119; ś 1089.

Koṇḍamūḍi
Pl.N
A.N; VV; Brihatphalayana Jayavarma Koṇḍamūdi Inscriptions EI.VI, No.31.

Koṇḍamūri
Pl.N
Baḍa Kannaḍa Niyōgi

Koṇḍapalli
Pl.N; Vijayawada Tq, Krishna Dt.
GV; VV
In Krishna District; once a stronghold of the Reddi kings; now famous for hand made toys.
SII, X, 504, ś 1235, SII, IV, 699, ś 1468; ISGO, 15, ś 1380.

Koṇḍapāṭi
Pl.N
A.N

Koṇḍapāṭuri
Pl. N
A.N

Koñḍapi
Pl.N; Kandukur, Prakasam Dt. IAP, Nalgonda II, No.8, 1088 AD.

Koṇḍaveeḍu
Pl.N; Narasaraopet Tq, Guntur Dt. Same as Kondaveeti
M.Dh; Ps.N; Vel.P ; SII, IV, 699, ś 1468 ; ISGO, 15, ś 1380.

Koṇḍaveeti
Pl.N; Narsaraopet Tq, Guntur Dt.
Vel.A; IVR,IV, 272, ś 1468.
Once the capital of the Reddy Kingdom. SII, IV, 699, ś 1468.

Kondēpūḍi
Pl.N; Guntur Tq & Dt.; Bhimavaram Tq, West Godavari Dt.
AN; EI, 31 : 77

Koṇḍu bhatla
Pe.N
TG

Koṇḍūri
Pl.N 'Koṇḍūrupura', IAP, Nalgonda I, No.18, AD 1087.
SV; ETI, p. 286, 8th Century AD.

Koṇḍūru
Pl.N; Pedda – Koṇḍūru, Tenali Tq, Guntur Dt.
AN; VV; SII, X, 174, ś 1092 ; 189, ś 1095.

Koṇijēṭi / Konjēṭi
Pl.N
Vy

Koṇiki
Pl.N; Ongole Tq, Prakasam Dt, ; Eluru Tq, West Godavari Dt. An elevated place or heap. ETI, p 284, 669 AD.
KN; A.N; SII, XVI, 325, 1638AD.

Kōnēṭi
Hydronymic
Ka; SII XVI, 187, 1553, AD.

Kongara
Pl.N; Kongaravāri palle, Chandragiri Tq, Chittoor Dt.

Konkēpūḍi
Pl.N
AN

Kontēṭi
Pl.N; 'Konēru', Guntur Tq & Dt.
Vel.P; Kanteti – vari – khandrika, Narasaraopeta Tq, Guntur Dt.

Konukanchi
Pl.N
Vel.; ISGO, 15, ś 1380.

Koppāka
Pl.N; Eluru Tq, West Godavari Dt., Anakapallin Tq, Visakhapatnam Dt.
AN

Koppale
Pl.N; Bhimavaram Tq, West Godavari Dt; Bandar Tq, Krishna Dt.
M.Dh.

Koppalli
Pl.N; 'Kōpalli' – Nalgonda Dt., CITD, 4; 34
GV

Koppa rāju
Pl.N; 'Kopale' Devarakonda Tq, Nalgonda Dt.
AN; Koppalle – Ramachandrapuram Tq, East Godavari Dt.

Kopparapu
Pl.N; Koppāram, SII X, 73, ś 1037. Narasannapeta Tq, Guntur Dt., Kakinada Tq
AN East Godavari Dt., ; SII, VI, 613, ś 1023; X, 271, ś 1145.

Kopparigām
Pl.N
M.Dh.; PD

Kopparti
Pl.N; Kopparti, Bapatla Tq, Guntur Dt.
AN; Ps.N; Koppartivari palle, Chandragiri Tq, Chittoor Dt.

Koppōlu
Pl.N ; Cuddapah Tq & Dt; Ongole Tq, Prakasam Dt, IVR, IV, 240, ś 1466.
Ps.N; IAP Cuddapah, II, 165, ś 1466.

Kōrāḍa
Pl.N
AN; VV; SII, IV, 1003, 1282.

Korimarla
Pl.N
AN

Korisapāṭi
Pl.N
Ps.N

Korivi
Pl.N; Kōrvi – Mahabubabad Tq, Warangal Dt., SII, X, 528, ś 1241
AN; Naḷgonda Dt, Koravi ; ETI, p.288, 892 - 922 AD ; SII, IV, 961 un-dated.

Korlapāṭi
Pl.N; Koṟṟaprōlu – SII X, 504, ś 1235 IA, 20 : 417.
AN; IA, 20 : 417.

Korrapāṭi
Pl.N; Koṟṟapādu, Sattenapalli Tq, Guntur Dt; Bhīṁavaram Tq, West Godavari Dt.
AN; Koṟṟapādu, Kamdapuram Tq, Cuddapah; IAP, Cuddapah, III, 89, ś 1662.

Kōrukonḍa
Pl.N ; Kōrukonḍa Tq, East Godavari Dt.; Korukonda, Vizianagaram Dt.
GV

Kōrumilli / Kōrupalli
Pl.N; Ramachndrapuram Tq, East Godavari Dt.
AN; IA, XIV, 50.

Kōsali
Pl.N
AN

Kōsuru
Pl.N
AN

Kōṭa
Pl.N; Fort, apparently after Dharaṇikōṭa, Guntur Dt., once capital of the Andhra Satavahanas.
VV; Vel. P; AD

Kōṭa bhattaru
Title
VY

Kōtama Rāju
Pl.N
AN

Kōṭamarti
Pl.N
TG

Kōṭapaḍu
Pl. N; Koilakuntla Tq, Kurnool Dt.
AN; IVR IV, 242, ś 1466.

Kōthi
Fort (Kōṭa)
M.Dh; Ps.N

Kōṭi
Hydronymic; river
AN

Kōtichintala
Pl.N
GV

Koṭikalapūḍi
Pl.N; Bezawada Tq, Krishna Dt; Darsi Tq, Prakasam Dt.
AN; VV ; SII, IV, 694, ś 1337

Kōṭipalli
Pl.N; Amdapuram Tq, East Godavari Dt.
M.Dh

Kōṭla
Pertaining to Kota = Fort
VV; Reddy

Komce
Pl.N IVR IV, No.164, ś 1450.

Kotra
Pl.N
KN; TG

Kottalanka
Pl.N ; Amlapuam Tq, East Godavari Dt.
AS

Kottalapalle
Pl.N
Ps.N; IAP Cuddapah, III, 157, ś 1507

Kottapalli
Pl.N ; Nalgonda Tq & Dt, IAP, Nalgonda I, No.70, ś 1173, Darsi Tq, Prakasam Dt,
Divi Tq, Krishna Dt. ; IVR IV, No. 496, ś 1496.
TG; GV; SV; Vel; Ps. N ; SII, XVI, 286, 1575AD

Kottaruvu
Pl.N
AN

Kottavālu
Employment; Kotwal; a high ranking watchman
Ps.N

Kotturi
Pl.N ; Srikakulam Tq & Dt.
KD; KK; PD ; D ; Dhavalapeta Grant of Uma varma, JHRS, X, p 143-144.

Koṭukūru
Pl.N
Ps. N

Kotwāla
Same as Kotwal (See above)
Ps. N

Kōvā
A sweet milk preparation
AN

Kōvela
Temple ; Pl.N, Kōvela – mūḍi ; Guntur Tq & Dt.
AN; VY

Kōvūru
Pl.N; Kovuru Tq, Nellore Dt, SII, X, 504, ś 1235
Bada Kannada ; IAP Cuddapah, II, 114, ś 1454; Medak, ś 936.

Kovvali
Pl.N; Eluru Tq, West Godavari Dt.
AN

Kovvūri
Pl.N
AN; VV

Kowlu
Tenentment
VV

Kowtā
Pl.N; Kowtāḷam – Adoni Tq, Kurnool Dt., ś 976, PCB, p 324
VV; TG ; Kowtā – vāri – Agrahāram, Nandigama Tq, Krishna Dt.

Kowtārapu
Pl.N; Kaule palli; Divi Tq, Krishna Dt.
Vel. P; EI, 3:82 H ff.

Kramadhāṭi
Title
'Krama' like Ghana and Jaṭa is a form in the recitation of the Vedas.

Krishna
Pe.N or the river Krishna
AN

Kṛovi
Pl.N
VV

Kṛovviḍi
Pl.N; Bhimavaram Tq, West Godavari Dt.
AN; SII, IV, 1193, ś 1050.

Kṛṣnam bhaṭla
Pe.N
Br.; ISGO, 15, ś 1380

Krushna vajhala
Pe.N
TG

Kruttivenṭi
Pl.N 'Kruttivennu', Bandar Tq, Krishna Dt.
AN

Kshirasāgara
Pe.N; Another name for Viṣṇu
M.Dh; VY

Kūci
Little in the sense of endearment ; Kūci, IAP,Nalgonda I, No.2, ś 894
AN; SII, XVI, 42, 1503 AD; ISGO, 15, ś 1380.

Kūci bhatla
Pe.N
AD; VV; SII, 1080, ś 1308; Ep. An. II, p 77, No.27.

Kūci manchi
Pe.N; Suryapet Tq; Nalgonda Dt.
AN; IAP Nalgonda, II, No.48, ś 1182.

Kūḍāli
Pl.N
AN

Kukkara
Pl.N
GV

Kulaśēkhara
Pe.N
Br.; SII, V, 1231, Srikurmam Inscription.

Kuṃchaṃ
A unit of measurement
Ps.N

Kuṃchanapalli
Pl.N
Ps.N; SII, IV, 709, ś 1480.

Kumḍanamaḍugu
Pl.N; Kundana – puram, Venkatagiri division, Nellore Dt.
Ps.N

Kuṃdurṭi
Pl.N; 'Kundūru', Narasaraopet tq, Guntur Dt.
AN

Kuṃdūru
Pl.N; 'Kundhrru', Narasaraopet Tq, Guntur Dt; Kundūru – Guntur Tq & Dt, E
AN; EI, 24 : 137 H.

Kuṃdurupi
Pl.N
IVR IV, 141, ś 1444.

Kummanūru
Pl.N
AN

Kummaragunṭla
Pl.N; IVR, IV, No.237, ś 1466.
SV; SII, XVII, 130, ś 1544 AD.

Kumpaṭi
Stove
Ep. An. VI, p.99, ś 1513.

Kūnapalli
Pl.N
VV; ISGO, 15, ś 1380.

Kūnaparāju
Pe.N
GV

Kūnapuli
Title; Kuna = little ; Puli = tiger
Ps.N; VV

Kundā
See Kundanam
VV

Kundāṃ
Pl.N; Pe. N. Venkatagiri division, Nellore Dt.

Kundēṭi
Kudēru – river in Ghandikota - sima
PD; VV; 'Kumdeti'- ISGO, 15, ś 1380.

Kunṭamukkala
Pl.N
AN

Kunṭimaddi
Pl.N
TG

Kuppa
A heap; ISGO, 15, ś 1380.
VV

Kuppāka
Pl.N
VV

Kuppam bhatla
Pe.N
KN

Kuppila
Pl.N
Ps.N

Kuppili
Pl.N; Srikakulam Dt.
SV

Kūrāḍa
AN; VB, Pl.N. Gudivada Tq, Krishna Dt., Kakinada Tq, East Godavari Dt.
JAHRS, 5:22 H.

Kūrapāṭi
Pl.N; Kurapādū – Guntur Dt.
AN; VV – SII, X, 368, ś 1181.

Kuravi
Pl.N
KK

Kūreḷḷa
Pl.N; Ramanapeta Tq, Nalgonda Dt.
TG; IAP, Nalgonda I, No. 91, ś 1217.

Kurikāla
Pl.N
Ps. N

Kurnutala
Pl.N
Ps.N

Kurti
Pl.N
ISGO, 15, ś 1380.

Kuruganṭi
Pl.N ; Kuruganṭi –vāri-khandrika, Nandigama Tq, Krishna Dt., Guntur Tq & Dt.
VV; Kurugallu, SVR, IV, 426, ś 1480; SII, X, 112, ś 1061; 109, ś 1063.
Kuru = small; Kurumagallu – SII, VI, 239, ś 1077; ibid, IV, 681, ś 1065.

Kurumaddāli
Pl.N; Gudivāḍa Tq, Krishna Dt.; Kuru = small; Maddāli (intra)
AN; IAP Mahabubnagar, 57, 11th 12th Centuries AD.

Kurumēṭi
Pl.N
KKV

Kuruvēmula
Pl.N; Karivēmula, Pattikonda Tq, Kurnool Dt.
TG

L

Lachchi rāju
Pe.N
AN

Lagaḍapāṭi.
Pl.N; Sattenapalli Tq, Guntur Dt.
Ps.N; Ka

Lakka pragaḍa
Pe.N Pl.N; Lakkavarapu – kota, Visakhapatnam Dt.
AN

Lakka rāju
Pe. N; Lakka a corrupted form of Lakshmi.
AN; Ps. N; Kh. SII, XVI, 16, 1396 AD; IAP Cuddapah, II, 28, ś 1318

Lakkaṃ rāju
Pe.N; Pl.N; Lakkavaram, Nandigāma Tq, Krishna Dt.
AN

Lakka vajhulu
Pe.N
V; IAP Warangal, 110, ś 1386 ; CTI, IV, No.50, ś 1386.

Lakshmaṇa vajhula
Pe.N
Occurs as a surname in the celebrated work 'Kridabhiramam'

Laṃbu
Title; stout; greatness
M.Dh

Lanka
Pl.N; Island
VV

Laṭṭala
Pl.N
Ps.N

Lēkha rāju
Pe.N Lekha = Letter; Raju = Pe.N, suffix.
AN

Lēḷḷapalle
Pl.N; Markapuram Tq, Prakasam Dt. IVR, IV, No, 460, ś 1486.
VV; SII, IV, 698, ś 1496.

Liṅgāla
Pl.N; Karimnagar Tq, & Dt., Achampēṭ Tq, Mahabūbnagar Dt; Koilakunṭḷa Tq, Kurnool Dt. ; Nugur Tq, East Godavari Dt.; Kaikalūr Tq, Krishna Dt.
Ps.N; IAP Mahabūbnagar Vol. I, No.170, ś 1089.

Liṅgamu
The icon of Śiva ; Lingaṃ – palle, Badvel Tq, Cuddpah Dt., Lingaṃ – vāri – palle,
GV Markāpuram Tq, Prakasam Dt.

Liṅgamuguṇṭa
Pl.N; Sattenapalli, Narasaraopeta Tq, Guntur Dt; Kandukur Tq, Prakasam Dt.;
Ps.N; SII, X, 504, ś 1235.

Liṅgana-makhi
Pe.N + Title (makhi = performer of a sacrifice)
V

Liṅga rāju
Pe.N
AN

Lōkā
Pl.N; Lōka-mūḍi, Kaikalur Tq, Krishna Dt.
M.Dh

Lōkam
Pl.N; world
KKV

Lolla
Pl.N; Ramachandrapuram Razole Tq's, E.G. Dt; IVR, IV, No. 128, ś 1442.
AN; VV: SII, IV, 699, ś 1468; ISGO, 15, ś 1380. ; Lakshmidhara, a celebrated musician in the court of the Gajapatis and of Krişnadēvarāya of Vijayanagar.

M

Māchana vajhula
Pe. N
VV

Māchavarapu
Pl.N; Māchavaram, Rāmachandrāpuram Tq, East Godavari Dt., Ongole Tq, Prakāsam Dt, Bezawada Tq, Krishna Dt.
NN; AN

Māchеrla
Pl.N; Mācerla Tq, Guntur Dt.
AN; Ep. An V, P. 112, No.21, ś 1518.

Māchi rāju
Pe.N; SII, X, 577, ś 1332
Ps.N; AN; Machiraju palli' – IAP Warangal, 79, un-dated.

Māchūri
Pl.N
AN

Mādala
Pl.N; Sattenapalli Tq, Guntur Dt.
SII VI, 196

Mādayyagāri
Pe.N; Mādannagāri -palle, Atmakur Tq, Nellore Dt.
SB

Maddāla
Pl.N; Maddāli, Gudur Tq, Nellore.
VV; AD

Maddāli
Pl.N; Peddamaddāli, Gudivāḍa Tq, Krishna Dt.
AN; SV ; I.A. May 1884 Vol. 13; 137.

Maddāli Tirumala
Pl.N
SV

Maddi
Pl.N; Flora (a tree) ; Bhimunipaṭnam Tq, Visakhapatnam Dt.
Ps.N

Māddi rāju
Pe.N
AN CTI, IV, No.60, line 24, ś 1529.

Maddikera
Pl.N
Ps.N

Maddikoṇḍa
Pl.N
AN

Maddipaṭla
Pl.N; Divi Tq, Krishna Dt.
KN

Maddirāla
Pl.N; Ongole Tq, Prakāsam Dt., Suryapet Tq, Nalgonda Dt.
KKV; Vel.P

Maddulapalli
Pl.N
TG

Maddulūri
Pl.N
Ps.N;
Niḍadavōlu, Tq, West Godavari Dt.

Maddūri
Pl.N; Sidhavatam Tq, Cuddapah Dt, IVR, IV, No.181 ś 1454
VV; Ps. N; IAP Cuddapah, III, 225 un-dated.

Mādhava bhaṭla
Pe.N, Pl.N; Mādhava-paṭṭanam, Kākināḍa Tq, East Gōdavāri Dt. ISGO, 16, 1458 AD.
TG; KKV; Mādhavaram Bezawada Tq, Krishna Dt. SII, V, 100, 1456 AD.

Mādhava peddi
Pe.N Pl. N ; Mādhava Paṭṭanam, (see above)
VV; SII, X, 387, un-dated.

Madhira
Pl.N; Madhira – pāḍu, Gannavaram Tq, Krishna Dt
VV

Madhunā pantula
Pe.N; Pl.N; Madhurāpuram, Dharmavaram Tq, Anantapuram Dt.
AD; Gannavaram Tq, Krishna Dt, IVR, IV, No.527, ś 1512.

Madhura-kavi
Title; a sweet poet; Title of Vanamamala Ramānuja Swamy,
AD; IAP Mahabubnagar, Vol. II, No.96, ś 1791.

Madhurantakam
Pl.N. Tamil Nāḍu Br.
SII, V, 139 ś 1129

Madhvāchāryula
Title; Teacher of the Madhvās
M.Dh

Madhvapaṭi
Title; Chief among the Madhvās
M.Dh.

Madhyārjunam
Pl.N
KN

Mādi rāju
Pe.N; Corruption of Mādhava
AN; Ps.N ; SII, XVI, 220, 1557 AD.

Māḍireḍḍi
Pe.N; Māḍireḍḍipalli, Hindpur Tq, Anantapur Dt. ; IVR, IV, No.16, ś 1309.

Madukumilli
Pl.N
AN

Māḍabhūṣhi
Title; 'Mādahūśi' – CTI, No.50, ś 1386
VY; SV; IAP, Warangal, 110, ś 1386.

Māḍapāṭi
Pl.N
AN

Maḍicherla
Pl.N; Chōḍavaram division, East Godavari Dt.
Ps.N

Maḍiki
Pl.N; Rāmachandrāpuram Tq, East Godavari Dt.
AN

Maḍipaḍiga
Pl.N
NY

Māḍugula
Pl.N; Palnad Tq, Guntur Dt, Viravalli Tq, Visakhapatnam Dt.
VV; TG

Maḍugūri
Pl.N
Br.; ISGO, 15, ś 1380.

Magallūri
Pl.N
AN

Māganṭi
Pl.N; Māgallu – Nandigama Tq, Krishna Dt, SII, X, 277, ś 1252

VV; AN; Mānugalu, IAP, Nalgonda, I, No.16, 1981AD; ISGO, 15, ś 1380.

Māgāpu
Temple ritual related
AN; Adi Saiva Pujari

Māgi
Pl.N
AN; Ps.N

Māgulūri
Pl.N
AN; SII, IV, 919 ś 1672.

Mahābāṣhyam
Scholarship; Great commentary
TG; SV

Mahādēva bhaṭṭaru
Pe.N; Mahādēvapuram, Sirivella Tq, Kurnool Dt, Kondukur Tq, Prakasam Dt.,
Polavaram division, East Godavari Dt. ; SII, X, ś 1204; No. 504, ś 1235.
GV

Mahaṃkāḷi
Pe.N after the deity; Maha (great) Kali
AN; TG; M.Dh, VV; Mahakali-bhatla occurs as a Pe.N in ISGO, 15, ś 1380.

Mahāpātruni
Office; Great among the patras – an office under the Gajapatis
PD; SII,IV, 1167, ś 1336; IVR, IV, No. 55, ś 1384.

Mahāvratayājula
Ritual
PD

Mahēndravāḍa
Pl. N; Rāmachandrāpuram Tq, East Godavari Dt.
AD; JHRS, 6:23.

Mahimalūru
Pl.N; Atmakur Tq, Nellore Dt.
AN; NI, Atmakur (38) ś 1139.

Mahjdhara
Pe.N
VNV SII, X; 66, ś 1033.

Mājēṭi
Pl.N; Majēru, Division Tq, Krishna Dt.
Vel; Ka

Makhāri
Pe.N; Makha is the 10th among the 27 Stars.
Daruka

Malakapalle
Pl.N; Nidadavolu Tq, West Godavari Dt.
AN

Malakapaṭṭaṇapu
Pl.N
KKV

Malapāka
Pl.N
VV

Malla jōsyula
Pe.N
VV

Malla pragaḍa
Pe.N
AN; SII, X; 407, ś 1188.

Malla vajhula
Pe.N
KN; IAP, Warangal, 110, ś 1386; CTI, IV; No. 50, ś 1386.

Mallāḍl
Pl.N; Sattenapalli Tq, Guntur Dt.
VV

Mallampalle
Pl.N; Divi Tq, Krishna Dt.
Arādhya

Mallapa rāju
Pe.N
AN; SII, X; 261, ś 1136.

Mallasamudram
Pl.N
VV

Mallavarapu
Pl.N; Mallavaram Kakinada Tq, East Godavari Dt., EI, V,No.10, ś 1024.
PNN; Ps.N; Mallavaram in Assamki – Sima, Ongole Tq, Prakasam Dt. IVR, IV; No.260, ś 1467.

Mallavōlu
Pl.N; Palnadu Tq, Guntur Dt, IAP, Nalgonda, I, No.148, 14th Century AD,
'Mallavrōlu' – Mallavaram, Pithapuram Tq, East Godavari Dt. EI, 5, 73
AN; Mallavrōlu – Bandar Tq, Krishna Dt., SII, X, 451, ś 1202.

Mallela
Pl.N; Madanapalli Tq, Chittor Dt, Tiruvuru Division, Krishna Dt.
VV; SII, XVI, 326, 1638AD ; IAP Cuddapah III, 166, un-dated.

Mallemaḍugula
Pl.N; Rajampeta Tq, Cuddapah.
Ps.N

Mallēpally
Pl.N; Deverakonda Tq, Nalgonda Dt.;
VV, IAP, Nalgonda, I, 56, ś 1157.; Nalgonda II, No.48, ś 1182.

Malli vajhula
Pe.N
PD

Mallikārjuna
Pe.N; after Śiva
LN

Mallu bhaṭla
Pe.N
VV; ISGO, 12, ś 1376.

Malrāju
Pe.N; Mallurāju, IVR, IV, 186, ś 1454.
AN

Malrāvu
Pe.N
AN

Malyāla
Pl.N
AN

Māmiḍāla
Pl.N
TG; GV

Māmiḍanna
Pe.N
AN

Māmiḍi
Mango tree; Guduru Tq, Nellore Dt.
AN; SII, X, 504, ś 1235.

Māmiḍi bhaṭla
Pe.N
VN

Māmiḍipalli
Pl.N; Rajam Tq, Srikakulam Dt.
VV; SA

Māmiḍipūḍi
Pl.N; Nellore Tq & Dt.
AN; Pu. D

Māmillapaḷḷi
Pl.N; Bapatla Tq, Guntur Dt; Gannavaram Tq, Krishna Dt;
AN; VN; TG; KN; Achhampet Tq, Mahabubnagar Dt, IAP Mahabubnagar Vol.171, ś 1100.

Māmjēṭi
Pl.N
Br.; ISGO 15, ś 1380.

Māmuḍūru
Pl.N; Gutti Tq, Anantapur Dt., Tanuku Tq, West Godavari Dt.
AD

Maṃgolni
Pl.N
Br.; CTI, IV, No. 50, ś 1386.

Māṃkāla
Pe.N
M

Māna
Pl.N
AN

Manā pragaḍa
Pe.N
AN

Mānavalli
Pl.N
MV

Mancena
Pe.N; Maṃchena – bhaṭṭu – Composer of the Inscription – IAP, Nalgonda,
Ps.N; I. No. 113, ś 1321.

Mancha vajhula
Pe.N; Manccanojhyalu IVR, IV, No.30, ś 1334,
VV; IAP Cuddapah, II, 34, ś 1334.

Mañchāla
Pl.N; Adoni Tq, Kurnool Dt, ś 815, PCB, p.324.
V; ARE, Hyderabad, 67, 406

Manchel̤la
Pl.N; Manchalla –Bapatla Tq, Guntur Dt,
AN; SII, V, 133, ś 1338.

Manchi bhaṭla
Pe.N; Related to Manicikonda – Nādu – Warangal Dt. ; ISGO 15, ś 1380.
KN; IA, July 1903, Grant of Kusumayūdha, 11th Century AD, Gotra: Maitrteya.

Manchi rāju
Pe.N
AN; Ps.N ; IAP Warangal, 54, ś 1139.

Manchikanṭi
Pl.N; 'Manchikollu' Palnadu Tq, Guntur Dt, IVR, IVR, IV, No.136, ś 1443.
AN; IAP, Cuddapah Dt, III, 87, un-dated; II, 84, ś 1443.

Manchikōṭa
Pl.N
AN

Mańchili
Pl.N; Tanuku Tq, West Godavarin Dt.
Saiva Pujari

Mańci
Title; a learned man; scholar
Ps.N

Mańdaḍapu
Pl.N; Maṃdaḍapu, Mandadam, Guntur Tq, Dt.
Ps.N; IVR, IV, No. 404, ś 1478. ; ISGO, 15, ś 1380.

Mańdāḍi
Pl.N; Palnadu Tq, Guntur Dt.
TG

Mańdagonḍi
Pl.N
TG

Mańdhā
Title
PD

Mańdhāta
Pe.N; one of the ŞhatchakravarthisV
V

Mańḍa
An assemblage; group
Ps.N

Mańḍa
Pl.N; Manḍapēta, Ramachandra Puram Tq, East Godavari Dt. Tanuku Tq, W.G. Dt.
Ps.N; VN; JAHRS, 6:17 H

Mańḍalaparti
Pl.N; 'Mandaparti' Tadepalligudem Tq, West Godavari Dt.
AN

Mańḍalēmula
Pl.N
TG

Mańḍalika
Title; Māndalika, ruler of a province
VV

Mańḍamula
Pl.N
AN

Manḍapāka
Pl.N; Tanuku Tq, West Godavari Dt.
AN; VN; VV

Mańḍapaṭi
Pl.N; Maṃdpāṭi, Guntur Tq & Dt ; Gudivada Tq, Krishna Dt.
AN; IVR, IV, 425, ś 1481.

Mańḍavilli
Pl.N; Kaikalur Tq, Krishna Dt.
VV

Mānēpalli
Pl.N; Markapuram Tq, Prakasam Dt, Hindupur Tq, Anantapur Dt.
SA; AD; SII, X, 395, ś 1183

Mangaḷagiri
Pl.N; Guntur Tq & Dt
AN; SII, XVI, 130, 1544 AD, ibid, IV, 709, ś 1480.

Mańgaḷaṃpalli
Pl.N; Mańgaḷapalli – Nalgonda Tq & Dt.
TG; Vel.

Mańgamāri
Pl.N
VV

Mangavilli
Pl.N
SV

Mańgipūḍi
Pl.N; Maṃginapūḍi – Darsi Tq, Prakasm Dt; Bandar Tq, Krishna Dt.
Vel.; SII, VI, 1084, ś 1304

Mańgōli
Pl.N; IAP Warangal,
Br.; 110, ś 1386

Mańgu
Pl.N; Mańgu palle, Atmaku Tq, Nellore Dt.
GV; VY

Mānikoṇda
Pl.N; Mannēru in Kandukur Tq, Nellore Dt, has a Sanskrit name

Maṇika
AN; NI, Kandukur (77), ś 1450; Gannavaram Tq, Krishna Dt.

Mañjulūri
Pl.N
AN

Mannava
Pl.N; Mannūru Tq, Guntur Dt.
AN; SII, VI, 121, ś 1041.

Mannēpalli
Pl.N; Darsi Tq, Prakasam Dt.
AN; NDI, Darsi; 48

Mannēṭikōṭa
Pl.N; Kondukur Tq, Prakaṣam Dt.
AN

Mantapūḍi
Pl.N
KK

Manthena
Pl.N; Karimnagar Dt, Mahadevapuram Tq, IAP, Karimnagar, No. 28, ś 1121
AN; VV; Kh ; earlier name Mantrakuta ; SII, V, 1166, ś 1948.

Mantrāla
Pl.N
VV

Mantravādi
Title; expert in sacred spell
VN

Mańtri
Office; Minister
AN; V

Mantri pragaḍa
Office; Minister
GV; AN; SII, V, 31, ś 1348, IAP Nalgonda, II, No.91, ś 1753.

Mānuka
Pl.N
Ps.N

Mānukōṭa
Pl.N
AN

Mānūri
Pl.N; Eluru Tq, West Godavari Dt.
M.Dh; V

Maṇimāmala
Pl.N
TG

Maṇugula
Pl.N
Ps.N

Marā vajhula
Pe.N
TG

Maramrāju
Pe.N
AN

Maraṃganṭi
Pl.N
VY

Māreḷḷa
Pl.N; Māreḷḷa – Kanigiri Tq, Nellore Dt. IVR IV, 375, ś 1476. Vayalpad Tq, Chittor Dt
AN; VV; Ps. N ; Darsi Tq, Prakasam Dt; SAP Mahabubnagar ; Vol. II, No.42, ś 1220.

Māreḷḷapūḍi
Pl.N; Marella – mūdi, Tadepalligudem Tq. West Godavari Dt.
VV

Mārēmalli
Pl.N
AD

Mārēmanḍa
Pl.N
M.Dh

Mārēpalle
Pl.N; Miryalaguda Tq, Nalgonda Dt.; Tiruvur Division, Krishna Dt.
V

Mārgapuri
Pl.N
Ps.N

Mariḍa
Pl.N
V

Marinkañṭi
Pl.N
SV; IAP Nalgonda, II, No. 108, un-dated.

Marla
Pl.N; Marla-pādu, Ongole Tq, Prakasam Dt.
KN; Marlā –palle, Srugavarapukota Tq, Vizianagaram Dt.

Maruḷāchārya
Pe.N
Dwaraka

Māruti
Pe.N; after Hanuman, the son of Vāyu – a marut.
AN

Māruṭūru
Pl.N; Narasaraopet Tq, Guntur Dt., ; Fenikala Māruṭūru – Maturu, Miryalaguda Tq,
AN; SII, VI, 1019, ś 1323; Nalgonda Dt, I , 61, AD 1197.

Maruvāḍa
Pl.N; Srikakulam Tq,
PD; SII, X, 271, ś 1145.

Maṟṟicheṭṭu
Flora – a tree
AN

Maṟṟipāṭi
Pl.N; Marri-pādu , Kovur Tq, Nellore Dt.
Ps.N

Maṟṟipūḍi.
Pl.N; Bapatla Tq, Guntur Dt.
AN; SII, VI, No. 124 ś 1094.

Maṟṟivāḍa
Pl.N; Chodavaram Division, East Godavari Dt. , Gannavaram Tq, Krishna Dt.
AN

Māṭēṭi.
Pl. N
GV

Mathaṃ (Maṭṭam)
Pl.N.; North Arcot Dt, Tiruttani Tq, Tamilnadu Dt; Kalahasti Tq, Chittoor Dt.
M.Dh; (A dwelling place for the ascetics)

Matsyagaṇṭi
Pl.N
KKV

Matsyapuri
Pl.N; Narasapuram Tq, West Godavari Dt.; Viravalli Tq, Visakhapatnam Dt.
SA

Maṭukumalli
Pl.N; Kakinada Tq, East Godavari Dt.
AN; ISGO, 50, ś 1406.

Matukupalli
Pl.N
V

Maṭli
Pl.N; IAP, Cuddapah, III, No.62, ś 1500.
Kh.

Maṭṭapalli
Pl.N; Huzurnagar Tq, Nalgonda Dt.
PD; IAP, Nalgonda, I, No.148, ś 14th Century AD.

Maṭṭegunṭa
Pl.N; Bapatla Tq, Guntur dt.
Ps.N

Mēdapaṭi.
Pl.N; 'Mēḍapāḍu', Kakinada, P. Ramachandrapuram Tq's , East Godavari Dt.
Ps.N; Narasapuram Tq, West Godavari Dt.

Mēdịpalli
Pl.N; Eluru Tq, West Godavari Dt.
GV; SV; TG; Ps. N; VV

Mēḍachervu
Pl.N
VV

Mēḍangi
Pl.N
AN

Mēḍapi
Pl.N; Markapuram Tq, Prakasam Dt.
Ps.N; SII, 9 -1 : 204.

Mēḍasāni
Pe.N
SII, V, 174, undated

Mēḍavarapu
Pl.N
AN; KKV

Mēḍicherla
Pl.N
Vel.

Mēḍidinne
Pl.N; Jammalamadugu Tq, Cuddapah Dt.
Ps.N

Mēḍikonḍūru
Pl.N; Sattenapalli Tq, Guntur Dt.
AN; IVR, IV, 426, ; ś 1480; EI, VI, No.15, ; ś 1109.

Mēḍūri
Pl.N; Gudivada Tq, Krishna Dt.; Tiruvur Division, Krishna Dt.
It is a 'Sthala' (administrative division) during the Vijayanagara period.
Vel; SII, IV, 981; ś 1440; IVR, IV, 123; ś 1440

Meesāla
Title: , Wishkers – a sign of power or authority.
Meesala Appayya – a character referred to in the work Kridābhirāmam.

Mēka
SII, X, 98, un-dated.

Mēlamēṣhara
Pl.N
KN

Mēḷḷacheruvu
Pl.N; Vayalpad Tq, Chittoor Dt, Huzurnagar Tq, Nalgonda Dt.; I, No.98 ś 1233.
Vel.; IAP Nalgonda, II, No. 116 undated.

Meḷḷavarapu
Pl.N
Vel

Meṅḍi.
Pl.N
PD

Merattūru
Pl.N
VV; Vel.

Meriṭala
Pl.N
TG

Mēru Great
Br.; SII, VI, 1231, (intra)

Meruṅgu
Better polished
Br.; SII, V, 1231, Srikurmam Inscription.

Mērusōmayājula
Pe.N; indicating the high (Mēru); Sōmayājula = sacrificer of Somayajña
VN

Meruvapūḍi.
Pl.N
AN

Metaku
Pl.N; (probably modern Medak)
Br.; Gotra : Kouṇḍinya ; ISGO, 15 ś 1380.

Meṭṭa
Pl.N; High place
VV

Meṭṭupalli
Pl. N ; Cumbam Tq, Kurnool Dt.
AN

Mikkivi
Pl. N
VN

Minnikanți.
Pl.N; 'Mrindikanti', Minnikalluj, Narasaraopet, Guntur Dt.
AN; SII, X, 76, un-dated.

Miriyāla
Pl.N; Palnadu Tq, Guntur Dt.; Ellavaram Division, East Godavari Dt.
A
N; 'Miriyampalli' - SII, X, 196, ś 1099.

Mirtipāți.
Pl.N; Rajahmundry Tq, East Godvari Dt.
Vel.

Missula
Pl.N
KN

Mițțadoḍḍi.
Pl.N
GV

Mițțipāți.
Pl.N
Vel.

Mōcherla
Pl.N; Kanigiri Tq, Prakasam Dt.A
N

Modali
Title – original or earlier
VV

Mōdēkurti
Pl.N; Medikurti, Vayalpad Tq, Chittoor Dt, & Razole Tq, East Godavari Dt.

Mōdukūri
Pl.N; Mrontukuru, Tendi Tq, Guntur Dt,
SII, X, 176, ś 1093.

Mōdumūḍi
Pl.N; Divi Tq, Krishna Dt.
AN

Mōganṭi.
Pl.N; Mōgallu, Bhimavaram Tq, West Godavari Dt.
Vel

Mōgiligida
Pl.N; 'Mōgili' – Chittor Tq & Dt.
GV; ARE, 1906 : 587.

Mokkapāṭi.
Pl.N
Vel; Ps.N; SII, X, 295, ś 1184.

Mokkarāla
Pl.N
TG

Mōkshagunḍam
Pl.N; Cumbum Tq, Kurnool Dt.
M

Mōparti
Pl.N, Ps. N; Moparru, Tenali
Tq, Guntur Dt,; Gudivada Tq, Krishna Dt,; Pulivendula Tq, Cuddapah Dt.; Ruled by Vinukonda Vallabhamatya, author of Kridabhiaramam.

Mōpidēvi
Pl.N; Divi Tq, Krishna Dt.
AN

Mōraṭūṛu
Pl.N
VV

Mōrta
Pl.N; Tanuku Tq, West Godavari Dt.
AN

Morusupalli
Pl.N
M.Dh

Mosalikanṭi.
Pl.N
VV

Motukuri
Pl.N;
Br.; Ep. An V, p.128, No. ś 1346

Movva
Pl.N; Divi Tq, Krishna Dt.
SA

Muchchukōṭa
Pl.N
AN

Mudda
Pl.N, Ps. N Muddapuram, Tadepalligudem Tq, W.G Dt.; Dhone Tq, Kurnool Dt.

Mudda rāju
Pe.N; See above
NN; IAP Cuddapah, III, 115, ś 1584.

Muddāli
Pl.N
Br.; Gotra: Maudgalya ; ISGO, 15, ś 1380

Muddu
Title; Kiss; likable
AD

Mudigoṅḍa
Pl.N; IAP , Warangal, 6; Mahabubnagar tq, Warangal Dt,; IA, July 1908, Grant of Kusumayudha IV, 11th Century AD
UA; GV; TG ; SII, VI, 200, Kuloyungs Choda R4.37.

Mudivarti
Pl.N; Kovuru Tq, Prakasam Dt.
AN

Mudra
Seal
Br.; SII, V, 1231, Śrikurmam Inscription.

Muduganṭi
Pl.N
TG

Mudunūru
Pl.N; Tadepalligudem Tq, West Godavari Dt; Pulivendula Tq, Cuddapah Dt., Gannavaram Tq, Krishna Dt.
AN; Ps. N; SII, X, 504, ś 1235.

Muḍikamṭi.
Pl.N;
IAP Nalgonda I, No. 93, ś 1121.

Muḍumbi
Pl.N
VY

Muḍumby
Pl.N
VY

Muḍiya
Pl.N
DD

Muḍiyam
Pl.N; Muḍiyamvāri palli, Vayalpadu Tq. Chittor Dt. Pedda-mudiyam, Jammalamadugu Tq, Cuddapah,
NN; IAP Cuddapah II, 224, ś 1473.

Mugulḷa
Pl.N; Tadepalligudem Tq, West Godavari Dt.
Ps.N

Mukkamāla

Pl.N; 'Mukṛōmala' Amalapuram Tq, East Godavari Dt, Tanuku Tq, W.G Dt.AN;

VV; Vel. V

Mukkapāṭi.

Pl.N; Gannavaram Tq, Krishna Dt.

Ps.N

Mukkavilli

Pl.N

VV

Mukkolani

Pl.N

Br.; Gōtra : Kausika ; ISGO, 15, ś 1380.

Mukku

Nose

TG; VN; Ps. N

Mukku (originally Nandi)Timmanna, author of Parijatapaharam, Court-poet of Sri Krishnadevaraya

Muktēvi

Pl.N

VY

Muktinūtalapāṭi.

Pl.N; Ongole Tq, Prakasam Dt.

AN

Mūla

Pl.N or one of the Stars in the Hindu calendar

PD

Mūla-ghaṭika

Original (mūla) place of learning (ghaṭika)

AN; SII, V, 1040 RY5 of Anantavarma.

Mulakalūri

Pl.N; Narasaraopet, Vinukonda Tq, Guntur Dt.
AN; ISGO, 15, ś 1380.

Mulpūru
Pl.N
AN; V

Mulugu
Pl.N
VA; VY

Mulukuṭla
Pl.NV
V; AN

Mulumūḍi.
Pl.N
AN

Mulupāka
Pl.N
AD

Muḷḷapūḍi.
Pl.N; Gudivada tq, Krishna Dt.
AN; VV

Mummaḍi.
Thrice or Third as in Mummaḍi Chōḷa
AN; SII, VI, 729.

Munagāla
Pl.N; Rajahmundry Tq, E. G Dt, Nandigama Tq, Krishna Dt, Kurnool Tq & Dt.
VV; M.Dh

Munagapāṭi.
Pl.N; Bezawada Tq, Krishna Dt.
Ps.N

Munamarti
Pl.N; 'Munamapu' Januku Tq, West Godavari Dt.
AN

Munimāṇikyam
Pe.N; Jain affiliation
AN

Munipalle
Pl.N
AN; Kanva; IAP, Medak, 1, ś 768.

Munji
Pl.N
M.Dh

Munjulūri
Pl.N; Mumjaluru – Bandar Tq, Krishna Dt, JAHRS, 5:109, Konda - muñjaluru,
Ongole Tq, Praksam Dt
AN; SII, V, 1, ś 1321.

Munnaṃgi
Pl.N
NV; SII, IV,699, ś 1468; ISGO,15, ś 1380.

Muntapūḍi.
Pl.N
V

Munuganṭi.
Pl.N
TG;GV

Munukuṭla
Pl.N
VV

Munupalle
Pl.N; Amalapuram Tq, East Godavari Dt; Nidadavolu Tq, West Godavari Dt.
LN

Muppaḷḷa
Pl.N; Sattenapalli, Vinukonda Tq's. Guntur Dt; Nandigama Tq, Krishna Dt.
AN; Ps. N ; SII, VI, 589, ś 1069; 420, ś 1190.

Muppavarapu
Pl.N; Nidadavolu Tq, West Godavari Dt.; Ongole Tq, Prakasam Dt.
M.Dh

Mūrti
Pl.N.; Mūrtivāripalle, Chandragiri Tq, Chittor Dt.
(Image; often found as a suffix to Pe.N)
M.Dh; Kh.; IVR, IV, 304, ś 1467.

Mūrtirāju
Pe.N
Ps.N; IVR, IV,No.301, ś 1470 = 1548 AD, SII, XVI, 166, 1548 AD.

Murukuṭla
Pl.N
KKV

Musunūri
Pl.N; Kavali tq, Nellore Dt; Nuzvid Tq, Krishna Dt.
AN; VV ; SII, IV, 1355, undated.

Mushṭi.
First indicating strength. Pl. N. Muṣṭūru, Dharmavaram Tq, Anantapur Dt.
VV; Madanapalli Tq, Chittoor Dt.

Mutta rāju
Pe.N; 'Muttarāju'; IVR, IV, No.40, ś 1348.
AN
Also the name of a caste - Mutta-rāju / Mudirāju meaning old (in time) Rāju

Muttenapalle
Pl.N; Narasaraopet Tq, Guntur Dt.
AN

Muttēvi
Pl.N
VY
AN; Ps. N ; SII, VI, 589, ś 1069; 420, ś 1190.

Mutukula
Pl.N; Markapuram, Kandukur Tq's, Prakasam Dt.
AN

Mutukūri
Pl.N; Palnad Tq, Guntur Dt, Nellore Tq & Dt, Muttukuru, Pulivendula Tq, Cuddapah Dt; Madaksira Tq, Anantapur Dt.
GV; IVR, IV,No.58, ś 1415.

Mutya
Pl.N or a one of the precious stones
KN

Mutyāla
Pl.N; Mutyala – palle, Narasapur Tq, West Godavari Dt.
AN; ISGO, 15, 1380.

Muṭnūri / Muṭlūri
Pl.N; Guntur Tq & Dt.
VV

Muvva
Pl.N
AN

Muvva
Pl.N
SA
Muvva can also be anklet-bell of Śiva of Tandava (dance) in view of the name of this particular sub-sect – Sivarchaka ; Archaka = Worshipper.

Mydavōlu
Pl.N
Ps.N

Mylavarapu
Pl.N; Mylavarapu-vāri – Gūḍem, Bhimavaram Tq, W.G. Dt. Jammalamadugu Tq, Ongole, Dasi Tq's, Prakasam Dt.; Cuddapah Dt.; ISGO, 15, ś 1380.
TG; M.Dh; AN; GV

Mynamupāṭi.
Pl.N; Maliyampudi; Ongole Tq, Prakasam Dt.
AN

Mynapalli
Pl.N
Vey

Mysūru
Pl.N; Mysore in Karnataka
AN

N

Nāchana

Pl.N; Also called Nācirāju Sōmana, the famous Telugu poet, author, 'Uttara Harivaṃsa' a Telugu Kāvya.

AN; IVR, IV, No.38, & No.154 ś 1451, un-dated of the time of Praudhdēvarāya.

Nadakudiṭi

Pl.N; Kakinada Tq, East Godavai Dt.

AN; Divi Tq, Krishna Dt.

Nādeḷḷa

Pl.N

A.N

Nādenḍla

Pl.N; Narasaraopet Tq, Guntur Dt; Nāḍiṃḍla Gōpa, E.G., VI, No.22, ś 1442.

VV; IVR, IV,No.301, ś 1470

Nādṇḍla

Pl.N

AN; SII, XVI, 72, 1521 AD.

Naḍigōṭa

Pl.N

GV

Naḍímniṭi.

Nadimi = middle ; Inti = house ; A house situated in the middle of a row.

Naḍiṃpalli

Pl.N; Repalli Tq, Guntur Dt., Puganur Tq, Chittor Dt; Kaugundi division, North Arcot, Tamil Nadu

AN

Nāga
Serpent, deity
KN

Naga bhaṭṭa
Pe.N; See Narasimhadevara
AD; Pl. N; Nagam –bhotla – palem, Darsi Tq, Prakasam Dt.

Nāga rāju
Pe.N; Pl.N.; Naga raju – palle, Udayagiri Tq, Nellore.
Ps.N

Nāga vajhula
Pe.N; See Pl. N. above.
Ps.N

Nāgadēvara
Pe.N
Ps.N; 'Nāgadēva' – SII, V, 1231, Śrikurmam Inscription.

Nāgalūru
Pl.N; 'Nāgūru' Pulivendula Tq, Cuddapah Dt.
Aradhya

Nāganamanchi
Pe.N
Ps.N

Nāgapūḍi
Pl.N
PD

Nāgavarapu
Pl.N; Bandar Tq, Krishna Dt.
KN

Nāgeḷḷa
Pl.N
GV

Nāgiḷḷa
Pl.N; 'Nāgaḷḷu', Bapatla Tq, Guntur Dt.
GV

Nāgula koṇḍa
Pl.N
Vy

Nāgulapāṭi.
Pl.N; Atmakur Tq, Nellore Dt; IAP, Nalgonda, II, No.64, ś 1225.
M.Dh; Nālgulapāḍu, Suryapeta Tq, Nalgonda Dt.

Nakkalapalli
Pl.N; Krishna Tq, Salem Dt, Tamil Nadu.
GV; AK

Nalagaḷḷa
Pl.N
Ps.N

Naldeege
Flora
AD

Nāli
Pl.N
Br.; ISGO, 15, ś 1380.

Nallacheruvu
Pl.N; Pulivendula Tq, Cuddapah Dt.
M.Dh.

Nallagerla
Pl.N; Tadepalligudem Tq, West Godavari Dt.
Ps.N

Nallagoṇḍa
Ps.N; Head-quarters of the district of the same name (Nalgonda)
Pl.N; Rajahmundry Tq, East Godavari Dt.

Nallan Chakravartula
Pe.N; after title
SV; IAP, Cuddapah, II, 31, ś 1326.

Nallari
Pl.N

Nallāru
Pl.N
VY

Nāmavarapu
Pl.N
GV

Nambūri
Pl.N; Guntur Tq & Dt.
AN; Vaishnava ; SII, IV, 702, ś 1440.

Namudūri
Pl.N; Nanduru, Bapatla Tq, Guntur Dt.
VV; It may be a corruption of Neminadha (Jain Teethankara), SII, X, 450, ś 1202

Naṃdyāla
Pl.N; IVR, IV, 237, ś 1466.

Nańdagiri
Pl.N; Nandagiri – kota, Ellavaram Division, East Godavari Dt.
M. Dh.

Nandamūru
Pl.N; Nidadavolu Tq, East Godavari Dt. Bandar Tq, Krishna Dt.
AN; SII, V, No.116, ś 1170.

Nandanavanam
Pl.N; The celestial garden of Indra. Kandukuri, Kanigiri Tq's, Prakasam Dt.
AN

Nandavarapu
Pl.N; Nandavaram, Adoni Tq, Kurnool Dt, SII, 9-i ; 279
TG; IAP Warangal, 110, ś 1386.

Nandi
Pe.N; Bull, The Vehicle of Śiva;
S; AN

Nandi, later Mukku Timmanna, a court poet of Śrikrishnadēvarāya. SII,IV, 702, ś 1440

Nandi bhaṭla
Pe.N
TG

Nandi rāju
Pe.N
Ps.N; AN

Nandigām
Pl.N; Nandigāma Tq,Krishna Dt; Bobili Tq,Visakhapatnam Dt.;Tekkali Tq, Srikakulam
Ps.N; IA, 7: 19.

Nandigāma
Pl.N; Bandar Tq, Nandigāma Tq, Krishna Dt. ; SII, IV, 741, ś 1183.
AN; Ps.N; IAP Cuddapah, I Dommari nandyala plates of Puṇyakumara, p.XXI.

Nandivāḍa
Pl.N; Gudivada Tq, Krishna Dt.
AN

Nandivelugu
Pl.N; Tenali Tq, Guntur Dt.
AS; SII, IV, 699, ś 1468; X, 509, ś 1236.

Nandula (of Nandi)
Pe.N
VV

Nandūri
Pl.N; Bapatla Tq, Guntur Dt.
AN; Ps.N; Ar; SV ; SII, X, 450, ś 1202.

Nannela
Pl.N
AN

Nārā
Pl.N; Nārāvāripalli, Chittoor Dt., Nara is a stumped form of Narayana.

Nāram bhaṭla
Pe.N
VV

Nārannagāru
Pe.N
AN
Naranna, a corruption of Narayana; Garu = honorific suffix

Nārapa rāju
Pe.N
AN; Ps.N

Narasimhadēvara
Pe.N; after the deity Narasimha - the forth Avatara (incarnation) of Viṣṇu.
A branch of the family later assumed the surname Nāgābhaṭala – evidently after the personal name of a pundit who gained renown in that line. Both the eponyms belong to AD.

Narayanabhaṭla
Pe.N
TG; ISGO, 13, ś 1378.

Nārāyananaṇaṃ
Pe.N
VY; TG; Vys

Nārāyaṇa
Pe.N
AD

Narēdla
Oxzen. Pl. N
VV

Nārla
Pl.N; Narlapuram, Dhone Tq, Kurnool Dt.
TG; There is a surname Nārla among the Kammas.

Nārlāpurapu
Pl.N
Ps.N

Narluvāḍa
Pl.N
AN

Nasirāvu
Pe.N
AD

Navuḍūri
Pl.N; Navuturu, Guntur Tq & Dt.
VV; SII, X, 459, ś 1210.

Nawābu
Title: Common among the Muslim rulers.
Pl.N; Nawābu – pēṭa, Ramachandrapuram Tq, E.G. Dt.; Nandigāma Tq, Krishna Dt, Nawābu-pālem, Tadepalligudem Tq, West Godavari Dt,
PD.

Nēdunūri
Pl.N; Amalapuram Tq, East Godavari Dt.
AN; 'Nrdunuri' – IAP Nalgonda, II No.108.

Neelam
Pl.N; Bodhan Tq, Nizamabad Dt, ARE, Hyderabad, 66, 310

Nēla bhaṭla
Pe.N
TG

Nēlaganṭi
Pl.N
Ar

Nēlakanṭi
Pl.N
Ps.N

Nēlanutala
Pl.N
TG

Nēlapaṭi
Pl.N
Ps.N

Nēlatūri
Pl.N; Proddutur Tq, Cuddapah Dt; Ramachandrapuram Tq, East Godavari Dt, Nidadavolu Tq, West Godavari Dt, Ongole Tq, Prakasam Dt.
AN; PD

Nellūri
Pl.N; Nellore – H.Q. of a district in A.P.
AN; IVR, IV, 447, ś 1483; NI, 1, ś 1112.

Nelluṭla
Pl.N; 'Nelluṭu' – IAP, Nalgonda, I, No. 36, AD 1112.
AN

Nemali
Fauna; Peacock. ; Nemali, Tiruttani Division, Tamil Nadu, Nandigama Tq, Krishna Dt.
GV; ARE, 1935 : 307.

Nemalikanṭi
Pl.N; Nemali-kollu, Sattenapalli Tq, Guntur Dt.
Niyogi

Nemalūri
Pl.N; Gudivada Tq, Krishna Dt.
VV

Nemaḷḷadinne
Pl.N; Jammalamadugu Tq, Cuddapah Dt
Ps.N

Nemāni
Nemana-a wooden spoon to pour ghee into the sacrificial fire.
PD; VV; TG; SII, X, 530, ś 1242.

Nemmāni
Pl.N
KK

Nemmikanṭi
Pl.N; Nema-kallu, Rayadurg Tq, Ballary Dt, Karnataka.
Vel.

Neppali
Pl.N
AN

Neppalle
Pl.N; Bezawada Tq, Krishna Dt.
VS

Nērel̤l̤a
Pl.N; Nellore – Vagu is a small attribute of Penna river. Ananatapur Dt.
VV; Ep. An V, p 99, ś 1321.

Nērel̤l̤apalli
Pl.N; Neredupalli, Kanigiri Tq, Prakasam Dt.
TG; SII, VI, 1004, ś 1301.

Netana bhaṭla
Pe.N
VV

Nētraganṭi
Pl.N; Netrakallu, IAP. Nalgonda, I, No. 16, AD 1081.
M.Dh.

Nēṭi
Ghee
VV; TG; Ps. N ; SII, X, 420, ś 1190.

Nibhānupuḍi
Pl.N; Gudivada Tq, Krishna Dt.
KN; AN

Nichchenameṭla
Pl.N; Koilakuntla Tq, Kurnool Dt.
AN

Niḍadavōlu
Pl.N; Niḍadavōlu Tq, West Godavari Dt, 'Niravadyapuramu' after to tile 'Niravadya' Western Chalukya Vijayaditya II (699-729 AD)
AN; SV ; SII, V, No. 124, ś 1228.

Niḍamānuru
Pl.N; Ongole Tq, Prakasam Dt.; Bezawada Tq, Krishna Dt.
AN

Niḍamarti
Pl.N; Tadepalligudem Tq, West Godavari Dt; Guntur Tq & Dt, Bandar Tq, Krishna Dt.
AN

Niḍavanameṭla
Pl.N; Nidasanametla, Ramachandrapuram Tq, East Godavari Dt.
GV

Niḍigonḍa
Pl.N; Janagaon Tq, Warangal Dt, IAP Warangal 58
Ps.N; IAP, Karimnagar Dt, 3,Vemulavada Chalukya Arikesare II.

Niḍumōlu
Pl.N; Divi Tq, Krishna
AN

Niḍumukkala
Pl.N; Guntur Tq & Dt.
AN; IVR, IV, No. 502, ś 1499

Nimaṣha-kavi
Title, the one poet who could turn out poetry in a minute (Nimisha)
AN

Nimma rāju
Pe.N
AN

Nimmageḍḍa
Pl.N; Divi Tq, Krishna Dt
VV

Nimmala
Pl.N; Nimmala – palem, Ellavaram Division, East Godavari
Aradhya; Saiva

Nippāṇi
Pl.N, in Karnataka
M.Dh.

Nirōgi
Title, having no disease.
VV

Nissankula
Title, having no obstruction. Pl. N. Nissankula – Durgam, Puttur division, Chittoor Dt.
Nissankula – Puram, Tiruttani division, Tamil Nadu.
AN

Niṣhṭala
Title; conformity or discipline
VV

Niṭṭa
Pl.N
VV

Niṭṭala
Pl.N
VV

Niṭṭuri
Pl.N; Nitturu, IVR, IV, No. 298, ś 1469; Tadiparti Tq, Anantapur Dt., Bellari Dt, Karnataka
AN; IAP, Cuddapah, II, 48, ś 1388.

Nịlam rāju
Pe.N
AN

Nookala
Pl.N
PD; KN; TG

Nōri
Pl.N
VV; ISGO, 15, ś 1380.

Nowdūri
Pl.N
SV

Nowlūri
Pl.N
AN

Nrusimhadēvara
Same as Narasimhadevara Nrusimha is sanskritization of Narasimha.

Nudurumāṭi.
Pl.N; 'Nudurumbadu' Nuduru-padu, Sattenapalli Tq, Guntur Dt.
VV

Nūjeḷḷa
Pl.N; Gudivada Tq, Krishna Dt.
VV

Nūka rāju
Pe.N
Ps.N

Nunēpalli
Pl.N
Ps.N

Nūtalapāṭi.
Pl.N; 'Nutalapadu', Chirala Tq, Prakasam Dt., EI, 18:311, Bapatla Tq, Guntur Dt;
Gudivada Tq, Krishna Dt.
Ps.N; TG ; IAP Karimnagar Dt., 1, ś 869; SII, X, 504, ś 1235.

Nūtamki
Pl.N; Nuttemki / Nuteki ; Nutakki, Guntur Tq, & Dt.
Niyogi; SII, X, 102, 1059, 142, ś 1080.

Nūtana-kavi
Title, New poet
AN

Nūti
Well – a water source
VV

Nyāpati
Title; shortened form of Nyapati; Judge
M. Dh.

Nyāsa vajhula
Leaning
TG
Nyasam = Śaranāgati; A concentrated form of Japa while chanting the mantras.

Nyayapati
Title; Judge; arbitrator of law; Nyayam = Dharma or law
GV

Nyṣhadham
Title; having mastered one of the five Mahakavyas in Sanskrit Srinadha translated the work into Telugu.
VV; AN

O

Ouḍḍepuḍi
Pl.N; Narasannapeta Tq, Guntur Dt.
AN; SII, X, 320, ś 1170.

Oḍḍre
Pl.N; a corruption of Oḍra Country modern Odissa
VV

Oṃgōlu
Pl.N; Prakasam District.
AN

Oṃṭieddu
Single Ox
PD; SII, V, 100, ś 1456AD

Oṃṭimāmiḍi
Pl.N; Single Mango tree
AN

Oṃtivelaga
Pl.N; Single Wood-apple tree
NN

Ō

Ōḍugūri
Pl.N
VV

Ōgēti
Pl. N; Hdronynimic. From Ōgēru
VV

Ōgirāla
Pl.N ; Also kind of food – offering to the Deity in temple.
AN;Vel; IAP, Mahabubnagar, Vol. II, No.15, ś 1202.

Ōkāṭu
Pl. N
AD

Ōleṭi \ Sri voleṭi
Pl. N ; Voleti – pālem, Kandukur Tq, Prakasam Dt.
AN ; AD

Ōmkāramu
Religious. Pl.N. Monkāram – Chendhu-gudem, Nandyal Tq, Kurnool Dt.
VV
The sacred syllable which is the seed of all mantras; AUM – the sound is a combination of 'A' which signifier Vishnu, 'U' Siva and 'M' signifying Brahma, the sound is called 'Pranava' (essence of life or 'Brahmans' (Maneka, P289).

Ōrugaṇṭi
Pl.N ; Modern Warangal H.Q of District, in A.P.
VV; M. PD; TG; AD ; SII, VI, 736, ś 1307.

P

Pabba rāju
Pe.N
AN

Pachcha
Yellow colour
Ps.N

Pachchaḷḷa
Edible pickles. Pl. N; Pachchaḷḷa Venkatāpuram, Cumbum Tq, Khammam Dt.
TG

Pachchameṭṭla
Pl.N
Kh

Pachchipāla
Unboiled-milk
VV

Paḍakaṅḍla
Pl.N ; Sirvel Tq, Kurnool Dt.
Ps. N

Padamanābhuni
Pe.N; Padmnābha = Visnu
VY

Padama-sōmayājula
Pe.N
PD

Paḍaviṭi
Pl.N
IVR, IV, 147 ś 1448

Padma-sōlala
A measuring unit (sola) with the adjective prefix padma signifying the goddess Lakshmi.
PD

Pādukala
Sandals
Apart from the significance of the Rāma-pādukās-at one time it was a mark of distinction or privilege to wear sandals.

Paduḷḷaparti
Pl.N
VV

Pagchamaṭṭa
Pl.N
AN

Pagiḍāla
Pl. N ; Pagidyala, Nandikotku Tq, Kurnool Dt.
Ps. N

Pākāla
Pl.N; Correctly Pākāla if pakala Kondukur Tq, Prakasam Dt,–a thatched dwelling place.
VV; Baḍa Kannaḍa Niyōgi

Pākalapāṭi.
Pl.N; pākalapādu, Sattenspslli Tq, Guntur Dt.
Kh; ARE, 1953; 327.

Pālaḍugu
Pl.N; 'Paladvu' Sattenapalli Tq, Guntur Dt
GV; AN; VV; ARE, 193 : 325

Pālagummi
Pl.N; Amalapuram (Razole Tq) East Godavari Dt.
AN

Pālakōḍeti
Pl.N; Pālakōḍēru – Bhimavaram Tq, West Godavari Dt
AN; SII, X, 288 ś 1160

Pālakonḍa
Pl.N
Br.; SII, V, 1248 ś 1393

Pālam
Pl.N
KN; IAP Cuddapah, II, 175, ś 1468.

Pālangi
Pl.N; Tanuku Tq, West Godavari Dt.
AN

Pālanka
Pl.N
KN

Pālanki
Pl.N; Pālanki – pādu, Divi Tq, Krishna Dt.
AD; Pālanki, Bhimavaram Tq, Visakhapatnam Dt.

Pālaparti
Pl.N; Gudivada Tq, Krishna Dt
AN; VV; SA; VN ; SII, IV, 758, un-dated; EI, XXV, p137, 146, ś 1280.

Pālapūḍi.
Pl.N
V

Pala vajhula
Pe.N
VN

Pālepu
Pl.N Pālem, Gutti Tq, Anantapur Dt.
AN; IVR, IV, 418, ś 1481.

Pālēṭi.
Pl.N; Pālēru – Krishna Dt, SII, X, 259, ś 1133. Kondukuru Tq, Nellore Dt,
Ps.N; NI , Kāndukur, No.30, IAP Cuddapah, III, 101, ś 1737.

Pāli
Pl.N
AN

Palivela
Pl.N; Razole Tq, East Godavari Dt.
GV; SII, V, No.111, ś 1099.

Paḷḷa
Fruits or teeth
VV

Palla
Pl.N
VV; TG

Palla – vajhula
Pe.N
Ps.N

Pallavi
An essential part of a musical concert along with Ragam and Tanam in Carnatic music.
VV

Palle
Pl.N; suffix
M.Dh

Palle bhaṭla
Title
Ps.N

Pallerlamūḍi
Pl.N; Nizivid Tq, Krishna Dt.
VY

Pallēṭi.
Ps.N, Pl.N; Pallēru in Palnadu Tq, Guntur Dt.

Palli
Village; Pl.N. suffix
TG

Palukūru
Pl.N; Kandukur Tq, Prakasam Dt.
AN; 'Pālakalūru', CP of AP, Vol. I, 193.

Pālūri
Pl.N
VV; AN; JAHRS, 6: 17

Pālutḷa
Pl.N
AN

Pāluvāyi
Pl.N; 'Pālavāya', Palnad Tq, Guntur Dt, Palavāya, Kalyanadurg Tq, Anantapuram Dt.
GV; ARE, 1930 : 21.
Bhanumati, a versatile Cine artist and Singer.

Pāma rāju
Pe.N
AN

Pāmarti
Pl.N; Pāmarru, Gudivada Tq, Krishna Dt, Ramachandrapuram Tq, E.G Dt.
V; EI, 5:142; IA, 8:76.

Pāṃdeḷḷapalli
Pl.N
Ps.N; TG

Pāṃḍrangi
Pl.N; Pandrangam, Gudur Tq, Nellore Dt.
AN; Pandrangi, Bhimunipatnam Tq, Visakhapatnam Dt.

Paṃḍrangu
Pl.N
GV; Also personal name – Pānduraṃgu (N.I.2 , 848AD)

Paṃḍravāḍa
Pl.N
AN

Pamiḍi.
Pl.N; from Bhamidi = Gold; perhaps the fertility of its soil.
TG; Pāmidi, Gutti Tq, Anantapur Dt., IVR, IV, 367, ś 1476.

Pāmiḍipāḍu
Pl.N; Atmakur Tq ;Nellore Dt.;Narsaraopet, Vinukonda Tq's, NI, Atmakur (55) ś1212
AN; SII, X, 135, ś 1077.

Pammi
Pl.N; Khammam Tq & Dt.
VV; IAP Karimnagar : 5

Pāmulapārti
Pl.N
AN

Pāmulapāṭi.
Pl.N; Pamulapādu, Guntur Tq & Dt ; & Nalgonda Tq & Dt
AN; SIḶ X, No.98, un-dated; No.181, ś 1094.

Pāmuru
Pl.N
Ps.N

Pānaṃgipalli
Pl.N; Ramachandrapuram Tq, East Godavari Dt.
AN

Panappākam
Pl.N; Tiruttani division, Tamil Nadu
VY

Paṇatala
Pl.N
Ps.N

Panchādi
Pl.N; SII, V, 1248 ś 1393.
Br.

Panchāgnula
Five-fires-Dakṣhnāgni; Gārhapatyam; Ahavaneyam; Sabbyam; Avapadhyam. Observance of penace amdist them.
VV; KN

Panchāngam
Consists of Thithi, Vara, Nakshtra, Yoga and Karana – its study.
VY

Pańdala
Pl.N; Pandala – Pāka, Ramachandrapuram Tq, East Godavari Dt.
KN

Pańdiḷḷapalli
Pl.N.
PS.N; TG
IAP Cuddapah, III, 103, ś 1828.

Panḍitārādhyula
Śaiva; IAP, Warangal, No.79, un-dated.
Title: one of the Āradhyas (venerable ones) among the Panḍita – threya (three panḍits = scholars) among the ardent Śaivite preceptors in Āndhra Dēśa.

Panganāmamula
A religious mark in the shape of either 'U' or 'V' worn by the traditional Vaishnavites
AN

Pāngulūri
Pl.N Pāngullūru, Ongole Tq, Prakasam Dt.
AN; SII, X, 577, ś 1332.

Paṇihāram
An ornament SV

Paṇkupāṭi
Pl.N
GV

Pannāla
Parts of the Vedas
TG; KN; M. Dh.

Pańtina
Pl.N
GV

Pańtula
From Maharashtrian pant meaning a pundit or teacher.
AN; AD; VNV; often found as a suffix to surnames.

Pańuganṭi
Pl.N; Present Panagal, Kollapuur Tq, Mahabūbnagar Dt, or Pānugallu, Nalgonda Tq & Dt.,
M.Dh; Ps. N; KKV; IAP Mahabūbnagar, Vol. II, No.73, ś 1581; SII X, 422, ś 1191.

Paṇyāla
Title – A praised one or Pl. N. Pāṇyam, Nandyal Tq; Kurnool Dt.
M.Dh

Paṇyāram
Title; Paṇi = businessman; Market place; one who has been praised.
VV

Pāpa rāju
Pe.N; Here Pāpa means snake in the sense of an Ādiśeṣha.
AN; IVR, IV, 181, ś 1454.

Pāpaṭla
Pl.N.; SII, VI, 677, ś 1352.

Pappu
Pl.N; Pappula –vāri – pālem. Udayagiri Tq, Nellore Dt. Edible item made of cereals like red gram, green gram etc.
PD; VY; VN; KK; Ep. An. II, p.77, Krāku Grant of Harihara II.

Pappūri
Pl.N; Pedda – Pappuru, Ananthapuram Tq & Dt,
SII, XVI, 6, 1132 AD.
Ka

Parachūri
Pl.N; Paruchūru, Bapatla Tq, Gunturu Dt.
VY; IVR, IV, 414, ś 1480

Paradā
Pl.N; Parandā Agraharā, Nalgonda Tq & Dt.
AD; IAP Nalgonda, I, No. 48, AD 1144.

Parakāla
Pl.N
AN; Ps. N; SII, IV, 280, ś 1495.

Paramātmuni
Pe.N; Supra – soul ; God
AN

Parāṃkusam
Title among the Vaiṣhnavites, IVR, IV, No.373, ś 1477
GV; VY; SV SII, XVI, 199, 1554 AD.

Pāranańdi
Pl.N
KN

Parānēni
Pe.N
M.Dh; AN

Parasa
Festiva gathering; a group of travelers; cattle fair
GV

Parāsaram
Pl.N; Parāsarapuram, Tiruttani division, Tamil Nāḍu.
Vy

Parasurāma – Pantula
Pe. N
AN

Para-vajhula
Pe.N
VV

Paravastu
Title
VY; CV

Parayutam
A type of Vedic study.
TG

Pārēpalli
Pl.N
AN; SII, V, 126, ś 1218.

Pārēpūdi.
Pl.N
VV

Paricherla
Pl.N
Kh

Parige
Pl.N; Paruvi, Hindupuram Tq, Anantapuram Dt
M.Dh.; EI, XXIV, p 234, 4225 AD.

Parikula
Pl.N
AD

Parimi
Pl.N; 'Parigi' Pedda-Parimi, Guntur Tq & Dt.
VV; AN; Ps. N ; SII, VI, No. 232 of the time of Krishnadevaraya.

Pariṭi.
Pl.N
PD; VN

Parlapāṭi.
Pl.N; Parla, Kurnool Tq & Dt.
Ps.N; IAP, Cuddapah, III, 138, un-dated.

Parṇasāla
Pl.N; A thatched house, Bhadrachalam Tq, Khammam Dt.
VY; IVR, IV, No.150, ś 1449.

Pārṣi
Desirous of victory
M.Dh.

Pārupalli
Pl.N; Sattenapalli Tq, Guntur Dt.
AN

Pārupūḍi
Pl.N; Gudivada Tq, Krishna Dt.
VV

Parvataṃ
Oronymic, a mountain, usually in the context of Śriparvata or Śrisailam.
Pl.N; Parvata-puram, Tiruvur Division, Krishna Dt.
AN

Pasarakoṅḍa
Pl.N
TG

Pasarlapāṭi.
Pl.N; Palnad Tq, Guntur Dt.
V

Pasiḍikonḍa
Pl.N
N

Pasumāmula
Pl.N; Pasuvēmula, Palnad Tq, Guntur Dt.
VV

Pasumarti
Pl.N; Pasumbarti, IVR, IV, 272, ś 1468
VV; KN; VYAN; SII, V, ś 1222.

Pasunūri
Pl.N
GV

Pasupula
Pl.N; Kurnool Tq & Dt.
NN

Pasupulēṭi.
Pl.N
IVR, IV, 322, ś 1471.

Pāta
Old
V

Pātakōṭa
Old Fort ; Ellavaram Division, East Godavari Dt.
Ps.N

Patangi
Kite; a bird
TG; Badagala Kannada

Pātapāṭi
Pl.N
Ps.N; Kh

Pathelkhāna
Office; Pathel = Police officer ; Khāna = residence
Ps.N

Pāṭibaḷḷa
Pl.N
AN, VV

Pāṭibanḍa
Pl.N; Sattenapalli Tq, Guntur Dt.
AN; SII, VI, 241, ś 1349.

Pāṭimaḷḷa
Pl.N
AN

Patrāyudu
Title - Paṭṭana + rāyuḍu - Ruler of a town
AD

Patri
A kind of leaf used in worship
M.Dh; TG

Pātruni
Title – minister under the Sūryavamsi Gajapatis of Orissa
VV

Paṭṭameṭṭa
Pl.N
AN

Paṭṭaswami
Title; Paṭṭana + swami - Lord of a town
Ps.N

Paṭṭisam
Pl.N; Polavaram Tq, West Godavari Dt.
VV; SII, X, 113, ś 1065, No. 116, ś 1067.

Paṭṭivardhanamu
Pl.N
TG

Pātulūru
Pl.N
SV

Pātūri
Pl.N; Pātūru, Bandar Tq, Krishna Dt.
V

Pātūru
Old Village 'Pātūru', Rajampet Tq, Cuddapah Dt.
AN; VV; IVR, IV, ś 1299.

Pavani
Pl.N; One of the five elements of nature - Air
AN

Pāvulūri
Pl.N
AN

Pedakūchi
Pe.N; pedda= elder, Kūchi = younger
VN

Peḍaparti
Pl.N
VV

Pedāpaṭi
Pl.N; Peddapāḍu, Bhadrachalam Tq, Khammam Dt.
AN; VY ; IVR, IV, No. 107, ś 1440.

Pedaprōlu
Pl.N
AN

Pedapūḍi
Pl.N; Tenali Tq, Narasannapet Tq, Guntur Dt., Kakinada Tq; E.G. Dt, EI, 4:303.
It is a common enough name of villages in the Telugu Country
VY; Ep. An. III pp. 38-39.

Peḍavanaganṭi
Pl.N
Ps.N

Peddāḍa
Pl.N; Kakinada Tq, East Godavari Dt.
AN; VV; Ka

Peddappa
Pe.N
PD

Peddi bhaṭla
Pe.N
VV; SII, VI, 1098, ś 1305; Ep. An II, p.77.

Peddinṭi.
Pedda + inṭi = Big + house
Ps.N; PD; Vel. P; VY; AD

Peddi rāju
Pe N
Ps.N; AN; IVR IV, 229, ś 1464

Peddi-sōmayājula
Pe.N
Vel.; SII, VI, 982, ś 1218.

Peetāmbaram
Yellow silk garment associated with Viṣṇu
AN; VY

Pēkēṭi.
Pl.N; 'Pēkēru', Ramachandrapuram Tq, E.G. Dt.; Tanuku Tq, West Godavari Dt.
AN; VN; SII, VI, 622 ś 1120; X, 263 ś 1140.

Pelapāla
Pl.N
AN

Peḷḷakūru
Pl.N; Chittoor Dt.

Peḷḷūri
Pl.N; Ongole Tq, Prakasam Dt.
AN; Ps. N ; NI, Ongole (101), ś 1194.

Pemma rāju
Pe.N; IVR, IV, No.237, ś 1466
Kh; AN; IAP Cuddapah II, 38, ś 1358.

Pemmasāni
Pe.N
IVR 317 ś 1471.

Penamakūri
Pl.N
AN

Pendēkanṭi.
Pl.N; Dharmavaram Tq, Anantapur Dt., Dhone Tq, Kurnool Dt.
Vy; Ep. An. V, 110 ś 1518, 'Pemdēkallu'.

Pendyāla
Pl.N; Nidadavolu Tq, West Godavari Dt; Nandigāma Tq, Krishna Dt.
VY; TG; AN; IAP Cuddapah, II, 74, ś 1436.

PeṇṭaSandy
Pl.N; suffix
VY

Peṇṭapāṭi
Pl.N; Pentapādu, Tadepalligudem Tq, West Godavari Dt.
VV.

Penugonḍa
Pl.N; IVR, IV, 214 . ś 1458.

Penumāka
Pl.N; Guntur Tq & Dt. Penuṃbāka
AN; SII, X, No. 395, ś 1183; No.459, ś 1210.

Penumaḷḷa
Pl.N; Penumaḷḷe, Amdapuram Tq, E.G Dist ; Kakinada Tq, E.G Dist.
AN

Penumarti
Pl.N; Rāpur Tq, Nellore Dt.; Kakinada Tq, East Godavari Dt.
Vel.; ISGO, 15, ś 1380.

Penumatsa
Pl.N; Gudivada Tq, Krishna Dt.
KG, Kh

Penupalli
Pl.N
AN

Pērala
Pl.N; Bapatla Tq, Guntur Dt.
AN

Pērama rāju
Pe.N
AN

Peramgūri
Pl.N
SV; IVR IV, 273, ś 1466.

Pēra pragaḍa
Pe.N
AN

Peravali
Pl.N; Tenali Tq, Guntur Dt. ; Tanuku Tq, West Godavari Dt.
VY; AN; SII, X, 138, ś 1078.

Peravana peddi
Pe.N; Pl. N. ; Peravena, Atmakur Tq, Nellore Dt.
Ps. N

Pēre pragaḍa
Pe.N
AN

Pēri
Title: Big; elderly; respectful
PD

Periyāla
Pl.N
Ps.N

Perrāju
Pe.N
AN

Perugupalli
Pl.N
VV

Pērukuntala
Pl.N
AN

Perumāḍi
Pl.N
Br.; Gotra: Bharadwaja , ISGO, 15, ś 1380.

Perumaḷḷa
Pe. N of Viṣṇu in Tamil. Pl. N Perumāḷḷa – pāḍu Rapur Tq, Nellore Dt.
AD

Pērūri
Pl.N; Gaṅga Pērūru – Siddhavatam Tq, Cuddapah Dt; Amalapuram Tq, East Godavari Dt,; Ramannapeta Tq, Nalgonda Dt; Pērūru – Cri, IV, No.12, CV.44 = 119
AD. AD; SII X, 569, ś 1319.

Pēru sōmayājula
Pe.N
Vel.

Pervela
Pl.N
TG

Pētēṭi.
Pl.N
SA

Peyyala
Pl.N
VNV; Gotra Mudgala ISGO, 15, ś 1380.

Peyyēṭi.
Pl.N
AN

Phakki
Pl.N ; Pḷaki < Pakki, Bobili Tq, Vizianagaram Dt.
AN; Ei, 12 ; 133 ; 31 : 131

Phārasi
< Parasika < Persian language or Profession; Gold-smith (Alchemist)
M.Dh.

Pichikalapāṭi.
Pl.N
VV

Pichikalapūḍi.
Pl.N; Pichchikala - Pāḍu, Bhadrachalam Tq, Khammam Dt.
AN

Piḍaparti
Pl.N; Piḍiparru, Tenali Tq, Guntur Dt.
VV; VS

Piḍugu
Title: Thunderbolt. Pl. N Piduguralla, Pidugu-palem, Kanigiri Tq, Prakasam Dt, IAP Nalgonda I, 95, ś 1223.
Ps.N; AN; occurs at the end of a personal name (E.I 27, 231-234, 625 – 650 AD)

Pilaka
Tuft of hair. As Śikha i.e., signifies an independent high position.
VV

Piḷkhāna
Pl. N
KKV

Piḷḷa
Comp. Tamil Piḷḷai
PD

Pillalamarri
Pl.N; Narasaraopet Tq, Guntur Dt. SII, VI, 622, ś 1170. Mahabubnagar Tq, & Dt.
VV; AN; Suryaraopet Tq, Nalgonda Dt. ; SII, XVII, 77, 1525 AD.

Pilli
Pl.Na; Pilli – pādu, Kaikalur Tq, Krishna Dt.
Ps.N; Kp

Pilluṭla
Pl.N; Palnad Tq, Guntur Dt.
VV; N; Ep. An. IV, pp.97-98 ś 1141

Pinapa
Pl.N; Pina < pinna = small
Ps.N

Pinapāṭi
Pl.N; Tenali Tq, Guntur Dt.
VV

Pindikūra
Food item - curry
Ps.N

Pindiprōlu
Pl.N
AN

Pingaḷi
Pl.N; Palnad Tq, Guntur Dt.
AN; SII X, 500, ś 1233, X,155 ś 1085.

Pinnama rāju
Pe. N
AN; Kh; Ps.N.

Pinnelli
Pl. N
TG

Pinnēni
Pe.N
AN
neni suffix is mostly associated with the personal names and surnames of the Kammas.

Pinninṭi.
Pinna (small) + Illu (house)
AD; VV

Pirātla
Pl.N
VV; SII, V; 1171, ś 1105

Pisapāṭi.
Pl.N
VV; SV

Pisupāṭi.
Pl.N
VV

Pōchina peddi
Pe.N
TG

Pōchi rāju
Pe. N; IVR, IV, No. 451, ś 1479
AN; SII, X, 480, ś 1218.

Poḍichēṭi.
Pl.N
GV

Podila
Pl.N; Podili – Prakasam Dt, SVR, IV, No.2921, ś 1469.
AN; AD; KN; VV; VY; IAP, Mahabūbnagar Vol. II, No. 87, ś 1479; No.80, un-dated.

Podili
Pl.N; Podili Tq, Prakasam Dt.
AD; IVR, IV, No.91, ś 1437.

Pōdūri
Pl.N
AN; VV

Pogāku
Tobacco
KKV

Pogaru
Haughty. Pl. N. Pogarūru, Gooty Tq, Anantapuram Dt.
AN

Pokkulūri
Pl.N; See below
M.Dh.; TG

Pokkunūri
Pl.N; Nandigama Tq, Krishna Dt.
AN

Pōla

Pl.N; Pōli, Rajahmundry Tq, Krishna Dt.

KN

Polā

Pragaḍa Pe.N

AN

Pōlama rāju

Pe.N; Pl.N.; Polamūru, Ramachandrapuram Tq, East Godavari Dt.

AN

Pōlavarapu

Pl.N; Prolavaram on the bank of Malāpahāri – now Pullēru in Krishna Dt. Darsi Tq, Prakasam Dt.; Amalapuram Tq, West Godavari Dt.

AN; IVR, IV, No.163, ś 1451.

Pōlūru

Pl.N; Pōlūri-vāri-Khandrika, Darsi Tq, Prakasam Dt.; Pōtūru – a nāyaṃkara sima during the period of Krishnadēvarāya.

AN; IVR, IV, No.111, ś 1439.

Pondūri

Pl.N; Poṃdūru, Ogole Tq, Prakasam Dt.

AN; IVR, IV, No.251, ś 1466.Pondūru in Śrikakulam district of AP is famous for Khadi or Khaddar cloth production.

SII, V, 128, ś 1240; CP of AP. Vol. I, p.180.

Ponna

Gold

Ps.N; SII, X, No. 395, ś 1183

Ponnāḍa

Pl. N; Ponna – vāḍada – Pithapuram Tq, East Godavari Dt.

AN E.I. V, p.70-74, ś 1024.

Ponnaganṭi.

Pl.N; Ponne-kallu, Guntur Tq & Dt.

AN

Ponnakaṇṭi
Pl.N; Kurnool Tq & Dt.
VV; AN

Ponnamalle
Pl.N
VY; SII, IV, 699, ś 1468.

Ponnapalli
Pl. N ; Krishna Dt, Divi-sima.
KN; AD

Ponnūru
Pl.N; Bapatla Tq, Guntur Dt.
AD; SII, VI, 121, ś 1041.

Ponugutāḍi
Pl.N
AN

Ponukumāṭi
Pl.N
VV

Ponukupāṭi
Pl.N; Sattenapalli Tq, Guntur Dt.
GV

Pōṇangi
Pl.N; Eluru Tq, West Godavari Dt.
AN; IA, 20; 418.

Pōpūri
Pl.N
VV

Pōpūru
Pl.N
Vel.

Pōranki
Pl.N; Bezawada Tq, Krishna Dt.
Vel.

Pōta
Pe.N. IAP Nalgonda II, No.41, ś 1171.

Pōta pragaḍa
Pe.N
AN; SII, X, No.107, ś 1061.

Pōta rāju
Pe.N
AN
Bammera Potanna or Pōtarāju was the author of Andhra Bhagavatam.

Poṭlacheruvu
Pl.N; Sangareddy, Medak Dt.
AN; Ponnaganti Telangana, 'Yayati charitra'.

Poṭnūri
Pl.N; Bhimunipatnam Tq, Visakhapatnam Dt.
Kp; SII, VI, 743, ś 1350.
Potnūru in Visakhapatnam district A.P., where Krishnadēvarāya planted a pillar of victory after his eastern campaign.

Pottapi
Pl.N; (1) Pottapi-nāḍu – a territorial division. Rajampeta Tq, Cuddapah Dt.
(2) A sub-division in Prōlu-nāḍu- EI,V. No.10 ś 1024;JAHRS,XI, Parts 1-2 ś 892
N; SVR, IV, No.63, ś 1423.

Poṭṭicherla
Pl.N
KN

Poṭṭuri
Pl.N; Guntur Tq & Dt.
Kh. An; SII X, 439, ś 1197.

Pōtukūchi
Pl.N; Pōtukuchchi-vāri-pālem, Eluru Tq, West Godavari Dt.
KN; Vel.

Pōtulahe-buffalo
Pl.N; Pōṭula-pāḍu, Podili Tq, Prakasam Dt.
Ps.N

Pōvuru
Pl.N
V

Prabhākara
Pe.N
Br.; IAP, Cuddapah Dt, III, No.26, ś 1700

Prabhala
A decorated flag-staff in the ritual procession of the deities in towns and villages. It can also be from 'Prabha' shinning.
VV; 'Pātaprabhalaviḍu', Badvel Tq, Cuddapah Dt.

Pragaḍa
Office; Mnister; IAP, Nalgonda, Vol. I, No.9, ś 986.
VN; Telaga; IAP, Mahabūbnagar Vol.I, No.148, 1137 AD; No.177, ś 977.

Praharāju
Pe.N
Ps.N

Prakhya
Title; Famous
VV

Prakki
Pl.N; Prakki - Lanka, Nidadavolu Tq, West Godavari Dt.
VV

Praḷayakāla
Title , Time of Deluge.
Br.; SII, XVI, 195, 1554 AD.

Pramida
Earthen-lamp particularly in association with religious ceremonies
Ps.N

Prāta
< pāta Old; Anterior
VV

Pratāpa
Title: Prowess or chivalry
VV

Pratāpagiri
Pl.N; IAP, Mahabubnagar Vol.II, No.35, ś 1548.
TG; IAP Karimnagar, 69, un-dated.

Prativāda-bhayankara
Title; A terror to the opposing parties in arguments
VY

Prattipāṭi.
Pl.N; Guntur Tq & Dt., Pedapuram Tq, E.G. Dt.; Tadepalligudem Tq, W.G. Dt.
AN; SII X, 449, ś 1202.

Pravā
Title; Flowing
VV

Prayāga
Pl.N; Now, Allahabad in U.P.
TG; SII, VI, 1139, ś 1203.

Pregaḍarāju
Title: Chief among the ministers
AN; ISGO, 76, ś 1448.

Prēta
Gobbling
VV; SII, IV, 924, Datable to 8th Century AD.

Prodduṭūri
Pl.N; Proddūṭūru Tq, Cuddapah Dt.
M.Dh.; IAP Cuddapah, iii, 139, ś 1800; IVR, IV, No.62, ś 1420.

Prōluganṭi
Pl.N
AN

Prouḍha -kavi
Title: matured poet
AN

Puchcha
Title; Sanskrit : Prucha = questioning
VV

Puchchakāyalapalle
Pl.N
Ps.N

Puchchalapalli
Pl.N
Reddy; Gudur Tq, Nellore Dt.

Puchchelapāṭi
Pl.N
SII, XIV, 256, 1463 AD.

Pūḍi peddi
Pl.N; Pūḍi, Sullurpet Tq, Nellore Dt.
DD; PD

Puguru
Pl.N
AD

Pūjyam
Title: worshipble
SA

Pūla
Flower
VV

Pulagurti
Pl.N; Narayanakhed Tq, Medak Dt. A.P
AN; Vel.; IAP Medak, 77, ś 1042.

Pulakhanadam
Pl.N; Niravalli Tq, Visakhapatnam Dt.

Pulakhanda
Pl.N
Br.; SII, VI, 204, ś 1145.

Pulanṭasāla
Pl.N
Vel.P

Pulapāka
Pl.N
GV.

Pulavarti
Pl.N; Pulaparru, Kakalur Tq, Krishna Dt.
VV; Telaga ; Pulaparti, Sarvasiddhi Tq, Visakhapatnam Dt.

Puli
Pl.N.; Ordinary meaning tiger. As such it can also be presumed as a title.
TG

Pulichēṭi
Pl.N
AN

Puligeḍḍa
Pl.N; Divi Tq, Krishna Dt
AN

Pulijāla
Pl.N; Nagarkarnool Tq, Mahabubbnagar Dt; ARE, Hyderabad 67, 406.

Pulikanṭi
M.N; Pulikallu, Palamamer Tq, Chittor Dt

Pulipāka / Pulupāka
Pl.N; Bezwada Tq, Krishna Dt.
AN; SII, IV, 773, un-dated.

Pulipāṭi.
Pl.N; Pūlipaḍu, Palnad Tq, Guntur Dt; Darsi Tq, Prakasam Dt.
Ps.N; ARE, 1930 : 24.

Pulla bhaṭla
Pe.N
TG

Pullakavi
Title (Poetry)
KK

Pullakuṭṭi
Pl.N
TD

Pulla pantula
Pe.N
AD

Pulle
Pl.N
VN

Pullela
Pl.N
VV

Pullēṭikurti
Pl.N; Pullēṭi-kurru, Razole Tq, East Godavai Dt.
SA; Pullēṭi-māgāṇi in Jagatāpi-Guṭṭi – Sịma, SVR, IV, 366, ś 1476
Famous for handloom saris

Pulupula
Pl.N 'Pulipaṭṭuru', Pulapaṭṭuru, Rajampeta Tq, Cuddapah Dt,
TG; ARE, 1930 : 106

Pulya
Pl.N
VN; ISGO, 15, ś 1380.

Punalūri
Pl. N
AN

Punḍla / Pulla
Pl.N; Bapatla Tq, Guntur Dt; Eluru Tq, West Godavari Dt;
AN; IAP Medak, 1, ś 768.

Punnama rāju
Pe.N; denoting the moon
GV

Punugu
A variety of perfume; Pl. N. ; Punugōti, Atmakur Tq, Nellore Dt.
Pu.D; V

Punyamūrtula
Title: Personification of Punya, Skt. holiness; virtue
AN

Puranam
Ps.N, TG; Pu.D; VV; KK
There are at least 18 Purāṇas as Hindu religious works. These families may be well versed in them in recitation, exposition etc.; IAP Cuddapah, II, 278, ś 1489, IAP Mahabūbnagar, II, No.11, ś 1194, ISGO 15, ś 1380.

Purāṇa-panḍa
Title; see purāṇa panḍa = pundit
AD

Puresangarāju
Pe.N
GV

Purighaḷḷa
Pl.N
TG

Puriheḷḷa
Pl.N
VY

Purijāla
Pl.N
GV; Puliujāla, Achampet Tq, Mehabubnagar Dt, A.P.

Purimeṭṭa
Pl.N
Br.; ISGO, 15, ś 1380.

Pūsapāṭi
Pl.N; Pūsa-pāḍu, Bapatla Tq, Guntur Dt.
AN; Kh; SII, XVI, 52, 1514 AD; X, 776, ś 1658.

Puṣhpagiri
Pl.N; Cuddapah Tq, & District
M; TD; IAP Cuddapah, I, No.91, (Rashtrakuta Krishna)

Puṣhṭi
Title: strong. Pe. N; Pustinathaya, IVR, IV, No. 71, ś 1430.
VV

Puṣpāla
Pl.N.;
IVR, IV, 154, ś 1451.

Pusuluri
Pl.N; Bapatla Tq, Guntur Dt, Kurnool Tq & Dt.
AN; Ps.N

Puṭrēvu
Pl.N
AN; VNN; SSI, X, 776, ś 1658.

Puṭṭacheruvu
Pl.N
AN

Puṭṭam rāju
Pe. N
AN

Puttaparti
Pl.N; Penugonda Tq, Anantapur Dt.
VY

Puttege
Pl.N
M.Dh

Puvvāḍa
Pl.N; Puvvāḍa Grant of Prōlaya Vēma of Konḍaviḍu,
AN; Ps.N, Vys.; ś 1346 AD. CP of AP, Vol. I, p.178

Puvye
Br.; ISGO, ś 1380.

Pyḍāla
Pl.N
MV

Pyḍighaṭala
Title; Golden - bells
AN; Ps.N

Pyḍimarri
Pl.N
TG

Pyḍimukkala
Pl.N; Pamiḍimukkala; Guidivada Tq, Krishna Dt.
AN

Pyḍipalli
Pl.N; Puttur Division, Chittor Dt.
Ps.N, Vys.
Pydi = gold; Pyda, a surname among the Vysyas.

Pyḍipāṭi
Pl.N; Ongole & Kandukur Tq's, Prakasam Dt.
AN; Ps. N; VV

Pyna
Pl.N
AD

R

Rāchakoṇḍa
Pl.N; A fort of Velmas of Velugonda in Nalgonda Dt.; Markapuram Tq, Prakasam Dt.
VV; TG; AN ; SII, 9-i ; 204 Nalgonda Tq & Dt.

Rāchamallu
Pe.N; after title, Royal wrestler
A.N

Rāchapāṭi
Pl.N
AN

Rāchapūḍi
Pl.N
AN; TG

Rācherla
Pl. N
AN; TG 'Rācheṛuvu' – IAP, Nalgonda, II, No.9 C.V.16.

Rāchirāju
Pe.N
AN IAP Cuddapah, II, 55, ś 1420

Rāchūri
Pl.N
AN; M.Dh; TG; GV

Radhṭtara
Name of a 'Gōtra'
AD: SII, X, 188, ś 1095.

Rāgadmṃpūḍi
Pl.N
VV

Rāghava
Pe.N; Pl.N; descendant of Raghu; another name for Rāma. Rāghava – puram, Bhadrachalam Tq, Khammam Dt & Kāmavarapu kōṭa Tq, East Godavari Dt.;
Rāghava-paṭnam, Peddapuram Tq, East Godavari Dt.; TG

Rāghava-bhaṭla
Pe.N
AD

Rāghavapūḍi.
Pl.N ; after Pe.N
Vel.

Rāghavarapu
Pl.N; See Rāghava (above)
KN

Raghunātha-bhaṭla
Pe.N, Pl.N; Raghudevapuram, Rajahmundry Tq, East Godavary Dt.
VN

Raghurāma-pātruni
Pe.N
Br.; SII, X, 587, ś 1376.

Rājanāla
Pl.N
V; Ka

Rājānam
Pl.N
AN

Rājasēkharuni
Pe.N
AN

Rājavarapu
Pl.N; Ellavaram division East Godavari Dt.
AN

Rājavōlu
Pl.N; Repalle Tq, Guntur Dt.; Nalgonda Dt; Rajahmundry Tq, East Godavari Dt.
AN; SII, V, 150, ś 1184; ISGO, 67, ś 1423; SII, X, 504, 1235, SII, VI, 240 of the times of Kulōthunga Chōḍa Gońka.

Raju (la)
A frequent surname and personal naṃe suffix among the Kṣhatriyās and Niyogi Brahmins
AD

Rājukoṃḍa
Pl.N
Br.; ISGO, 15, ś 1380.

Rājyam
Kingdom
PD

Rākuditi
Pl.N
VY; SII, IV, 995, ś 1011.

Rāḷḷabańḍi
Pl.N
VV

Rāḷḷapalli
Pl.N; Anantapur Tq, Chittoor Dt.; Kanigiri Tq, Prakasam Dt.
VV

Rāmābhaktula
Devotees of Rāma
AD

Rāma-bhaṭla
Pe.N; Raṃbhaṭlalapālem, Repalle Tq, Guntur Dt.
VNV; SII, V, 1228, ś 1425; IAP Cuddapah III, 196 un-dated.

Rāmachandruni
Pe.N
VV; PD; AN

Rāmadāsu
Pe.N
KK

Rāmaḍugula
Pl.N; 'Rāmaduke' – Palnad Tq, Guntur Dt. TMER, 1929-30, No. 84
TG; AD; IAP Warangal, 110, ś 1386; CTI, IV, No.50, ś 1386.

Rāmaguṇḍam
Pl.N
GV

Rāmakṛṣnam – bhaṭla
Pe.N
Br.; ISGO, 15, ś 1380.

Rāmakūri
Pl.N; Ongole Tq, Prakasam Dt.
AN; SII, VI, 640, ś 1073.

Rāmānujala
Pe.N; Rāmānuja, the celebrated Vasishnavite pontiff.
PD

Rāmā-pantula
Pe.N
VN

Rāmā-pragaḍa
Pe.N
AN

Rāmarājapuram
Pl.N; after Pe.N
V

Rama rāju
Pe.N, Pl.N; Rāmarāju – lanka, Razole Tq, East Godavari Dt.
AN; GV

Rāmavarapu
Pl.N; Bhadrachalam Tq, East Godavari Dt.
KN; GV

Rāmā-vajhula
Pe.N
VV

Rāmāyaṇam
Itihasa.
Pl.N; Rāmāyaṇaṃ – khanḍrika, Podili Tq, Prakasam Dt. Baḍa Kannada
Niyōgi

Raṃ-bhaṭla
Pe.N
PD; Rambhaṭṭu – Mahāpātra, ISGO, 68, ś 1425.

Rāmēswarapu
Pl.N; Razole Tq, East Godavari Dt ; Tanuku Tq, West Godavari Dt.
Rāmēswaram, Prodduturu Tq, Cuddapah Dt. IVR, IV, No. 69, ś 1430.
SA; IAP Cuddapah, III, 143, un-dated ; II, 55, ś 1420

Raṃpa
Pl.N; Chodavaram Division, East Godavari Dt.
D

Raṃpāla
Pl.N
AN

Raṃpalli
Pl.N
KN; AN

Raṇapaṭla
Pl.N
GV

Rangā bhaṭla
Pe.N
Vel.

Ranga rāju
Pe.N
GV

Rangā vajhula
Pe.N
VV; VNV

Rāṇi
Title: Queen
PD

Rāpāka
Pl.N; Bhadrachalam Tq, Khammam Dt; Rajahmundry Tq, East Godavri Dt.
AN; TG

Rāpalli
Pl.N
KN

Rāparti
Pl.N; Pithapuram Tq, East Godavari Dt.
Ps.N; SII, VI, No. 692, ś 1186.

Rāpūḍi
Pl.N
AN

Rāpuru
Pl.N; Nellore Dt.
TD; NI, R(49) ś 1559.

Raseed-khāna
Receipt (Revenue House) ;
Pl.N. Raṣid – Puram, Kanigiri Tq, Prakasam Dt.
KKV

Rāvāḍa
Pl.N; Anakapalli Tq, Visakhapatnam Dt.
PD

Rāvi
A tree – Botanical name = *Ficus religiosa*; Sanskrit = Aśwatha
VV; Ps.N; Reddy; Ka; IAP, Nalgonda, No.1, ś 829, IVR, IV, 251, ś 1466.

Rāviganṭi
Pl.N
KKV

Rāvinūtala
Pl.N; Ongole Tq, Prakasam Dt.
AN; IVR, IV No.200, ś 1456.

Rāvipāṭi
Pl.N; Tadepalligudem Tq, W. G Dt; Bapatla Tq, Guntur Dt. Cumbum Tq, Kurnool Dt.
Kh; V; ISGO, 78, 16th Century AD; SII, X, No.738, un-dated.

Rāviprōlu
Pl.N
VV; IAP Medak, 5, ś 901.

Rāvula
Title: Rao. Pl. N. Rāvulu-pālem, Razole Tq, East Godavari Dt.
AN

Rāvuri
Pl.N; Narasaraopet, Guntur Dt.
AN; AD; Ps.N; VV; KN; S

Rāyabhāram
Office; Ambassadorship
AN; Ps. N 'Rāyabari' – IAP, Nalgonda, 3, ś 978.

Rāyabhari
Office: Ambassador
M.Dh

Rāyalachervu
Pl. N
AN

Rāyanapāṭi
Pl.N; Bezawada Tq, Krishna Dt.
AN

Rāyani-pregaḍa
Pe.N
N

Rāyaprōlu
Pl.N
TG; GV; IAP Warangal, 110, ś 1386.

Rāyasaṃ
Office; writer in a king's court
AN; SII, IV, 686, ś 1502.

Rāyavarapu
Pl.N; Rayavaram – Markapur Tq, Prakasam Dt ; Bandar Tq, Krishna Dt.
AN; 'Rayavaram' – IVR, IV, No.22, ś 1325, SII, VI, 777, ś 1383.

Rebba pregaḍa
Pe.N
AN

Reḍḍi
Name of a caste. Derived from Rāṣhtrakuta
Ps.N; SII, VI, 622, ś 1120.

Reḍḍi gunta
Pl.N; Reddigūḍem, Sattenapalli Tq, Guntur Dt.
KKV

Rēgaḍamilli
Pl.N
Ps.N

Rēgi / Rēgu
A fruit; Rēga Agrahāram, Srungavarapukota Tq, Vizianagaram Dt.
KK; Rēga, Vizianagaram Tq & Dt.

Rēgulageḍḍa
Pl.N; Palnad Tq, Guntur Dt.
VV; ARE, 1930: 51.

Rēkapalli
Pl.N; Bhadrachalam Tq, Khammam Dt.
VV

Rēmaṇi
If viewed as an adjective - Moon
VV

Rēmavarapu
Pl.N
KN

Rēmeḷḷa
Pl.N; Rēmalle, Nuzvid division, Krishna Dt.
VV; Gotra : Kāsyapa – ISSGO, 15, ś 1380.

Rēmmarasu
Pe.N
AN

Ṛenṭachintala
Pl.N
TG; VV

Renṭāla
Pl.N
Ps.N; N

Rēpalli
Pl.N; Repalli Tq, Guntur Dt.
KN

Rētūri
Pl.N; Bapatla Tq, Guntur Dt.
AN; 'Renturu' SII, IV, 702, ś 1440; 297, ś 1164.

Rēvalageḍḍa
Pl.N
Renuka

Revaṇa-siddhācharya
Pl.N
Rēnuka;
'Rēvaṇa - nāyaka' – SII, IV, 667, ś 1054.

Rēvanūri
Pl.N
NN; ISGO, 33, ś 1387.

Rēvuri
Pl.N; Markapur Tq, Prakasam Dt.
VV; AN; IVR, IV, No. 150, ś 1448; SII, X, 241, ś 1107.

Rōjukhardu
Occupation; employment
M.Dh

Rōjukurti
Pl.N; Roza, Kurnool Tq & Dt.
M.Dh.

Romṇpicherla
Pl.N; Vayalpad Tq, Chittor Dt; Narasaraopet Tq, Guntur Dt.
VY, Ka ; SII, VI, 636, ś 1073; X, 406, ś 1187

Romṇpiguṇṭla
Pl.N
Ps.N

Rōṇanki
Pl.N. Srikakulam Tq & Dt. EI, 28 : 62

Rōsanūru
Pl.NA
N

Roṭṭi
Bread
V

Rōyyuru
Pl.N; Bezwada Tq, Krishna Dt.
V

Rudrā bhatla
Pe.N, Pl.N; Rudravaram, Ongole Tq, Prakasam Dt; Bandar Tq, Krishna

Dt.
VV; SII, X, 577, ś 1332 , IAP Mahabubnagar Vol. I, No.136, undated.

Rudra rāju
Pe.N; 'Rudravaram' – Manthani Tq, Karimnagar Dt.AN ;
Kh; Rudresvaram – Warangal Tq & Dt, - IAP, Warangal , 94.

Rudrapāka
Pl.N; 'Dūdrapāka' , Kaikalur Tq, Krishna Dt.
SA

Rudrā vajhala
Pe.N
TG

Rūpākula
Pl.N
VV

Rūpanaguṇṭla
Pl.N; Rūpanagudi – Bellary Dt, Karnataka ; Koilakuntla Tq, Kurnool Dt.
Ps.N; SII, XVI, 223, 1557AD.

Ryāli
Pl.N; Razole Tq, East Godavari Dt.
AN; Vel. P

S

Sabari
Hydronymic; Name of a river which joins Godavari
KKs

Sādhu
Humble person; a mendicant like Sanyasi, Byragi
Appropriate; best
Vel.; TG; M; ISGO 15, ś 1380.

Sādhuvalli
Pl.N
V

Sāgi
Pl.N
N; TG; Kh

Sāgi rāju
Pe.N
AN; Kh

Sahasranāmamula
Thousand names in the context of deities such as Lalita and Viṣṇu.
Vel.; SII, X, 422, ś 1191.

Śākavalli
Pl.N
V

Śākhamūri
Pl.N
Ps.N; SII, IV, 709, ś 1480.

Sakinēṭi.
Pe.N; Sakinēṭi – palli, Razole Tq, East Godavari Dt.
Kh

Śalapāka
Pl.N; Kakinada Tq, East Godavari Dt.
TG; AN

Sāligramaṃ
Religious icon; A stone form of Nārāyaṇa; A stone containing the representative chakras of Brahma and other deities.
KK

Sālūri
Pl.N; Sālur, Vizianagaram.

Sāḷva
Hawk; the name of a dynasty that rular over Vijayanagara
The surname of the famous minister Timmarasu.
AN; Sāḷuva, EI, VI, No.22, ś 1442, IAP, Cuddapah III, 127, un-dated.

Sālwa pantula
Pe.N
M.Dh

Sāmanchi
Pl.N
KKV

Sāmanthapūḍi
Pe.N; Darsi Tq, Prakasam Dt.
Kh

Sāmavēdam
One of the Four Vedas, the other three being Rg.; Yajur; Adharvana
VV; TG; KN; ISGO, 15, ś 1380.

Sāmavēdula
(of Sāmavēdam)
VV; AD; SII, X, 577, ś 1332.

Samayamantri
Office; a minister in time and need
AN

Saṃbara
Pe.N
PD

Sāṃba rāju
Pe.N
Ps.N; AN

Sāṃbhi rāju
Pe.N
AN

Sāmbhu
Pe.N
PD

Sāmi rāju
(Correctly Swamiraju)
Pe.N
AN

Śāṃjį
(Correctly Shyamji)
Pe.N
M.Dh

Saṃkusāla
Pl.N
AN

Sammeṭa
Kh; IVR, IV, No.37.

Saṃpara
Pe.N; Kakinada Tq, East Godavari Dt.
AN; EI, 4 ; 83

Sāmrājyam
Empire
GV

Samudrāla
(of Samudra) , Pl.N; Samudrāla-vāri-khanḍrika
TG; SV

Samudram
Sea
Ps.N

Sāmudrikaṃ
Title indicating expertise in Palmistry
M.Dh.

Saṃyapa rāju
Pe.N
Kh

Śanagala
A ceral
TG

Śanagavarapu
Pl.N
TG; SII, IV, 709, ś 1480.

Śānaṃpūḍi
Pl.N; Vinukonda Tq, Guntur Dt; Kandukur Tq, Prakasam Dt.
Ps.N

Sandēpūḍi
Pl.N; Bapatla Tq, Guntur Dt
AN

Sandhyāvandanaṃ
Brahmin, Ritual of offering oblations in the morning and evening 'pratah – sāyaṃ sandhya'

Saṅgaṃ
Pl.N; The meeting point of two or three rivers.
V; E.G.: Kundali Sangamam; Sangam in Srikakulam Dt.

Saṅginapu
Pl.N
VV

Śanivārapu
Saturday
VV

Śankara
Pe.N 'Saṃkara' Gōtra : Gowtama, ISGO, 15, ś 1380.
AN

Śankaragallani
Pe.N
SV

Śankaramanchi
Pe.N
Vel.P

Sankīrtanaṃ
Singing in praise; IVR, IV, 285, ś 146 (9) = 1547 AD.

Śaṅkhavaram
Pl.N; Badvel Tq, Cuddapah Dt, ; Udagiri Tq, Nellore Dt, ; Tuni Tq, E.G Dt.
VY; IAP, Cuddapah, II, 197 ś 1470.

Sannidhānam
In attendance; near the place either in royal court or temple.
TG

Sannidhi
In the presence
AD

Sannidhi-rāju
Pe.N. See Sannidhi
AN; Vel. P

Śāntalūri
Pl.N; Narasaraopet Tq. Guntur Dt.
SV; IVR, IV, No. 224, ś 1462.

Sārangu
Pe.N
An; M.Dh; IAP, Mahabubnagar, Vol. II, No.59, ś 1389.

Sarasvatula
(of Sarasvati) ; See below.
Pe.N; IAP, Nalgonda, I, No.91, line 73, ś 1214.
TG; VN

Saraswati
Pe.N; Goddess of learning. Pl.N. Saraswati-vilāsa-puram, Puttur division, Chittor Dt.
V; Ka; SAP, Cuddapah, II, 93, ś 1449.

Saripāka
Pl.N
VV

Sāripalli
Pl.N; Vizianagaram Tq & Dt.
PD; Ps.N

Sāripeḷḷa
Pl.N; Pe. N; Pithapuram Tq, East Godavari Dt.
AN; PD; IA, 14 : 55.

Sarla
A corrupt form of cherla Hydronymic
PD

Sar-rāju
Pe.N; a corrupt form of Sarva - rāju
AN

Sārańgu
Pl.N; Sārangapuram
M.Dh; AN; NDI, CP 17.

Satyāṣhāḍha
Br. Gōtra: 'Saṭhamarṣhaṇa', ISGO, 15, ś 1380. Now this is a Gōtra name.

Satakūri
Pl.N
Br.; Gōtrā: Kāśyapa, ISGO 15, ś 1380.

Sarvā
Pl.N
VV

Sarvā pregaḍa
Pe.N
AN

Sarvasiddhi
Pl.N; after a title.
AN

Sarvēpalli
Pl.N; Nellore Tq & Dt.; AN; N.I, Udayagiri. (21)

Śasirāvu
Pe.N
AD

Śāstrula
Title: Knowledge of Śāstrās
V

Salāka
Small stick; a needle
TG

Sātavilli
Pl.N
KK

Śathagōpaṃ
Religious; A crown embellished with the feet of God, which is placed on the head of the devotees visiting the temple.
SV, SII, XVI, 130, 1544AD.

Satram
The choultry where strangers and travelers are fed free for a short time. Inn or hostel.
(SII - V, 1118, 1083 AD)
Ps.N. TD

Sātulūri
Pl.N; Narsaraopeta, Guntur Dt
SV; SII, X, p.97 ś 1057.

Sattenapalli
Pl.N; Sattenapalli Tq, Guntur Dt.
VV; Ps.N; SII, X, 199, ś 1104.

Satti rāju
Pe.N; Satti – apabramsa of Satya
AN; SII, X, 749, ś 1505

Satyavāḍa
Pl.N; Tanuku Tq, West Godavari Dt; Ramachandrapuram Tq, East Godavari District.
KN; KKV

Satyavādi
Title: one who stands or argues for truth
SII, IV, 1316, ś 1063.

Satyavōlu
Pl.N; Eluru Tq, West Godavari Dt; Kavali Tq, Nellore Dt.
AN

Savaram
Ka; SII, XVI, 231, 1558 AD.

Sāviḍi.
The front portion of a house
Ps.N

Savitāla
Pl.N
KN

Seedēpalli
Pl.N
Vel.

Seemanapalli
Pl.N
Vel.

Seepali
Pl.N
VY

Seetakkala
Pe.N
PD

Seetam rāju
Pe.N
AN

Seetēpalli
Pl.N
Vel.

Seeti rāju
Pe.N
AN

Sēnādhipathyam
Office: Commandership of the army
VY

Sēnāpati
Office: Commander of the army
VV; SII, V, 1231, Eastern Ganga Anaṇgabhịma

Śēṣhamu
Title: The result; the unrevealed; food offered to the deity.
AN; SII, XVI, 9, 1397 AD; IAP Cuddapah Dt; III 93, ś 1643.

Śēṣhamu bhaṭṭaru
Title: see Seshamu
VY

Śēṭṭalūri
Pl.N
VY

Ṣhaddarsanaṃ
Title : Knowledge of the 6 Darśanās. They are 1. Nyāya, 2. Vaisēṣhika, 3. Sāṃkhya, 4. Yōga, 5. Mịmāmsa, 6. Vēdānta.
PD; ISGO, 15, ś 1380.

Ṣhāhukāru
Occupation; Merchant
VV

Shetchakravarthula
Title: 6 Chakravartis. They are : 1. Harischandra ; 2. Nala; 3. Purukutsa; 4. Purūrava; 5. Sagara ; 6. Kārtavịrya

Śiddalūri
Pl.N
GV

Siddhi
Attainment
Br.; ISGO, 15, ś 1380.

Siddhi rāju
Pe.N; IVR, IV, No.460, ś 1486
AN; IVR, IV, No.709, ś 1480

Śikha
Tuft, in the sense of importance; chief
PD

Śikharam
Top position
AN

Simańapalli
Pl.N
VV

Siṃbha bhaṭla
Pe.N
Ps.N

Siṃhādri
Pl.N; the location of the famous Vaishnavite shrine of Śri Varāhalakshminarasiṃha at Simhāchalam, Visakhapatnam district, A.P.
SV; IVR, IV, 100, ś 1438.

Siṃham bhaṭla
Pe.N
VN; 'Singa-bhaṭla', SII, IV, No.699, ś 1468.

Siṃhampūḍi.
Pl.N
KN

Siṅgampalli
Pl.N
AN

Siṅga rāju
Pe.N; SII, X, 746, ś 1417
AN; IAP, Cuddapah Dt., III, No.13, ś 1716.

Singā vajhula
Pe.N, Pl.N; Singavaram, Bhadrachalam Tq, East Godavari Dt
KN; SII, V, 10, ś 1326.

Siṅgītam
(correctly Sangeetam) ; music
M.Dh.; If Pl. N in Zahirabạd Tq, Medak Dt., A.P.

Singūri
Pl.N:
Br.; SII, VI, 1171, ś 1519.

Śiragavarapu
Pl.N
M.Dh.

Śirapagandḍla
Pl.N; Sisanapalle, Bhadrachalam Tq, East Godavari Dt.
TG

Śirasenagandḍla
Pl.N
TG

Śiripalli
Pl.N
GV

Siri pregaḍa
Pe.N
SV

Siripurapu
Pl.N; Ramachandrapuram Tq, East Godavari Dt., EI, 4 : 96
AN; SV; Kaikalur Tq, Krishna Dt, ARE, 1947; A-5, Gajapahinagaram Tq, Vizianagram Dt

Siriveḷḷa
Pl.N; Sirvel Tq, Kurnool Dt.
GV

Sirivūri
Pl.N
Kh

Śiṣhṭa
Title: excellent; best
PD; KN

Śiṣhṭlā
Title: see Śiṣhṭa
KN; IAP Warangal, 110, ś 1386.

Śiṣhtlā vajhula
Pe N
PD

Śiṣhṭu
Title : excellent; best; an office.
TG; KN; SII, V, 1240, ś 1267.

Śiva
Pe. N
KN; ISGO, 15,1380.

Śivakōṭi
Pl.N; Śivakōḍu, Razole Tq, East Godavari Dist.
Vel.P

Śivala
Pl.N; Ramachandrapuram Tq, East Godavari Dist.
VV

Śivalaṅka
Pl.N
AN

Śivalenka
Pe.N; (Servant = Lenka) of Śiva.
SB

Śivannapalli
Pl.N
VV

Śiva rāju
Pe.N
AN

Śivuḍu
Pe.N
M

Smrāri
Pe.N
VS

Sōdanapalli
Pl.N
AN

Sōlasa
Pl.N; Gotra: Bhāradvāja
Br.; ISGO 15, ś 1380.

Sōmana
Pe.N
TG

Sōmanchi
Pe.N
VV

Sōmapūḍi
Pl.N
VV

Sōma rāju
Pe.N
AN

Sōmāsi
Pe.N
Ps.N

Sōmā vajhula
Pe.N
VN

Sōmayājula
Religious ritual; one who performed the Sōma Yāga.
Pl.N; Sōmayājula – palle, Kadiri Tq, Anantapur Dt.
VV; DD; AD; KK; VN; SII, VI, 982, ś 1218; X 435, ś 1197.

Sōṃ bhaṭla
Pe.N
VV

Sondūru
Pl.N
M.Dh

Sonṭi
A spice variety
VV

Śrēṣhṭī
Title : The best among the Vysyas (merchants). The Telugu version is Setti. Here, the general meaning : the best has to be reckoned.
TG

Śṛibāṣhyam
Name of a religious treatise; expertise in it.
SV; IAP, Cuddapah, II, 220, ś 1473.

Śridhara
Pe.N; after Viṣṇu ; Pl.N; Śridharaghaṭṭa; Rayadurg Tq, Bellary Dt, Karnataka.
VV; Ps.N; SII, IV, 1089, un-dated ; X, 235, ś 1028.

Śridharamalle
Pl.N; Correctly 'Śridhanamalle' Sullurpet Tq, Nellore Dt.
Baḍa Kannada

Śrigiri
Pl.N; Śriśailam, Nandikottur Tq, Kurnool Dt.
AN

Śrigiri rāju
Pe.N
AN

Srikākulapu
Pl.N; Śrikakulam Tq & Dt.
Vel.P; SII, IV, 758, ś 1183.

Śrikanṭam
Pe. N after Śva, Pl. N ; Śrikantha – puram, Hindupur Tq, Anantapur Dt,; 'Śrikantha – paṇḍita' – IAP, Nalgonda I, No.17, AD, 1081. Recipient of a grant.
AV; AS

Śrikāram
Title: The auspicious beginning
Ps.N

Śrikoṅḍa
Pl.N
TG

Śrimattirumala
Pl.N
SV

Śrinivāsula
Pe.N; after Viṣṇu
VY

Śripāda
Religious; worshippers of Śri Cakra. Pl. N; Pl. N. Śripāda – Nellore, Chittor Tq, Dt.
VV

Śripādanna
(Śri Pāda + anna = brother); see Śri Pāda
AN

Śriparāsara
Pe.N; after the sage Parāsara
SV; SII, X, 554, ś 1275.

Śripati
Pe.N; after Viṣṇu
AN; SII, V, 146, ś 1220; IAP Cuddapah, 111, 228, ś 1715.

Śripati Panditāradhyula,
Pe.N; Religious Teacher. SII, VI, 1124, ś 1310.

Śrịperumbudhūr
Pl.N: Chingalput Dt, in Tamilnadu
(Late Prime Minister of India, Rajiv Gandhi assassinated here)
GV; SVR, IV, 490, ś 1499.

Śrịrāma
Pe.N
Br.; SII, V, 1231, Śrikurmam Inscription.

Śrịrāmakavacham
Religious
KK
Śrị Rāma, the 7th Avatara of Viṣṇu. Kavacham in the normal sense means a protective shield or armour worn over the body. But in the present context it means a talisman. Important or the first words of a Mantra written on a leaf or similar substance are embodied in cover and worn on the muscle of the hand. Apparently such a talisman is prepared by the *Upāsikas* of such deities, here for example of the Rāma.

Śrịrāmēswara – bhaṭla
Pe.N
Br,; SII, X, 422, ś 1191.

Śrįrangam
Pl.N; Srirangapuram, Bapatla Tq, Guntur.
DD; 'Srįraṃga', Ep. An VI, 98, No.22, ś 1513.

Śrįvōleṭi.
Pl.N; with the honorific prefix 'Śrį'
AN

Śrungāra – kavi
Title: Srungāra is one of the nine (9) Rasas ; Kavi = poet
AN

Śrungāram
Occupation – decorating the deity
VY; IAP Mahabūbnagar, II, No.15, ś 1202.

Śruṣhṭu
Fully; completely; sumptuous
TG

Sthānam
Position; place; IVR, IV, 318, ś 1471, SII, VI,165, ś 1204.
Ps.N

Subruveeti
Pl.N
M

Sūdarsanaṃ
Sudarsana; lovely in appearance; pleasing to eyes; the discus of Viṣnu and Krishna.
Ps.N; SV ; SII, XVI, 158, 1547 AD. ; IVR, IV, No.285, ś 146(9).

Suddāla
Pl.N
AN

Suddapalli
Pl.N
VV

Sūkara
Pig; in the sense of the 3rd incarnation or Avatara of Viṣṇu
AN

Sūkūru
Pl.N
KKV

Sundaragiri
Pl.N
GV

Sundarapalli
Pl.N
AN

Sunkakaraṇaṃ
Employment; Sunkaṃ = Tax; Karaṇaṃ; a village level revenue official.
AN

Surābāyi
Pe.N
AN

Surabhi
Pl.N; The name of the divine Cow
KK; IAP Mahabubnagar, Vol. II, No.15, ś 1202.

Sūrampūḍi.
Pl.N
AN

Sūrapa rāju
Pe.N
PS.N; SII, X, 261 ś 1136.

Sūravarapu
Pl. N ; Bhadrachalam Tq, East Godavari Dt., Nuzivid division, Krishna Dt.
VV; TG; AN

Sūrāvajhula
Pe.N
VV

Sūri
Title: Pundit
TG

Sūri bhaṭla
Pe.N
Vel; TG

Sūrikuchchi
Pe. N
VV; SII, VI, 622, ś 1120

Sūripeddi
Pe.N
Vel.; SII, X, 247, ś 1130.

Sūrisōmayājula
Pe.N
KK

Sūryadēvara
Pe.N after the Sun god
AN; SII, V,1233, ś 1193.

Sūsarāvu
Pe.N
VY

Susarla
Pl.N
VV; TG; KN; VN; M.Dh.

Suvāṇam
Royal kitchen (in charge of)
V

Swarṇa
Pl.N; Gold, Bapatla Tq.; Guntur Dt.
SA

Swayampāka (Kula)
Cooking by oneself as an *āchāra*.
TG

Swayamprakāsaṃ
Title: Shiny by self
PD

T

Tachchuūru
Pl.N
VY

Taḍakamaḷḷa
Pl.N
GV; Taḍakamaḍla – IAP Nalgonda, II, No.83, ś 1466.

Tāḍēpalli
Pl.N; Guntur Tq & Dt; Tadepalligudam Tq, East Godavari Dt,;
AN; VV; Gōtra : Hārita ; SII, X, 459, ś 1210 ; ISGO 15, ś 1380.

Tāḍigaḍapa
Pl.N
LN

Tāḍikelapūḍi
Pl.N; Eluru Tq, West Godavari Dt.
AN; SII, V, 195, ś 1126.

Tāḍikoṅḍa
Pl.N; Guntur Tq & Dt. ;
AN; KK; SII, X, 492, ś 1225.

Tāḍimaḷḷa
Pl.N
LN

Tāḍimēti
Pl.N; Tadimēḍu ; Sullurpeta Tq, Nellore Dt.
AN

Tādimaḍa
Pl.N; Manthani Tq, Karimnagar Dt.
AN

Tādināḍa
Pl.N Kaikalur Tq, Krishna Dt.
AN; EI, 29; 5777.

Tātiparti
Pl.N; Tadiparti Tq, Anantapur Dt.; Tanuku Tq, West Godavari Dt.
VV

Tāḍiparti
Pl.N; Tadiparti Tq, Anantapur Dt.
VY; IVR IV, 182, ś 1453.IVR, IV, No.72, ś 1431.

Tāḍi Pūṃdi
Pl.N
Br.; Gōtra: N.A; ISGO,15, ś 1380.

Tāḍūri
Pl.N; Tāḍūr – Tiruttani division, Tamil Nadu, Gunapasapuram of Inscriptions.
AN; M.Dh; SII, VI, 600, ś 1087; CP of AP Vol. I p.243.

Tāḍuvāyi
Pl.N; IAP, Nalgonda I,No. 94,ś 1222,Sattenapalli Tq, Guntur Dt; Peddapuram Tq,EG Dt
AN; SII, VI, 236, ś 1104 ; X, No.199, ś 1104; 489, ś 1222.

Takkellapāṭi
Pl.N; Takkellapadu, Ongole Tq, Prakasam Dt; Guntur TQ & Dt.
AN; GV; EI, XVIII. P.III, ś 1350. Sattenapalli Tq, Guntur Dt.

Tallaṃki
Pl.N
AN; SII, IV, 282, ś 1436.

Tāḷḷapāka
Pl.N; Rajampet Tq, Cuddapah Dt.
NN; SII, XVI9, 31, 1433 AD, Annamayya the Vaggēyakara, Pada-kavita-pitāmaha.

Tallapa rāju
Pe.N
AN

Tallā pragaḍa
Pe.N; Pl.N; Tallāpuram, Tadepalligudem Tq, West Godavari Dt.
AN; SII, X, 577, ś 1332. IAP Mahabubnagar Vol. I, No.172, ś 1113.

Talla vajhula
Pe.N, Pl.N See above
VV; IAP Warangal, 110, ś 1386.

Tallem rāju
Pe.N, Pl.N see above
AN

Tāllūri
Pl.N; Satteṇapalli Tq, Guntur Dt; Nandigama Tq, Krishna Dt.
Ps.N; SII, IV, 709, ś 1480.

Tellūri
Pl.N
Br.; SAP, Cuddapah, III, 84, ś 1800

Tamarāpalli
Pl.N; Tāmarāpalli, Srikakulam Tq & Dt.
AN; KNV; SII, V, 1290, ś 1152.

Taṃdra
Pl.N
TG

Tāmarāḍa
Pl.N; Tanuku Tq, West Godavari Dt.,
Br.; ARE 1925 : A – 4.

Tamirasa
Pl.N; Gudivada Tq, Krishna Dt.
AN; GV

Tamiri
Pl.N
AN

Tamma
Pl.N; Tamma-varam, Kakinada Tq, East Godavari Dt.
VV; 'Tammalūru' – C.P. of A.P. Vol. I, p. 180.

Tāmāḍa
Pl.N; Chipurupalli Tq, Vizianagaram Dt.
Br.

Tāmmara
Pl.N
Ps.N

Tāmmavarapu
Pl.N
AN

Tammi
Pl.N; Tammiteru (river) near Eluru, West Godavari Dt.
VV; SII, X, 407, ś 1188.

Tammi rāju
Pe.N
GV

Taṃpeḷḷa
Pl.N
AD

Tānḍra
Pl.N
TG; IAP Mahabūbnagar Vol.II, No.92, 16th Century AD.

Tangeḷḷa
Pl.N
VV; Kandukur Tq, Prakasam Dt., SII, VI, 248, ś 1437; SII X, 565, ś 1317

Taṅgirāla
Pl.N; Vinukonda Tq, Guntur Dt.
VV

Ṭangutūri
Pl.N; Taṃgatūru, Rajenpet Tq, Cuddapah Dt, Ongole Tq, Prakasam Dt.
AN; Ps.N; IAP Cuddapah; III, 137, ś 1656.

Tanikeḷḷa
Pl.N
VV

Tantravahi
Title or occupation : Tantra = crafty, Vahi = account
AN; GV

Taṇuku
Pl.N; Tanuku Tq, East Godavari Dt.
AN; KN; SII, IV, 1298, CV 46.

Tāra kavi
Title pertaining to poetry ; Tāra = Star; Kavi = poet
AN

Tareniganṭi
Pl.N
TG

Tarigoṅḍa
Pl.N; Tarugoṃda Vayalpad Tq, Chittoor Dt; IVR, IV, 191, ś 1454.
N

Tarigoppula
Pl.N; Ganavaram Tq, Krishna Dt.
GV; AN

Taripeḷḷa
Pl.N
AD

Tātā
Old man; grand father
PD; VN, VNV; ISGO, 11, ś 1377.

Tātaṃki
Pl.N; 'Tādaṃki' Gannavaram Tq, Krishna Dt.
AN

Tātapalli
Pl.N
PD

Tātapūḍi
Pl.N
AD

Tatavarti
Pl.N; 'Tati-varru', Gudivada Tq, Krishna Dt.
AN

Tāṭikoṅḍa
Pl. N ; Mahabūbnagar Tq & Dt.,
VY

Tāṭikōṭa
Pl.N; Ellavaram division, East Godavari Dt.
M.Dh

Tāṭipaḷḷa
Fruit
PD

Tāṭiparti
Pl.N; Kalahasti Tq, Chittoor Dt; Tekkali Tq, Srikakulam Dt.
VV; SII, IV, 799, un-dated.

Tāṭi rāju
Pe.N
AN

Taṭṭa
Basket
VY

Teḍḍepu
Pl.N
AN

Teerdhāla
Holy place associated with water. Pl.N. Tįrtham, Polamaneri Tq. Chittor Dt.
VV

Tejōmūrtula
Pe.N
KN; SII, X, 577 ś 1332.

Ṭēkumaḷḷa
Pl.N; Present Tekmal in Andole Tq, Medak Dt., A.P.
VV; M.Dh.; 'Tēkumbēḍa sthala' – IAP Medak, 135, ś 1230.

Ṭēkupalli
Pl.N; Medaḷi Tq, Mahabūbnagar Dt, Divi Tq, Krishna Dt.
VV; M.Dh

Telakapalli
Pl.N
V

Tēlaprōli
Pl.N
Br.; Gōtra : Bhāradvāja; ISGO, 15, ś 1380.

Telidevara
Pe.N
AN

Telikacherla
Pl.N; Tadepalligudem Tq, West Godavari Dt.
KN

Telikarcherla Kandāḍy
Pl.N; See above
SV

Telikepalli
Pl.N; Tēliki, Pulivendula Tq, Cuddapah Dt.
TG

Tēḷḷa
Scorpion
Pl.N.; Tēḷḷa – pāḍu, Badvel Tq, Cuddapah Dt; Tēḷḷa – puri, Siruvel Tq, Kurnool Dt.
Ka

Teṃjerla
Pl.N
VV

Teṃpalli
Pl.N; Chittoor Tq & Dt.
KN; SII, 3: 16

Tenāli
Pl.N; Tenali Tq & Dt.
Ps.N; SII, X, 112, ś 1065

Tenēṭi.
Pl.N
AD

Tenmaṭham
Pl.N
SV

Tennēṭi.
Pl.N 'Tennēru', Bezwada Tq, Krishna Dt.
VV; AN
Viswanadham Freedom fighter, Parliamentarian. ; Hemalata Novelist

Terāla
Pl.N; Palnad Tq ; Guntur Dt.
KN; CTI, IV, No.35, ś 1213.

Tātali
Pl.N
AN

Tiguḷḷa
Pl.N
Ps.N

Tikkavarapu
Pl.N
Reddy; SII, X, 504, ś 1235.

Tilaka
An auspicious mark on the forehead; Tilak
Maharastra Chitpavan Brahmin

Timma rāju
Pe.N; Timma – rāju peta, Rajampet Tq, Cuddapah Dt. ; Pl. N ; Timma-puram, Puttur Tq, Chitoor Dt; Ellavarm division, E.G Dt, Vindukonda Tq, Guntur Dt.
GV; Ps. N; AN; IVR, IV, No. 173, ś 1448.

Timma vajhula
Pe.N, Pl.N; Timma-samudram Tq, Cuddapah Dt ; Timmā-puram, Cumbum Tq, Kurnool Dt.
Br.

Tippā bhaṭla
Pe.N; Tippalūru, Kamdapuram Tq, Cuddapah Dt.
VV; Tippabhaṭlavāri palle, Penugonda Tq, Anantapur Dt. ; EI; 27:23 ft.

Tippa vajhula
Pe.N; Tamil nadu, Tippāpuram, Nugur Tq, East Godavari Dt.
TG; KNV; Tippanūru, Pattikonda Tq, Kurnool Dt.

Tịrthāla
Pl.N; Tịrtham, Polamanagar Tq, Chittoor Dt.
VV

Tirukkovalūru
Pl.N
Vy

Tirukuchchi
Pl.N in South Arcot district in Tamil Nadu
Ps.N

Tirukūri
Pl.N
AN

Tirumala
Pl.N; Abode of Venkateswara (Balaji) in Chittoor district, A.P.
VY; IAP Cuddapah II, 177, ś 1467.

Tirumala Bukkapaṭṭaṇapu
Pl.N; Tirumala – Chandragiri Tq, Chittoor Dt.
VY; Bukkapaṭṭṇaṃ, Penugonda Tq, Anantapur Dt.

Tirumala Pallērlamūḍi
Pl.N
VY

Tirumala Pañchāngam
Pl.N + expertise in Almanac.
SV

Tirumala peddinṭi.
Pl.N; Big or reputed family (house) in Tirumala
VY

Tirumala Pragaḍa
Pl.N
GV

Tirumala Upparapalli
Pl.N
VY

Tirumala rāju
Pe.N
AN

Tirumāmiḍi
Pl.N
AD

Tirunaghali
Pl.N
VY

Tirupati
Pl.N; Abode of Venkateswara (Balaji) in Chittor district, A.P.
TG

Tiruvāyipēṭa
Pl.N
CV

Tiruvūru
Pl.N; Tiruviuru division, Krishna Dt.
AN

Tōdēru
Pl.N
Ps.N

Togararāṭi.
Pl.N; Togarchēḍu – Nandyal Tq – Kurnool Dt.
KN; Togarāmūḍi, Sullurpet Tq, Nellore Dt.

Tōgummi
Pl.N; Nidadavolu Tq, West Godavari Dt.
SV

Tōlēṭi
Pl.N; 'Toteru' Bhimavaram Tq, West Godavari Dt.
Ps.N, VB ; SII, XVI, 14, 1388 AD; ibid, V, 147, ś 1222.

Tonḍapi
Pl.N; Sattenapalli Tq, Guntur Dt
AN; SII, V, 147, ś 1222.

Tōnṭaśomayājula
Pe.N
V; Tomṭa – sōmayājula; Gōtra : Kauṇḍnya; ISGO, 15, ś 1380.

Tonṭipāṭi
Pl.N
Ps.N

Tōpalli
Pl.N; 'Tempalli', Gannavaram Tq, Krishna Dt.
VV

Tōpella
Pl.N
VV

Tōṭa
Garden
AD
The prefix 'Arāma' to the Dravida Brahmin sect itself means Garden. Hence they are also referred to as Tōṭa Dravidas.

Tōṭapalli
Pl.N; Peddapuram Tq, East Godavari Dt; Parvatipuram Tq, Vizianagaram Dt.
AN; TG

Toyyēṭi.
Pl.N; Toyyēru, Chodavaram division, East Godavari Dt.
Vel.; IAP Cuddapah III, 162, ś 1667.

Tripurari bhaṭla
Pe.N; IAP, Nalgonda I, No.81, Lines 62-63, ś 1196.
TG; SII, V, 114, ś 1480.

Tūbāṭi.
Pl.N; Tūmāḍu, Kondukur Tq, Prakasam Dt.
AN; SII, IV, 709, ś 1480.

Tulasi
Plant; sacred basil. Pl.N Tulasi-pākalu, Bhadrachalam division, East Godavari Dt.
VV

Tummaguṇṭa
Pl.N; Tummalaguṇṭa, Chandragiri Tq, Chittoor Dt; Kanigiri Tq, Prakasam Dt.
Ps.N
There is a separate Dravida Brahmana sect associated with this Pl. N
Tummala palli
Pl.N; Peddapuram Tq, East Godavari Dt.
AN; GV; KN, Ps.N

Tumarāḍa
Pl.N; Bobbili Tq, Vizianagaram Dt.
VV

Tummapūḍi
Pl.N; Tenali Tq, Guntur Dt.
SV; IAP Cuddapah Dt. III, No.3, 15th Century A.D.

Tumma rāju
Pe.N
Ps.N

Tummarugōṭi
Pl.N
GV

Tūmu
Drainage water way
GV

Tumulūru
Pl.N; Tumaṭūru, Atmakuru Tq, Kurnool Dt, Tenali Tq, Guntur Dt;
VV; AN; IVR, IV, No.7, ś 1292

Tungaturti
Pl.N
KK

Tupurāṇi
Pl.N
VY

Turaga
Horse
AN

Turlapāṭi
Pl.N; Turla-pāḍu, Bapatla Tq, Guntur Dt; Nandigama Tq, Krishna Dt.
AN

Turumeḷḷa
Pl.N; Markapuram Tq, Prakasam Dt; Tenali Tq, Guntur Dt.
AN; IAP Cuddapah, II, 27 (Times of Prodhadevaraya of Vijayanagara)

Tutupalli
Pl. N
TG

Tùḍi
Pl. N Tāḍi, Anakapalli Tq, Visakhapatnam Dt.
V

U

Uḍāli
Pl.N
Pu.D

Uḍatala
Squirrel. Pl N. Udata-vari-palle/palem, Gudur Tq, Nellore Dt.
GV

Udayagiri
Pl.N; Udayagiri Tq; Nellore Dt.
Ps; KK; V; TG; Ka; IVR IV, No. ś 1299.

Udbhaṭa
Best; a great man; Chivalrous; Sun.
N

Udbhata ārādhyula
Pe.N; Name of a Śaiva teacher or preceptor
AN; LN; Śiva purōhita

Uddi
Equal
N

Udgāvi
Pl.N
M.Dh.

Ūdumūḍi
Pl.N; Razole Tq, East Godavari Dt.

Ūlapalli / Ulapaṭṭi
Pl.N; Ūlapādu, Punganur Tq, Chittoor Dt;
AN; Vel. Niyōgi; / Vel.

Ulichi
Pl.N; Ongole Tq, Prakasam Dt.
AN

Ulimiri
Pl.N: Ulimeḷḷa - Pulivendula Tq, Cuddapah Dt.
VNV; IAP Cuddapah , II, No.150, Vijayanagar Period, Isvara Nayaka.

Ulipi
Pl.N
Kh

Ullaganṭi
Pl.N
Ps.

Ullipālemu
Pl.N; Divi Tq, Krishna Dt.
AN

Ulugunḍam
Pl.N
M.Dh

Umāpati
Pe.N after Śiva
V; IVR, IV, No. 402, ś 1479.

Ummettala
Pl.N; Ummetta, Ellavaram division, East Godavari Dt.
M.Dh.

Unḍavalli
Pl.N: Guntur Tq, & Dt. : SII, X, 162, ś 1089.
TG: V; IAP Mahabūbnagar, Vol. I, No. 114, 1107 AD.

Uṅḍi
Pl.N; Bhimavaram Tq, West Godavari Dist.
SA

Unḍukonḍala
Pl.N
SA

Uṅdurti
Pl.N; Nalgonda Dt.
Ps.; IAP Warangal, 110, ś 1386; CTI IV, No. 50, ś 1386.

Unnaṃ
Pl.N
AN

Unnava
Pl.N; Guntur Tq & Dt.
AN; SII, VI, 120, ś 1197.

Upāḍhayula
Teacher
PD; TG; KN; VV; Vel

Upadhrashṭa
Religious; a supervisor who overseas and corrects any commission or omissions in the conduct of an Yajña or sacrifice.
VNV; ISGO, 15, ś 1380

Upamāka / Upmāka
Pl.N; Visakhapatnam Dt.
AD

Uppala
Pl.N; IVR IV, No. 237, ś 1466
AN; Ps; V; KK ; SII, XVI, 130, 1544 AD.

Uppalam
Pl.N
Vel.

Uppalpāṭi
Pl.N; Ellavaram division, East Godavari Dt; Kamavarapu Kota Tq, West Godavari Dt.
AN; Ps; Kh ; SII, VI, 236, ś 1104, ibid iv, 709 ś 1480; X 509, ś 1236.

Upparapalle
Pl.N
SV

Uppu
Common salt
KK, M.Dh, Ka; ETI, p.238, ś 1084.

Uppūḍi
Pl.N; Amalapuram Tq, East Godavari Dt; Repalle Tq, Krishna Dt.
Vel.

Uppuguṇḍūri / Uppumangulūri
Pl.N
AN; / KN

Uppulūri
Pl.N; Bhimavaram Tq, W. G. Dt. 'Bōyala-uppalūru' Koilakunta Tq., Kurnool Dt,
AN; M. Dh; Ka; Vel.; SII, VI, 228, ś 1119; ISGO, 15, ś 1380.

Uppunūtala
Pl.N
IAP, Nalgonda, I, 62, ś 1124.

Ūrakaraṇam
Occupation
AN; Ka; Ps.N

Ure
Pl.N
GV

Usulamarti
Pl.N
AN

Ūṭa
Hydronymic; water source
Ka

Ūṭapālem
Pl.N; Ellavaram division, East Godavari Dt.
N

Ūṭala
Pl.N; Chodavaram division, East Godavari Dt.
TG

Utpala
Tree or Plant
SV; VY

Uttraēśvarapu
Pl.N
Br.Gotra; Kāśyapa; ISGO, 15, ś 1380.

Ūtukuru
Pl.N; Saṭtenapalle Tq, Guntur Dt.; Makatal Tq, Mahabubnagar; Miryalaguda Tq, Nalgonda Dt., IAP, Nalgonda I, 126, ś 1030
GV; KN; NN; AN; IAP Cuddapah, III, 206, ś 1569; II, 13, ś 1382.

Utupalli
Pl.N
AN

V

Vaḍala
Pl.N
GV

Vaḍali
Pl.N
VY

Vaḍāli
Pl.N; Tanuku Tq, West Godavari Dt. , Kakinada Tq, Krishna Dt.
VV

Vāḍapalli
Pl.N; Chodavaram division, East Godavari Dt, Miryalaguda Tq, Nalgonda Dt., IAP Nalgonda I, No.142, un-dated.
VV; AN; Ad. N; VY ; SII, V, 131; ś 12318 ; IAP, Nalgonda, II, No.33.

Vāḍaparti
Pl.N
Ps.N

Vāḍarēvu
Pl.N; Rēvu = port ; correctly Vōḍa-rēvu
AN

Vadaṃguṇṭla
Pl.N

Vaḍḍapaṭla
Pl.N
AN

Vaḍḍāri
Pl.N

Vaḍḍegacherla
Pl.N
Ps.N

Vaḍḍi.
Pl.N
VV; Kp ; ISGO, 15, ś 1380.

Vaḍḍiparti
Pl.N; Vaddiparru, Razole Tq, Godavari Dt, Narasapuram Tq, West Godavari Dt.
AN

Vaddi rāju
Pe.N
Ps.

Vaḍḍūri
Pl.N
AN

Vādēla
Pl.N
TG

Vādhūla
Name of a 'Gōtra' Ep. An. V, p.128, ś 1346. Here the donee's father's name is given as Vādhūla Tippaya and his gōtra as Vyādhula.
VV; VY; SII, V, 1231, Eastern Ganga Anangabhịma.

Vaḍlamāni
Pl.N; Vardhamānapuram – Vaḍḍamāna, Nagarkarnul Tq Mahabūbnagar Dt, Anumakonda Inscription – MAS, No.13, No.3
PD; SII, IV, 709, ś 1480.

Vaḍlamannāṭi
Pl.N; Bandar Tq, Krishna Dt.
AN

Vaḍlamūḍi
Pl.N; Vaḍlapūdi – Bapatla Tq, Guntur Dt.
AN; Kh.

Vadre
Pl.N
VV

Vādrēvu
Pl.N; port; correction of Vōḍarēvu. Vādrēvu palle, Razole Tq, East Godavari Dt.
AN

Vaḍugūri
Pl.N; Cinna – Vaḍugūru, Gutti Tq, Anantapur Dt.
VN; IVR, IV,350, 1474

Vaḍūri
Pl.N
Ps.N

Vaḍḍāḍi
Pl.N; Chodavaram Tq, Visakhapatnam Dt.
AN; SII VI, 794, ś 1297.

Vaḍḍamānu
Pl.N; Nandikotkur Tq, Kurnool Tq.; Guntur Tq & Dt., SII, X, 279, ś 1153.
Ps.N; SII, IX, Part I, No.121, ś 980.

Vahi
Occupation; Accountant
Ps.N

Vāhinịpati
Title or Occupation : Commander (Pati) of army (Vāhini)
VN

Vaidyula
Doctor,
G.V; SII, VI, 1006, ś 1311.

Vajapeyājula
Religious; performance of the Vajapēya sacrifice or Yajña.
Vel.

Vajhu
<ojjaTeacher
AN

Vākāda vajhula
Pe.N; Pl.N. 'Vākāda', Kakinada Tq, East Godavari Dt.
AD

Vākāti
Pl.N; Vākāḍu, Gudur Tq, Nellore Dt.

Vakkalanka
Pl.N; Amalapuram Tq, East Godavari Dt.
AN

Vāliparti
Pl.N
Kh

Valivēṭī
Pl.N; Tenali Tq., Guntur Dt.
VV; SII, X, 6, ś 965.

Vallabha rāju
Pe.N
AN

Vallabha vajhula
Pe.N
KN

Vallabha-Jōsyula
Pe.N; 'Vallabha' – Lord, Master.
Vel.; 'Vallabha - Sōmayājula', SII, IV, 699, ś 1468.

Vallam bhaṭla
Pe.N; Pl. N. Vallam – paṭla, Tiruvur division, Krishna Dt.
Ps.N; SII, X, 766, ś 1600.

Vallūru
Pl.N; Cuddapah Tq & Dt SII X, No.448, ś 1279, Bapatla Tq, Guntur Dt;

AN; Cuddapah Tq & Dt, IVR, IV, 353, ś 1475, SII, XVI, 281, 1572 AD.

Vama rāju
Pe.N
AN

Vanaṃ
Pl.N; Garden
Ps

Vanamāmale
Pl.N
VY; IAP, Mahabūbnagar, Vol II, No. 96, ś 1791.

Vānapalli
Pl.N; Rajol Tq, East Godavari Dt.
Ps.N; EI, 17 : 334.

Vānapāmula
Pl.N; after a type of snake
TG

Vānasa
Pl.N
Br.; SII, V, 1042, ś 1061

Vanḍamūri
Pl.N
AN

Vandi rāju
Pe.N
AN

Vangala
Pl.N
TG; SV; SII, XVI, 130, 1544AD; IAP, Cuddapah Dt, III, No.79, undated.

Vangara
Pl.N; Tekkali, Rājam Tq's , Srikakulam Dt.
TG; EI, 25: 281.

Vaṅgavēṭi
Pl.N
VV

Vangēpurapu
Pl.N
VY

Vangipurapu
Pl.N; Vangipuram, Bapatla Tq, Guntur Dt.
Ps.N; IVR, IV, No.404, ś 1478

Vangoṅḍa
Pl.N
AN

Vangurapu
Pl.N
AN

Vangūri
Pl.N; Alampuram Tq, Mahabūbnagar Dt.
AN ; IAP, Mahabūbnagar Dt., Vol. I, No.2, 600 AD, Vol., No.31, ś 1298.

Vanka
Pl.N
VV

Vankadaḷaṃ
Pl.N
GV

Vankamāmiḍi
Pl.N
Ps.N

Vankāyala
Pl.N; after Brinjal. See below
VN

Vankayāla bhaṭla
Pe.N; See below
VN

Vankāyalapāṭi
Pl.N; Vaṃkāyalapāḍu, Narasaraopet Tq, Guntur Dt.
AN; SII, XVI, 130, 1544 AD; ISGO, 73, Prataparudra Gajapati.

Vankēswarapu
Pl.N
Ps.N

Vannela
Pl.N
PD

Vāpa
Pl.N
Ps.N

Varada
Title: protector; one of the names of Viṣṇu
AD; SII, V, 1262, ś 1288.

Varagāni
Pl.N; Bapatla Tq, Guntur Dt.
Ps.N

Varāha bhaṭla
Pe.N
PD

Varāhagiri
Pl.N
AD; Ps.N

Varāhapaṭnam
Pl.N
VY

Vāraṇāsi
Pl.N; Benaras; CTI, IV, No.50, ś 1386.
Vel; KN; TG; KK; SII, XVI, 190, 1554 AD; IAP Warangal, 110, ś 1386.

Vardha-kavi
Title: poetry
NN

Vardhamāna
Pl.N 'Vardhamāna puram' (Now Vadama). Tellkaliplates of Umavarma, EI, XXVII.No.47, Palakonda Tq, Srikakulam Dt.
Ps.N

Varigonḍa
Pl.N; Nellore Tq & Dt.
AN

Vajhula
<ojjaTeacher; Vazzalavāripalem, Venkatagiri Tq, Nellore Dt.
PN; VV; Ps.N; AD

Vāsa
Pl.N
KN

Vasantarāvu
Pe.N
KKV

Vasantavāḍa
Pl.N; Razole Tq, East Godavari Dt.
AN

Vāsi rāju
Pe.N
Baḍagala Kannda

Vatsavāyi
Pl.N; Nandigama Tq, Krishna Dt.
Kh

Vaṭṭi.
Pl.N
AN

Vaṭṭipalli
Pl.N
TG

Vāvila kolanu
Pl.N
GV

Vāvilāla
Pl.N; Tiruvuru Tq, Krishna Dt.
TG; Reddy; IAP Mahabūbnagar, Vol. II, No.10, ś 1193.

Vāvilla
Pl.N; Vāvilḷapāṭi ; IVR, IV, No.129, ś 1442.
Ph.D

Vāyu vēgula
Title: As speedy as the air
PD

Vēda rāju
Pe.N
Ps.N

Vedāla
Pl.N or Title
Vel; VY; Ps.N

Vēdaṃ
Title: Veda. Pl. N; Kalahasti division, Chittoor Dt.
Pu.D; TG; Vēdaṃvāri Khanḍrika, Puttur division, Chittoor Dt.

Vēḍaṃgi
Pl.N
AN

Vēdaṃpūḍi.
Pl.N
AN

Vēdana bhaṭla
Pe.N
VN

Vēdāṇtaṃ
Title: Generally, philosophy. Pl.N.Vēdāntapuram, Polavaram division, E.G. Dt.
VV; TG; KN ; ISGO, 15, ś 1380.

Vēdāri
Title: Enemy of Vēda
VS

Vēdavalli
Pl.N
AN

Vēdula
Title: Pertaining to Vēda
PD; TG; VV

Vedurucherla
Pl.N; Vedullacheruvu, Kalahasti division, Chittoor Dt.
Kn; IAP, Cuddapah, I, No.134, (Vaidumba dynasty)

Vedurumūḍi.
Pl.N
M.Dh.

Veeṇa
Title: The stringed musical instrument
M. Dh

Veetūri
Pl.N
TG

Vēgeḷḷa
Pl.N
Kh

Vēgenḍla
Pl.N
Ps.N

Vēgēṭi
Pl.N
VV

Vēgi nāṭi
Pl.N; A territorial division in Andhra. Pedda-Vēgi, Eluru Tq, West Godavari Dt.
VN

Vēgi rāju
Pe.N; After vēṅgi, the capital of the Eastern Chāḷukyas; can also be after 'Vēgu' = spy
AN; Kh

Vēgunḍlapāṭi
Pl.N
AN

Veladi
Pl.N
AN

Velidi
Pl.N; Nandigama Tq, Krishna Dt.
VV

Velagalēṭi
Pl.N; Velagaṭēru, Bezwada Tq, Krishna Dt.
AN

Velagapāḍu
Pl.N; Kamavarapukota Tq, West Godavari Dt.
Kh

Velagapuḍi
Pl.N; Guntur Tq & Dt.
Ps.N; AN; SII, X, 395, ś 1183.

Vēlāla
Pl.N
M.Dh; GV

Velamakanni
Pl.N
TG

Velamūri
Pl.N
VV

Velavelapalli
Pl.N; Amalapuram Tq, East Godavari Dt.
SA

Velicerla
Pl. NTG; ISGO 72, ś 1443.

Velichēṭi.
Pl.N; 'Velivēru', Razole Tq, East Godavari Dt.
AN

Velidimarla
Pl.N
GV

Velidinḍi.
Pl.N
GV

Veligaṇḍla
Pl.N
Br.; CTI, IV, No.32, ś 1181

Velivela
Pl.N; Narasapur Tq, West Godavari Dt.
AN

Veliventi
Pe.N
KN

Velivēṭi
Pl.N; Velivennu, Nidadavolu Tq, West Godavari Dt.
VV

Vellāla
Pl.N; Nandikotkur Tq, Kurnool Dt.
M; IAP, Cuddapah Dt. II, III, No. 62, ś 1500.

Vellaṃchēṭi
Pl.N
Ps.N

Vellaṃki
Pl.N; Nandigama Tq, Krishna Dt; Bhimunipatnam Tq, Visakhapatnam Dt.TG;
AN; V; IAP, Karimnagar Dt. 25, ś 1092.

Vellaṃṭi.
Pl.N
Ps.N

Velluṭla
Pl.N
AN

Veluganṭi
Pl.N; Veligallu, Madanapalli Tq, Chittoor Dt.
AN

Velumpalli
Pl.N
VV

Velunūri
Pl.N
VV

Vēlūri
Pl.N; Veluru Tq ; Krishna Dt; Narasaraopeta Tq, Guntur Dt.
TG; 'Veṛuru' IVR, IV, No. 139, ś 1443.

Veluvali
Pl.N
AN; Ps.N

Vēmakōṭi
Pl.N; Vēmula – kōta, Markapuram Tq, Prakasam Dt.
AD; SII, V, 1236, ś 1199

Vēmanārdhyula
Pe. NAr

Vēma rāju
Pe.N
AN

Vēmavarapu
Pl.N; Amalapuram, Tuni Tq's, East Godavari Dt. Bezawada Tq, Krishna Dt.
AN

Vembāḷam Ambāḷaṃ
Pl.N
SV

Veṃpali
Pl.N
NN; SII, X, 363, ś 1191.

Veṃparāla
Pl.N; Darsi Tq, Prakasam Dt.
VV

Veṃpaṭi.
Pl.N; Veṃpādu, Nuzvid division, Krishna Dt.
VV

Vēmu
Pl.N; Vēmuturu, Chodavaram division, East Godavari Dt.
VV

Vēmuganṭi
Pl.N
M.Dh

Vēmula
Pl. N; IAP, Nalgonda, I No. 17, A.D. 1081 ; IVR, IV, No. 39, s 1347.
GV ; Ka ; IAP, Cuddapah, III, 174, ś 1603 ; SII, XVI, 28, 1576 AD.

Vēmulakoṅḍa
Pl.N ; Chodavaram division, East Godavari Dt. Koilakunta Tq, Kurnool Dt.
Ps.N; GV; VN

Vēmulapāṭi.
Pe.N
TG

Vēmūri
Pl.N; Tenali Tq; Guntur Dt.
VV; AN; TG; SII, X, 86, ś 1050 ; Ep. An. P.44

Veṃpaṭi.
Pl.N; Vempalli, Madanapalli Tq, Chittoor Dt.
AN

Vēna rāju
Pe.N
AN

Veṅdurti
Pl.N
AN

Vennelakanṭi.
Pl.N
AN

Vēnneṭi.
Pl.N
AN

Venṭra Pregaḍa
Pl.N; Gudivada Tq, Krishna Dt.
AN

Veṇuturla
Pl.N; Pedda – venturla, Kaikaluru Tq, Kurnool Dt.
Ps.N; IAP, Cuddapah Dt., III, No. 76, ś 1612.

Veṇuturupalli
Pl.N; Venturumilli, Gudivada Tq, Krishna Dt.
AN

Vēpa
Pl.N; Name of a tree
VV

Vēpachēdula
Pl.N
Ps.N

Vētūri
Pl.N
VV; GV

Vēvūri
Pl.N
Kh.

Vidhala
Pl.N
GV

Vijāpurapu
Pe.N
M.Dh

Vikrāla
Pl.N
VY

Vindamūri
Pl.N
VV

Vindūri
Pl.N
Ps.N

Vinja
Pl.N; Vinja –varapu – pāḍu ; Ellavaram division, East Godavari Dt.
AN

Vinjamūri
Pl.N; Udayagiri Tq, Nellore Dt.
AN; GV; DV; TG; Vel.

Vinjanampāṭi.
Pl.N; 'Vinjaram', Polavaram division, East Godavari Dt.
AN

Vinjarapu
Pl.N
VY

Vinnakōṭa
Pl.N; Gudivada Tq, Krishna Dt.
AN; Ps. N; Drujjavaram Inscription of Anavema.

Vinukoṅḍa
Pl.N; Vinukonda Tq, Krishna Dt.; Guntur Dt.
VY; AN; SVR, IV, 448, ś 1484; SII, VI, 248, ś 1437.Br.

Vipparti
Pl.N; 'Viripara' Narasaraopet Tq, Guntur Dt.; Mydavolu platen of Sivaskonda varma
Ps.N; AN; EI, VÍ, pp. 8J-88; SII, IV, 763, ś 1158; X, 484, ś 1221.

Vippaṭapu
Pe.N
Ps.N

Vịraghanṭala
Title; hero-bells
VV

Vịram bhaṭla
Pe N
VV

Vịram rāju
Pe N
Ps.N

Viriyāla
Pe.N
GV

Virridinḍi.
Pe.N
TG

Vīru bhaṭla
Pe N
VV

Viṣhnu bhaṭla
Pe.N
VV

Viṣhnu vajhula
Pe.N
TG

Vissā
Pl.N; Vissā – puram, Bhadrachalam Tq, East Godavari dt.
AN; Vissā – Kōḍēru, Bhimavaram Tq, West Godavari Dt.

Viśśā pragaḍa
Pe.N; See above
AN

Vissa vajhula
Pe.N; See above
KN

Vissam rāju
Pe.N; See above
GV; AN; Ps. N

Viśwanādha – bhaṭla
Pe.N
Br.; SII, X, 422, ś 1191

Viśwanādha / Viśvanādham
Pe.N
VV; PD

Viśvwārādhya
Title: worshipful in or by the world.
SK

Viśwāsari
Pe.N
AN

Viṭhala
Pl.N; Viṭṭalapuram, Hospeta Tq, Ballary Dt; Karnataka, Vithāpalle, Hindupur Tq.
TG; Ananthapur Dt ; Vithalam, Vayalpad Tq, Chittoor Dt.

Viṭhaṃ rāju
Pe.N
AN

Viṭhapu
Pl.N; Viṭhalaṃ, Vithalāpuram, Darsi Tq, Prakasam Dt.
V; IVR IV, 304, ś 1458.

Vruddula
Vrudda = Aged; old
PD

Vydula
Profession; Vydya = Doctor
GV

Vyjarsu
Pl.NG
V

Vyākanṭi.
Pl.N
Ps.N

Vyākaraṇam
Title: expertise in Grammar
TG

Y

Yābalūri
Pl.N
AN

Yādāṭi.
Pl.N
Ps.N; IAP, Cuddapah Dt, III, No.20, ś 1813

Yādavāni
Pl.N
TG

Yaḍavilli
Pl.N; Narasaraopeta, Guntur Dt.
TG; ISGO, 15, 1380

Yaddanapūḍi
Pl.N; Narasaraopeta, Guntur Dt.
A.N; SII, X, 73, ś 1037

Yaga rāju
Pe.N

AN

Yajnanna bhaṭla
Pe.NV; Yajñanna- bhaṭla, Gotra: Kounḍinya , ISGO, 15, ś 1380.

Yajña vajhula
Title: Yajña = sacrifice ; Vajhula = teacher
Ps.N

Yāmijāla
Pl.N
TG; GV

Yānḍalūri
Pl.N
IVR, IV, 210 ś 1548.

Yānamaṇḍra
Pl.N
VV; ISGO, 15, ś 1380.

Yanumula palli
Pl.N
GV

Yārlageḍḍa
Pl.N. Ellavaram division, East Godavari Dt., Divi Tq, Krishna Dt.
Ka; SSI, VI, 83, 1704AD; 79, ś 1718.

Yarra pātruni
Pe.N
Ps.N.

Yasantarāvu
Pe.N
M.Dh

Yātagiri
Pl.N
M.Dh.

Yati rāju
Pe. N after Rāmānuja. SVR, IV, No. 237, ś 1466.
SV; SSI, XVI, 130, 1544 AD.

Yēlēśvaram
Pl.N; Devarakonda Tq, Nalgonda Dt.
VV

Yelamarti
Pl.N
M.Dh.

Yellājōsyula
Pe.N
Vel;TG

Yellam bhaṭla
Pe.N
Vel.TG

Yellāyi
Pe.N
DD

Yeṃpaṭala
Pl.N
Br.; ISGO, 15, ś 1380.

Yemparēla
Pl.N
Br.; Gōtra : Bhāradvāja; ISGO, 15, ś 1380.

Yepuṭṭila
Pl.N
Br.; IVR 27, ś 1331

Yētū
Pl.N
Br.; ISGO, 15, ś 1380

Yudraṅki
Pl.N
AN

Bibliography

(i) **EPIGRAPHY**

Butterworth and Vēnugōpālachețty (Eds): *Inscriptions on Copperplates and Stones in the Nellore District* (in 3 Vols.) Madras, 1905.

Hanumantha Rao, B.S.L. : Buddhist Inscriptions of Andhra Pradesh, (Ananda Buddha Vihara Trust, Secunderabad).

Mukuṇda Rāo, N. (Ed.) *Siṃhāchalam Temple Inscriptions*, (Simhachalam, 1987).

Mukuṇda Rāo, N. and Rāmachndra Mūrty, N.S. (Eds.) *Inscriptions of Andhra Pradesh – Medak District*, (Epigraphical Series No.24, Dept., of Archeology & Museums, Hyderabad, 2001).

Parabrahma Śāstry, P.V. (i) (Ed.) : *Select Epigraphs of Andhra Pradesh*, (Archeological Series No.31, Hyderabad, 1965).

" (ii) (Ed): *Inscriptions of Andhra Pradesh, Karimnagar District* (Epigraphical Series No.8, Hyderabad, 1974).

" (iii) (Ed): *Inscriptions of Andhra Pradesh, Cuddapah District*, Parts I(1977); II(1978); III(1981) (Epigraphical Series Nos.12,13,15) Hyderabad).

" (iv) (Ed) : *Inscriptions of Andhra Pradesh, Nalgonda District*, Vol. I, (Epigraphical Series No.21, Hyderabad, 1992).

" (v) (Ed) : *Inscriptions of the Vijayanagar Rulers*, Vol. IV, Telugu Inscriptions (1351-1665 AD), (Indian Council of Historical Research, Bangalore, 2009).

Rāmachandra Mūrty, N.S. and Jōgi Nāiḍu, P (Ed.) : *Inscriptions of Andhra Pradesh, Mahabūbnagar district,* Vols. I & II (Epigraphical Series Nos.25 and 26, Dept., of Archeology & Museums, Hyderabad, 2003).

Rādhā Krishna Būdarāju, *Early Telugu Inscriptions, upto 1100 A.D.* (Andhra Pradesh Sahitya Akademi, Hyderabad, 1971)

Rangāchārya, V : *A Topographical List of the Inscriptions of the Madras Presidency* (in 3 Vols.) (First published 1919; Asian Educational Services, New Delhi, Reprint, 1985).

Ramēśan, N : *Copper Plate Inscriptions of Andhra Pradesh Government Museum,* Vol. I (A.P. Government Archaeological Series No.6, Hyderabad, 1962).

Ramēśan, N and Mukunda Row (Eds.), *Temple Inscriptions of Andhra Pradesh,* Vol. 1, Śrikākuḷam District (Hyderabad, 1980).

Robert Sewell : *The Historical Inscriptions of Southern India* (Madras, 1932: AES, Reprint, 1983).

Śāstry, B.N.: *Tripurāntaka Dēvālaya Śāsanamulu,* (Musi Publications, Hyderabad, 1991).

Matyāla Vamsa Charitra – *Śāsanamulu* (Valigonda, 1994).

Kayastha Rajulu (*Śāsanamulu*) (Musi Publications, Hyderabad, 1991).

Śāsanasamputi Part 1-2, (Hyderabad, 1989).

Mukhalinga Dēvālaya Charitra – *Śāsanamulu* (Musi Publications, Hyderabad, 1985).

South Indian Inscriptions, Vols. IV, V, X, XVI.

Subbarāyalu, Y and Toru Matsui : *A Concordance of the Names in the Chola Inscriptions*, (Madurai, 1978).

I, (Epigraphical Series No.21, Hyderabad, 1992).

Subrahmaṇyam, R : *Inscriptions of the Sūryavamsi Gajapathis of Orissa,* (Agam Prakashan Delhi, 1986).

Sōmaśekhara Śarma, Mallampalli (Ed. Subrahmaṇyam, R) : *Corpus of Inscriptions in the Telangana Districts,* Part IV, (Archeological Series No.32, Dept. of Archeology and Museums, Hyderabad, 1973).

Venkaṭaramaṇayya, N (Ed): *Inscriptions of Andhra Pradesh – Warangal District* (Epigraphical Series No.6 , Hyderabad, 1974).

Venkaṭaramaṇayya, Nēlatūri (Ed.): *Inscriptions of Andhra Pradesh – Nalgonda District,* Vol. II, (Epigraphical Series No.23, Hyderabad, 1994).

(ii) Dictionaries, Directories, Encyclopaedias, Gazetteers, Glossaries; Lexicons and Nighanṭus

Alphabetical List of Villages in the Taluks and Districts of the Madras Presidency (Madras, 1933, Asian Educational Services, New Delhi, Reprint, 1992).

Āndhra Deśa charitrā Bhūgōḷa Sarvasvamu, vols. (Hyderabad) Telugu.

Andhra Pradesh District Gazetteers (Series).

Birudurāju, Rāmarāju et al.: *Telugu Samśkruti,* vol. II (Hyderabad, 1988).

Brown, Charles Philip: *English – Telugu Dictionary,* (Reprint of 1853 Edition, Fifth Reprint, Potti Sreeramulu Telugu University, Hyderabad, 2000).

Burrow, T and Emeneau, M.B.: *Dravidian Etymological Dictionary,* (Oxford, 1961). *Dravidian Etymological Dictionary* – Supplement, (Oxford,1968).

Īśvara Dattu, Kuṃdūri : *Śasana Sabda Kōśamu (Inscriptional Glossary of Andhra Pradesh,* (A.P. Sahitya Akademi, Hyderabad 1967).

Kittel, F: *A Kannada English Dictionary* (Mangalore, 1894; Asian Educational Series Ninth Reprint, 1999).

Krishan Lal Khera : *Directory of Personal Names in the Indian History*, from the earliest to 1947, (Munshiram Manoharlal, New Delhi, 2002).

Mahādēva Śāstry, Kōraḍa (Ed.): *Telugu Desya Vyutpatti Nighanṭuvu (An Etymological Dictionary of Native Telugu)*, (Dravidian University, Kuppam 2003) Telugu.

Maclean, C. D : *Glossary of Madras Presidency*, (First Published 1893, Asian Educational Services New Delhi, Reprint, 1982).

Menaka Gandhi, *Hindu Names* (Penguin Books, New Delhi, 1993).

Rādhakrishna, Būdarāju et al. (Ed.): *Telugu – Telugu Nighantuvu* (Dictionary), (Telugu Akademi, Hyderabad Reprint, 2007).

Reddy, G.N.: *Telugu Paryāyapada Nighanṭuvu (Dictionary of Synonyms in Telugu)*, (Visālāndhra Publishing House, Hyderabad, 1998) Telugu.

Sangraha Āndhra Vijñana Kōśamu, vols. (Hyderabad), Telugu.

Sītārāmāchāryulu, B :, *Śābdhāratnākaramu* (Madras, 1937), Telugu.

Shibani Roy – S.H.M. Rizvi: *Encyclopaedia of Indian Surnames*, (B.R. Publishing Corporation, Delhi, 2002).

Subbrāyuḍu, Mahaṃkāḷi (Śābdārdha Chaṃdrika (Telugu) (Vavilla Press, Madras, 1969).

Subrahmaṇyam, Rāyaprōlu, et al. *Telugu Saṃkruti*, vol. I, (Hyderabad, 1983).

Venkata Śeshayya, Vetsā: *Sanskrit – Andhra Nighantuvu*, (First Publilshed 1893; Prachee Reprint, Hyderabad, 1995).

(iii) CATALOGUES OF SURNAMES

(Caste-wise)

Ananta Padmanābham, Dwivēdula, *Ārama Drāviḍa Vamśa Charitra* (Śankhavaram, 1992)

Arthur Anthony MacDonnell and Arthur Berriedace Keith; *Vedic Index of Names and Subjects* (Motilal Banarsidass, Varanasi, 1958).

Ranga Rao, Sādinēni, (Comp) *Kammavāri Iḷḷa Pērlu, Vāduka Gōtramulu,* Venkaṭappayya, velagā (Ed.) (Second Impression, Tenali, 2008).

Reḍḍi Nādu, vol. I, No.7, (Hyderabad, February, 1997), pp.36-37.

Satyanārāyaṇa Gupta, Garre (Comp.): *Ārya Vaiśya Gōtramulu ... Iṃṭi Pērlu* (Vijayawada, 1981).

Śrikanth Kumār, Chillagaṭṭu, *Kāpulu: Sāmajika Rājakiya Viśleṣhaṇa* (Vijayawada, 2007), pp 31-51.

Vajrapāṇi: *Brāhmanula Iniṭi Pērlu* (Bharaṇi Publications, Vijayawada, 2008).

Venkaṭa Nārāyaṇa, Pāvulūri, (Comp.): *Kammavāri Inṭi Pērlu – Gōtramulu* (Pāvulūri, Publications, Guntur, 2007).

Venkaṭa Śastry Musunūri (Comp.) *Viprula Inḍla Pērlu – Śākhalu – Gōtramulu – Pravaralu.* (Deepak Book Centre, Rajahmundry, 1980).

Virāchāryulu, P.B : *Viśwabrāhmana Gōtramulu* (Rōhini Publications, Rajahmundry, 1995).

(iv) RELATED AND RELEVANT

Books & Articles

Agarwala, V.S.: *India as Known to Pāṇini,* (1953).

Ārudra, *Samagra Āndhra Sāhityaṃ,* Vols. (Telugu).

Bālagangādhara Rao, Yārlagaḍḍa; (i) *Nāma Vijnānamu (Onomastics)* (ii) *Inṭi Pērlu* (Mangalagiri, 2001), (Vijayawada 2002), Telugu.

Changa Reddy, D.: *Kutuṃba Nāmālu – Grāma Nāmālu .....*

(Śravanti, April, 1979) Telugu.

Chitrarekha Gupta: *The Brahmanas of India: A Study Based on Inscriptions* (Delhi, 1983).

Datta Bhabataran : *A Linguistic Study of Personal Names and Surnames in Bengali* (University of Calcutta, 1981).

Doorai rangaswamy, M.A.: *The Surnames of the Cankam Age literary & Tribal* (University of Madras, 1968).

Īswara Dattu, Kuṃdūrị : *Prācịnāndhra Chāritraka Bhūgoḷamu,* (A.P. Sahitya Akademi, Hyderabad, Second impression, 1979).

Mahadēva Śastry, K.: *'Personal Names in Old Telugu'* – (Dr. R.P.Sethu Pillai, Silver Jubilee Felicitation Vol. Madras, 1961). pp 181-184.

Mallikārjun Maḍivalappa, Kulburgi: *Kannada Onomastics,* (English Translation by Sadanand Kanwalli of 'Kannaḍa Nāmavijñana'), (Place Names Society of India, Mysorem 1997).

Murty, M.L.K (Ed.) *Pre and Protohistory of Andhra Pradesh upto 500 B.C.* (Dravidian University, A.P. 2003).

Mangalam, S.J.: *Historical Geography and Toponomy of Andhra Pradesh* (Sundeep Prakashan, New Delhi, 1986).

Pratāpa Reddy, S.: *Āndhrula Sānghika Charitra, (The social history of Andhras).* Orient Lazman, (Hyderabad, 1996) Telugu.

Rāmachandra Mūrty, S.S.: *A study of Telugu Place – Names* (Agam Kala Prakashan, Delhi, 1985).

Śarma, I.K. (Ed.): *Early Historic Andhra Pradesh 500 B.C – AD 624.* (Tulika Books, New Delhi, 2008).

Satyavati, Tēḷḷa, *Teluguvari Inṭi Pērlu* (G.R.Publications, Guntur, 1987) Telugu.

Tej Ram Sharma: *Personal and Geographical Names in the Gupta Inscriptions.* (Concept Publishing Company, Delhi, 1978).

Tewari, S.P.: *Cultural Heritage of Personal-names and Sanskrit Literature* (Agam Kala Prakashan, Delhi, 1981).

Varahālarāju, Buddhirāju : *Śri Āndhra Kṣhtriya Vaṃśa Ratnākaramu,* (Bhatnavilli, 1980) Telugu.

Venkata Śastry, *Cheḷḷapiḷḷa, Kadhalu, Gādhalu* – Vol. I, (Second Impression, Kadiyam, 1958). Vol. III, (First Impression, 1960) Telugu.

Venkatappaya, Vēlagā et al. (Ed): *Luminaries of 20th Century; Iravay yo Śatābdi Telugu Velugulu;* Part I & II, (Poṭṭi Śrirāmulu Telugu University, Hyderabad, 2005) Telugu.

Vishnu Namboodiri, Nattarivum, Namapatnavum – *Folk Knowledge and Onomatology,* (D.C Books, Kottayam, 2010), Malayāḷam.

(v) JOURNALS

Bhārati (Telugu).

Epigraphia Āndhrica, Vols. (Dept. of Archaeology & Museums, Hyderabad).

Epigraphia Indica Vols.

Indian Antiquary Vols. (A Journal of Oriented Research).

Itihas (Journal of the Andhra Pradesh State Archives & Research Institute, Hyderabad).

Journal of Andhra Historical Research Society (Rajahmundry).

Proceedings of the Andhra Pradesh History Congress.

Studies in Indian Epigraphy (Bhāratiya Purābhilēkha Patrika, Mysore).

Studies in Indian Place Names (Bhāratiya Sthalanāma Patrikā, Mysore).